Get Free

and

Stay Free

Stories of Inmates Who Found
Freedom Inside and Out

Yokefellowship Prison Ministry

Helping at-risk youth, inmates, and returning citizens

yoke themselves to Christ for salvation and changed lives.

David M. Lewis

Print ISBN: 978-0-9908685-8-3

Printed in the United States of America

Endorsements

In the Proverbs of the Old Testament, we are challenged to expand our wisdom, knowledge, and understanding of life. In this book of interviews led by Dave Lewis, we hear genuine testimonials from men and women who have been through hell and back. Over the 50+ years of my active prison ministry, I have sometimes referred to the jail and prison experience as small "h"—hell—being the front porch of the large "H"—Hell. No one has ever disagreed with this.

These returned citizens from prison after many years, humbly open their journeys to us for the glory of God. We get to feel their deep pain and abuse. We see what caused them to start a positive reflection about life leading toward needed repentance. We learn of the forgiveness based on Atonement from God in Christ, even turning from Islam after seeing a genuine born-again Christian up close while becoming a cellmate. In comparison, the shallow so-called jailhouse religionists may return time after time. We come to see how trauma in early childhood can lead kids into gangs, and how petty use of toy guns can lead to unintended consequences, even deaths and a sentence of life inside. We realize that the worst thing any of us may do is not the total value of our life. I wholeheartedly recommend that you read all these heart-searching stories. I have known and loved most of these folks for years. Like Doug stated at the end of his interview, "Thank you for wanting to listen to my story." God of mercy and grace takes the time to listen and care about your story also, thankfully.

Chaplain John L. Rush
Former Executive Director of Yokefellowship Prison Ministry, Founder of New Person Ministry and Co-Founder of Justice & Mercy, Inc.

From the world of the forlorn, from the world of the lost and suicidal, David Lewis chronicles the long and agonizing journey of 11 incarcerated individuals, through faith in God, from the depths of hopelessness to freedom—freedom from the physical constraints of a prison cell as well as freedom from the chains of sin. David Lewis does this not by writing about the individual but by letting the individual describe his or her metamorphosis in their own words through one-on-one questioning, by posing insightful but fair questions.

Mr. Lewis poses no "gotcha" questions, he makes no moral judgments. He elicits the compelling story of each individual by moving from the larger picture of the person's background and why the person was incarcerated to the intensely personal depths of his or her human condition. He is able to draw out their determined commitment to the search for freedom and to God and how it changed each life. Each interview is a moving story of how the individual finds the Lord and gives their life to Jesus.

The word picture painted by the inmate chronicles their agonizing decades-long search in each case. The stories are so personal that one must surely give thanks to the good works of David Lewis and the many members of Yokefellowship Prison Ministry who helped make those journeys possible. Each day by their caring and mentoring, the Yokefellowship Prison Ministry is giving in God's name hope to the hopeless and salvation to the souls of the lost. More importantly, the reader is awarded an opportunity to examine and gain insight into his or her own struggle.

Ernest D. Preate, Jr., Esquire
Former Pennsylvania Attorney General

Get Free and Stay Free: Stories of Inmates Who Found Freedom Inside and Out paints the story of the amazing grace of God working in the lives of those who seek Him and find Him. This book gives examples of people who were trapped in sin and bondage and became free because they understood God's love for them, even in desperate times.

I've visited many prisons—county, state, and federal—and have spoken with many inmates and prison officials. I've spoken with many judges who sentenced convicted criminals to prison and to inmates, some of whom were unfortunately wrongfully convicted. If the public officials of Pennsylvania would apply the principles of this book it would have the potential to save between $500 million and $1 billion in incarceration costs and lower the recidivism rate by at least 25%. This book should be freely given to police officers, sheriffs, county and state prisons, rescue missions, and other locations where convicted felons are gathered.

The message in this book is the way, the truth, and the life for every person who wants to enjoy the blessings of God on his or her life.

Until the age of 50, I was strongly opposed to helping felons get it right. I was only interested in locking them up longer and punishing them harder. In the last 25 years, I have crisscrossed Pennsylvania, talking to the rich and the poor, and I now realize unless we help those who've fallen behind, our ability to live to the fullest will always be littered with crime.

Dr. Tom Zeager
Co-founder and President of Justice & Mercy, Inc.

Contents

Endorsements 4

Forward 11

Preface 14

Introduction 17

Chapter 1: Freddie Nole 21

Chapter 2: Keith Rodrigues 44

Chapter 3: Charity Sampsell 74

Chapter 4: Zachery Brooks and Tamir Hodges 105

Chapter 5: Lewis Lee 134

Chapter 6: Jeff Galitzky 168

Chapter 7:Jack Schrader 193

Chapter 8: Randall Schieck 220

Chapter 9: Marsha Curry-Nixon 255

Chapter 10: Doug Hollis 286

Appendix 319

Resources 322

About the Author 323

Forward

It's not what happens to you,
but how you react to it that matters.

Epictetus

About four years before he was elected president, U.S. Senator John F. Kennedy authored a book entitled "Profiles in Courage," which gives accounts of eight U.S. Senators who performed acts of bravery in the performance of their duties. The book you are about to read contains biographical narratives of 11 individuals. The experiences of these individuals provide a stark contrast to the experiences described by Senator Kennedy. While the Senators all sat in an office of prominence, receiving respect and admiration, these 11 individuals were not high-ranking elected officials but were all at one time or another convicted, incarcerated inmates. Their willingness to provide a public, candid and poignant account of their lives, in essence, "baring their souls," to guide other people in similar difficult or tragic situations shows both their commitment to the messages they provide and their mettle. The title "Profiles in Courage" would likewise be an apropos title for this book.

The book is a collection of interviews of the 11, providing detailed accounts of their backgrounds and upbringing, their crimes, and their incarceration, and doesn't sugar coat. They speak of coming from broken homes, with dysfunctional families. There is drug or alcohol abuse. Some were victims and/or perpetrators of violence and/or sexual abuse. Eventually, they were arrested for serious crimes and received extensive sentences, even life sentences in some cases. Fortunately, there is much more to their stories.

The thrust of these messages is that these 11 individuals made great changes in their lives and are now able to be productive members of society, helping others, particularly those who are in desperate need of guidance. Unfortunately, many in society see convicted criminals as useless and worthless, committing crimes when they are out on the street, and eating up taxpayers' money if they are incarcerated. A warden once told me about a phone call he received from the mother of a newly incarcerated inmate. The mother implored the warden to protect her son. The warden responded by stating that it's his job to protect all inmates, and they would do their best to maintain her son's safety. The woman then responded, "Well, my Johnny is not like the rest of the people in prison, he's not a criminal. Please look after him." While it is true that certain convicted criminals are career, hardened criminals or persons of violence requiring extensive jail sentences so that the community may be protected, many others can and do become useful members of society if given a chance.

Unfortunately, many convicted criminals also view themselves as useless. They view their circumstances as hopeless. As a result, some continue to abuse drugs or alcohol, don't try to change, and just give up. Others seek to remain in prison, becoming institutionalized. Still, others eventually commit suicide. The 11 storytellers in this book stand out as those who have overcome the societal stigma of being convicted criminals and their low self-esteem. They did not quit on themselves. You will also see that there were family members that never quit on them, even while the inmate languished in jail for many years. Yokefellowship Prison Ministry, a prison ministry instrumental in their turnaround, did not give up on them either, visiting with them and providing needed encouragement. The 11 sought, fought for, and obtained a better life.

The 11 storytellers have been rehabilitated. This is not a book about rehabilitation; however, it is a book about redemption. Most importantly, in addition to the help and encouragement they received from their families, Yokefellowship Prison Ministry, and even other inmates, the primary ingredient for the change in their lives was the development of their faith in Jesus Christ. By having the commitment and courage to change their ways, yield, giving up their lives to follow God, they became overcomers. They now have a message to share with others. In essence, the message is "with Christ anything is possible." As you read through these accounts, you will find yourself marveling at the changes, cheering for their success, while wondering how it could have gotten so bad in the first place. I applaud their courage to come forth to show the world a stark illustration of what their lives were, to provide hope to others for what one can become through a commitment to Jesus Christ, and to have the confidence in themselves to make the necessary changes, to never give up, even in the face of adversity. I say to the 11, well done.

Scott E. Lash, Judge
Court of Common Pleas, Berks County, Pennsylvania

Preface

In 1955 D. Elton Trueblood (1900-1994), a Quaker author, speaker, and theologian addressed chaplains from federal prisons across the nation in Washington, D.C. Trueblood believed being a Christian meant being yoked with Christ (Matthew 11:28-30).

Trueblood told the chaplains, "Separation from the world for a while is justified if new life emerges. But Yokefellows know that new life does not emerge of itself. New life comes only if there is a consistent and loving effort to embody the divine potential in each person made in God's image. That is why we work; we are trying to combine a warm heart and a clear head. We are well aware of the possibility of failure, but we never give up because the prize is one of real magnitude. If one person is truly changed, all of the effort expended is worthwhile."

Two chaplains, one from Tacoma, Washington, and one from Lewisburg, Pennsylvania, established Yokefellow groups in their prisons. At the start of the COVID pandemic in March 2020, Yokefellowship in Pennsylvania had over 300 Yokefellow volunteers visiting inmates in 44 Pennsylvania institutions. The mission of Yokefellowship Prison Ministry is "Helping at-risk youth, inmates, and returning citizens yoke themselves to Christ for salvation and changed lives."

John Rush, the executive director of Yokefellowship Prison Ministry (YPM) at the time, spoke at a pastor's meeting while I was serving as pastor of New Hanover United Methodist Church. I had a loved one caught up in the criminal justice system as an inmate and then as a "returning citizen" on parole. I asked John what I could do to help. He answered that there was not that much I could do to help my family member, but I could help others in similar situations. He got me a place on a Citizens Advisory Committee on Probation and Parole. I began visiting inmates at Graterford State Correctional Institution and learned more. I joined the board of directors of YPM.

As I have worked on this book, I have gained more insights into prison, crime, criminal justice, prison ministries, and the way the Holy Spirit moves and changes the lives of people who have committed crimes, been convicted, experienced fears and trials of incarceration and found freedom inside and out.

Just as the pandemic had shut down prison visitation, a friend and Pennsylvania Department of Corrections employee, Rich Jacobs, came to me with a vision he had for sharing stories in books and podcasts. Rich's goal was to use the accounts of those who had "gotten free and stayed free" to encourage currently and formerly incarcerated people and others in similar situations of brokenness. This book would consist of interviews with people who had been ministered to by YPM.

Rich Jacobs and his "Get Free and Stay Free" ministry have provided the impetus, model, resources, encouragement, and advice that have brought these salvation stories to print. Rich is one of those corrections employees who does his job not only for the pay and benefits but out of his commitment to Christ and his respect for the inmates he works with and comes to know very well.

John Rush, former Yokefellowship Prison Ministry executive director, connected me to many persons interviewed in this book, reviewed each chapter, and gave me wise counsel. My beloved life partner, Nancy

Lewis, affirmed the power in these stories by the tears in her eyes after she first read them. And then, she put her grammatical know-how and literary skills to work with corrections and suggested changes. Her final editing was exhaustive and precise, and her technological leadership and marketing skills greatly strengthened this project.

And thanks to the men and women who told their stories openly, honestly, and humbly. Who would agree to include their most sinful, foolish, shameful, embarrassing, tragic life decisions in a book other than people who had repented and accepted the forgiveness that comes through the cross of Christ? They will carry certain regrets and guilt to their graves. These redeemed men and women cannot change the past, but they have been "yoked to Christ for salvation and a changed life," and they are grateful and joyous "new creations."

David M. Lewis
Chair of the Board, Yokefellowship Prison Ministry

Introduction

I did not interview a random sample of "returned citizens" (former inmates who have been released) for this book. I interviewed men and women who had regained not only their physical freedom but their spiritual freedom. These are people who give credit for that freedom to Jesus Christ. These are imperfect people who have seen the dark side of themselves and the world and yearn to be more like Christ.

I asked probing questions of these men and women. These former inmates know what it feels like to lose the daily opportunities, comforts, and freedoms many enjoy and take for granted. Having now secured those opportunities, comforts, and freedoms, these "returning citizens" do not take them for granted.

Jesus proclaimed the Gospel, the Good News about God's love for us, by word and deed. If you want to teach eternal truth, do it as Jesus did—show the truth by the way you live. If you want to understand how God saves and changes men and women who have lost their spiritual freedom and physical freedom but then "get free and stay free," listen to the stories of these inmates getting free and staying free.

I asked questions, and the men and women in this book told their stories. They told their stories humbly and honestly. They were not defensive, seeking to protect their reputations. They talked about the poverty, abuse, neglect, poor role models, and addiction in their lives, but they did not blame those difficulties for their choices. Instead, they took responsibility for the choices they made. Imperfect as the criminal justice system may be, they did not blame that imperfection for their incarceration. Though racism undoubtedly impacted some of their sentences and experiences, they did not use racism to excuse their criminal behavior. Some of these men and women would probably never have gone to prison if they had not been addicted to drugs and alcohol, but they own up to their poor decisions and do not say, "The addiction made me do it."

As you listen to these stories, patterns emerge. Some experiences contribute to the poor choices people make: poverty, physical and sexual abuse, addiction, gang culture, negative peer pressure, the yearning for material things money can buy, the sex drive, the lack of healthy, consistent parenting, buried hurts you learn to lie about and ignore, the absence of a healthy spiritual foundation. These are the harsh experiences of life and temptations that plague all of us. "For all have sinned and fall short of the glory of God" (Romans 3:23). The difference between people convicted of crimes and incarcerated and the rest of us is that inmates must search for spiritual freedom while physically confined. The stories in this book come from people who have successfully gained their physical and spiritual freedom. There is so much for us to learn from them.

A Biblical reflection follows each chapter. The men and women who tell their stories do not see the Bible as a telescope to focus on other people and organizations to determine what is wrong with them but see the Bible as a mirror to take account of themselves. "How can you say to your brother, 'Brother, let me take the speck out of your eye,' when you fail to see the plank in your eye? You hypocrite, first take the plank out of your eye, and then you will see clearly to remove the speck from your brother's eye." (Luke 6:42 NIV) The focus of people interviewed in this book is on the plank in their own eyes. As inmates, these men and women used the Bible and prayer to discern just what their plank might be and what they needed to do to bring about its removal. So these reflections come from their experience with Scripture and what the Holy Spirit has said to them.

As I listened to these "returned citizen" stories, it became apparent that other stories should be told. Their spouses, children, families, and friends have a story to tell. Judges, attorneys, and law enforcement have stories to tell. Corrections officers, chaplains, and prison staff have stories to tell. And these inmates' victims and their families also have important stories to tell.

These stories of "salvation and changed lives" will encourage and provide practical help for inmates and returned citizens. I hope Yokefellowship Prison Ministry volunteers and other Christian prison ministry volunteers will feel affirmed in their service and use this book to recruit others to this vital work. I hope families of inmates will find comfort from these victories. I hope others who work in criminal justice will gain insight and motivation to do the challenging work assigned to them.

There is a tendency to judge people by their felonies or by the color of the inmate uniform they wear. But that is not how God sees people. In I Samuel 16:1-13, the prophet has been called to anoint the next king of Israel. God gives Samuel this advice, "The Lord does not look at the things people look at. People look at the outward appearance, but the Lord looks at the heart." (1Samuel 16:7b-c NIV) When we ask questions and listen carefully, we attempt to see what the Lord sees, not the outward appearance but the human heart.

I had two predominant impressions as I asked questions and learned from those whose stories are recorded here. The first impression is that as you learn about the experiences and development of another person, your empathy increases. If I had grown up in that environment, what choices would I have made? What would I be like? The second impression is that our past, no matter how difficult and confusing, does not have the power to imprison us forever. When we each take responsibility for the choices we have made and trust that Jesus came for us, we can escape the prison of our past and "get free and stay free."

I feel privileged to have gotten a glimpse of some broken, grateful, humble hearts who have responded to that amazing grace. Thankful for what they have received, they are determined to help others. As you read these stories, I trust that those same hearts will bless yours.

David M. Lewis
Yokefellowship Prison Ministry

Chapter 1
Freddie Nole

John Freddie Nole is a pleasant, calm, and gentle man, but Freddie Nole has not lived a pleasant, calm, and gentle life. Freddie spent parts of five years in youth detention centers between the ages of 8 and 17 and then 49 years in Pennsylvania correctional institutions. That's just about 54 out of 67 years of his life, without being free to walk where he wanted, to do what he wanted, to sleep when he wanted. But Freddie Nole has a story to tell about transformation, a story about becoming genuinely free.

YPM
Freddie, where did you grow up, and who was your family?

Freddie
I grew up in South Philadelphia. I was the third oldest of 12 children. My earliest memories are from when we lived in South Philadelphia. I had a godmother who raised me until I was about 5. She lived in the same neighborhood as my family. Then my family moved three or four

times. I never saw my godmother again. We lived on Marshall Street for three or four years before I got into trouble and was sent away.

YPM

Were you a happy boy? What were you like? Tell me about your early life.

Freddie

I didn't know what life was when I was young. With so many people living in the same way in the neighborhood that I was raised in, it was hard to make a distinction. There were always needs. My concept of needs took me out in the street doing all kinds of things—playing hooky from school, stealing stuff off store steps in the morning—thinking that I needed to help supply food and stuff for my family. So, school never was a big part of my life. My mom tried to discipline me as much as she could, but the streets were a little more influential in my life than anything else. But, as I said, I had a lot of sisters and brothers.

YPM

Did your mom and dad give you moral direction? Did they tell you what was right and wrong? Did they take you to church?

Freddie

No. The only church I remember going to was with my godmother. She was the biggest influence on my life as far as the church was concerned. And I remember her praying with me at night and taking me to church with her on a regular basis. But when I moved away, there was no real sense of church in my life other than what I might have occasionally initiated on my own.

YPM

Did your mom and dad figure it out if you stole something and brought it home to help out? Did they say it was wrong or just take what you gave them? Did you get any feedback from them?

Freddie

Well, I was a hustler. I used to go out early in the morning and do what we called "trash picking." You know, I would collect papers and bottles, so I was always doing things like that. So, I put a front on all the illegal stuff I was doing. But I stayed in trouble. My mom was always coming to a police station somewhere to get me. She would ask me what was going on. And I would lie until I was blue in the face, that it wasn't me, that it was the gang, and I was just one of the people they singled out.

YPM

Between the ages of 8 and 17, you spent five years in youth detention facilities. What was that like for a young kid, an adolescent?

Freddie

I was being shaped into that life. I started going to the youth detention center in Philadelphia when I was 8 years old. I was picked up for truancy, curfew violations, and gang-related activities. I would sometimes spend three or four months in the youth detention center waiting to go to hearings and stuff like that. So finally, when I was about 8 years old, I guess they had already had enough of me, and since my mom was still having kids at the time, they just took me away. My father was the one that had to deliver me to a youth center called Shallcross in Philadelphia, Pennsylvania.

I stayed at Shallcross until I was about 10. I stayed there for about a year and a half. I came home with no real instructions. I was put right back into my mom's care. I was absorbed once again into the makeup of my neighborhood, which was very poor.

YPM

What kind of school student were you?

Freddie

Oh, I was poor in school. When I finally got locked up in 1971, I had to take a test. The only subject where I was as high as a fifth-grade level might've been math. My reading was very poor, and my writing was almost non-existent.

YPM

When you were a teenager, who were your friends? Who was influencing you as you got to be 16, 17?

Freddie

I was more of an influencer than a lot of the guys that I hung around. But in our neighborhood growing up, risk taking was more or less a badge of honor. I didn't have any problems risking anything to do what I thought I needed to do for my family and neighborhood. So, I did burglaries. I stole off racks on Ninth Street. I would go into stores and shoplift. I did it all. Even though we all have a sense of right and wrong, I was getting away with it.

YPM

You were doing wrong, but you weren't getting consequences?

Freddie

Right. This is no badge of honor, but whenever I did something that was against the law, and I was alone, I was alright; I never got caught. But, whenever I did stuff with other people, I always wound up getting caught. Or if they got caught, I got told on. I never got caught for any of the things that I did by myself.

YPM
What was the big event in your life that led to a life term?

Freddie
Well, some friends of mine wanted to go to a skating party. And I thought, I don't have the money for it. But in candy stores back then, they used to have change boxes. You could go in, pick up the paper, pick up a few pieces of candy, and just throw the money in the box. So, this day I just figured we could run into the local candy store, snatch the change box, which would give us pennies or whatever, to go to the skating rink. Nothing would be said. Well, it didn't quite go that way.

We went into the store. I had a toy gun at the time. It was an old plastic, snub-nosed 38. We went into the store, and the owner was standing there. I handed the gun to one friend. The other friend and I ran around the counter, snatched the change box, and ran out. I held him at bay with the toy gun. The store owner came a little bit behind us, but he couldn't catch us. He was nearly 80 years old. We didn't think about his age or that this would result in anything tragic. At least I didn't.

Later, we heard that he had died from an aortic aneurysm and that they were looking for my co-defendants and me. Needless to say, that reverberated through the neighborhood. I left the neighborhood and went to stay with my father. My father and mother had been separated for about seven, eight years at this time. I stayed in North Philadelphia with my father without telling him anything. I was on the run for about seven months. This happened in February of 1969. My two co-defendants got caught in April of 1969. I wound up getting caught in September of 1969, but I was the only one that received a life sentence.

YPM

You received a life sentence, and you were holding a toy gun?

Freddie

Well, it wasn't that. I think it was because I got caught last.

YPM

The store owner died from an aortic aneurysm chasing you, and you were charged with murder?

Freddie

Yeah. They charged me with murder in the first degree. My sentence was life without parole. There was no parole back then for homicide. There's no parole for life sentences in Pennsylvania even now, whether it's a first degree or second degree.

YPM

Did they put you in prison right away?

Freddie

I went straight to the House of Corrections. They called it "The Creek."

YPM

So now you're 17 years old, and you're in prison. Talk about how you were emotionally? How did you feel? Were you sad, scared, angry? What was your basic emotional approach to the reality of being in prison for life?

Freddie

Well, first of all, I had already been indoctrinated while I was at the House of Corrections in 1967. Then in September 1969, once they certified me to stand trial as an adult, I was moved to Holmesburg. While at Holmesburg, I began educating myself, leaning on older prisoners for understanding the law.

I told my story to a few confidants that I had come across at Holmesburg. When they transferred me from the Creek to Holmesburg in November 1969, they sent me with about 20 other juveniles that had been convicted and certified to stand trial as adults. So, we had a little clique that kind of insulated us from the more brutal stuff that prisons were known for at the time. I was able to educate myself a little bit and learn about the law somewhat. I never thought about my sentence being as long as it was. I thought that if I behaved within a certain period, the craziness of my sentence might warrant me to be released. Maybe I will get out after 15, 16, or 17 years. And the thing about this is, that was the norm back then. Life sentence prisoners were getting out in the 70s.

YPM

When I asked you how you felt, you described what you did. You went right into survival mode. You were thinking about what you needed to do to get out, and you found a group of people to help you. Of course, everyone is different, but weren't you afraid? Were you angry at this shocking life sentence? Or were you just not in touch with your emotions?

Freddie

I think I was in shock mode because I didn't believe that they could give me what they did, even though I didn't know the law. My co-defendants weren't tried as adults. They only did juvenile time. One did 11 months, and one did 18 months. I never believed that this sentence would hold up. I knew that people who committed homicide and robbery got a different verdict. So I was more or less in shock mode and disbelief that this would be my fate.

YPM

You didn't have any clue that it wasn't going to be 17 years—it was going to be 49 years. You were a young man who had grown up in the correctional system, and you knew how to function in that environment. You're an inmate, and you're living your life. Year after year goes by, what sort of person were you? We are talking about transformation and who you were then and now. Were you a good guy? Were you trustworthy? You were living in an incarcerated community. What was your role in the community?

Freddie

When I got to Graterford SCI (State Correctional Institution) in 1971, I was interested in improving myself. My real mode at that time was to learn and better myself so that if I did have a chance to get out, I would be one of the people that they could say, "Well, yeah, if we let him out, he's good." I did get along with people, but I did not associate with guys my age, but older guys could teach me different things. I was eager to learn, and I participated in stuff. I never got involved in the everyday underground stuff. I mean, I had my occasional days where I went to the speakeasy on the block and maybe bought a bottle of wine or smoked a joint here and there. I always believed if I went up the ladder of success long enough, it would be better. Plus, you had people in prison; if you didn't have something to offer of substance, they didn't want you around.

I used to have a lot of old heads tell me, "Don't sit here and act like this is the end of your life. You have to do something. This doesn't have to be the end of everything for you. You're young; get something on your mind." That kind of language was constantly impressed upon me by the people I associated with. I associated with a lot of guys that I didn't know beforehand, but when I got to prison, I realized I had known some of their people. I knew their sons. I knew their daughters.

I knew their nephews and nieces. I knew their mothers. People that I never knew on the street, who had been incarcerated for years and years before I grew up. They were still in prison, but they had talents.

YPM

Were there people on the outside that you missed? Were there people that you loved, people you thought about? Were there things about the outside that you yearned for?

Freddie

I did miss my family because there were so many things that I never did as a family. I told my wife, Susan, that I only remember celebrating maybe one or two Christmases at home with my family. All the rest of them—all the holidays that normally would come and go—I only remember them because I was in prison and locked up somewhere,

YPM

As the years went by, what was happening to you? Were you getting bitter? Were you just resigned to it? What happened to you over time?

Freddie

I started growing up. I mean, I started realizing that if anything was going to happen to me, I had to make myself noteworthy enough for it to come my way, for the opportunities to be given to me. Don't get me wrong. I had a lot of breaks when I was in prison. Mr. Earnest ran the dental lab at that time. They used to make prosthetics for people in prison. I would work for him in my second year of being incarcerated. I put in to get into his dental lab. I still didn't have the education, but I was getting better. You know, I hadn't gone to school to get my GED yet, but I was getting better. I had started reading. I would read parts of the Bible over and over again until I understood them. I started learning how to write. Guys in prison were helping me. Mr. Earnest gave me a job. I did bite blocks and trays. As I was learning that process, I learned other techniques, choosing teeth, ordering teeth, making out purchase orders. He saw me as being interested in that and gave me a clerk job. Whenever I was given the opportunity to show myself more responsible, I went for it.

YPM

You're describing hard work—you were trying to earn your way out of prison. At what point did you begin to change in terms of your faith life, your belief in God and Christ? Turning to someone outside yourself for forgiveness, for grace? Did that happen gradually?

Freddie

Well, it was gradual. When I first got to Graterford in 1971, I didn't participate in any religious services. They were still building the chapel. We would meet, we were having our services in the school area. I didn't participate that much. I started participating in the church around 1975. I just went to part of the service, and then they brought in programs. Now and then, I would go down and participate in the studies. I got involved in the prison, doing social things, and in 1976, they gave me the chairmanship of the lifer's organization. I had gotten my GED in 1974 and graduated, and I was taking college courses in prison with Villanova University.

YPM

You're a 25-year-old guy in prison for life. You are maturing. You are learning to read. How was your faith developing? If what happened to you happened to me, I think I'd be angry. I'd be resentful. I'd be bitter about the penalty.

Freddie

It might be hard for people to understand why I wasn't that way. Or if I was that way, it was subtle anger. But you got to realize I never had a life on the street. Even though I had a relationship with my son's mom, it only lasted for a couple of months. It wasn't like a long-term relationship. We met, we got involved, and then I got in trouble.

YPM

So, you had a son before you went to prison?

Freddie

No, he was born while I was in prison. I went to prison in September, and he was born in November.

YPM

So, here's a boy you fathered, but you never got to know him. You couldn't raise him. You couldn't have been the father that he needed.

Freddie

No, not at that time. I couldn't raise him, but I did get to know him. At age 5, he could come to the prison for visits. And throughout the years, my mother and my wife, Susan, brought him to visit me. There were a few years when I didn't see him because I was being moved around the state, and then he joined the military. But when he got out, he started visiting me again.

Once I started going to church, I realized that my life had to change significantly, I mean change. This is what reading the Bible and being in the church provided for me. I started being involved in the church—performing, talking, putting on religious programs, designing religious programs for the services. I was sitting in church with some friends. Back then, family members and friends could come into the church and worship with us. I was sitting there one day, and it was like God said to me, "Alright, I'm ready for you now. Now is the time I want you."

I was looking around thinking that somebody was saying something to me, because the way it came to me was like, somebody in the back of me was saying something just loud enough that I could hear. I kept looking around. We had the service, and a lady named Sister Meyer called us up. She said, "I know there are people in this church right now who God has spoken to. He's waiting for you to come up here and announce that you are ready to live your life in accordance with what He desires for you."

And then I just got up. I just got up and walked up front, and I told her, "I'm here to accept the Lord Jesus Christ as my Savior." I said, "I heard him speaking to me today." She said, "I knew you did. And I was waiting for you." That's when I accepted the Lord. Later I was baptized, and I never looked back.

YPM

How did giving your life to Christ change your life?

Freddie

It only changed my life to a point. I could dedicate myself to reading the Bible, but I wasn't making it as applicable as it should have been. When I was at Graterford, I was in charge of a lot of programs. Although it didn't make me feel better than anybody, it made me feel equal to the people that were my captors. They didn't like that. You know, I didn't have the humbleness, you understand, of the position that I was in. And that reaped a lot of harsh benefits. Finally, in 1989, they transferred me to the Huntingdon institution. That's where God, really, really became an emphasis in my life. When I say that I had to humble myself and realize who was in control of my physical and spiritual life, it made me humble, and I got a different attitude.

YPM

You met a woman who was visiting in prison, is that correct? And then eventually you married her?

Freddie

My wife, Susan, and I met through a volunteer program in 1982. She would come in with her church, Prince of Peace, at the time. They would come in and volunteer with us on developing programs, assisting us in re-entry, and helping guys find jobs.

YPM

You met her at Graterford, and then they moved you?

Freddie

They didn't move me until after we were married for five years.

YPM

Were you married in a ceremony in the prison?

Freddie

Right, we were married in the visiting room in 1984. We had a friend of ours named Ann Deiterly. She had just gotten her ministry license. We were good friends, and she agreed to come in and marry us.

YPM

What kept your marriage together? How did you two care for your relationship from 1984 to 2019?

Freddie

We let God do it. This is God. Pastor, I need to tell you some things that show that my wife and I rely on God heavily because of all the things he has brought me through. When I was transferred out of Graterford, it was like another life sentence for me. I had been accused of grabbing a child in the visiting room in a play area. We had several inmates operating in that area with about 12 female volunteers from outside. Someone called this in a month or two after this incident had allegedly happened. To make a long story short, the jail believed that I was the one that did it. I talked to the state police. Rather than letting me have my hearing at Graterford, the day I spoke to the state police, they transferred me to Huntingdon. The day I got to Huntingdon, they put me on suicide watch and put me in the hole where I couldn't have contact with anybody.

YPM

Were you thinking of suicide?

Freddie

No, this was more or less the prison's way of keeping me out of contact with people who knew and believed I didn't do this. There were a lot of questions about how it happened and how it came about. There were questions that the administration at the time didn't want to answer. I was in the hole for 90 days trying to prove my innocence. I did prove it to some extent, but Huntingdon didn't want to release the misconduct because they feared a lawsuit. What they did was—even though I was only under administrative custody and having this continuously investigated—they finally released me from administrative custody in October 1989 with time served. They didn't restrict visits from me. They didn't put me in further confinement. They gave me all the privileges that I would have been entitled to as a regular person in the general population. I existed like that for seven years.

YPM

How far away was Susan?

Freddie

Well, she was over 155 miles away from me.

YPM

How did you manage that?

Freddie

Here's the God part. Susan already had her degree, but she went back to school and got a certificate in programming. God gave her a job shortly after she graduated. That helped in our financial situation. He provided for my wife those seven years that I was at Huntingdon, and during that time, I was transferred to other institutions in the western part of the state. He provided her with the means of receiving my phone calls daily and coming to see me every other week.

YPM

Did Susan drive 300 miles round trip on weekend visits?

Freddie

It depended on where I was. When I was in Pittsburgh, it was 600 miles, and at Huntingdon, it was a 400 miles round trip. They would give us six visits a month, and she would come on a Friday, Saturday, and Sunday, then go back home Sunday after visits were over. So we did that for seven years.

YPM

You didn't get out of prison until 2019, so you still had another 20 years, but you held your faith; you held firm.

Freddie

Susan and I prayed, and we believed that God had something for us. I never believed that I would die in prison. I used to tell her that I'm not going to die in prison. I don't know how it will happen. I was fighting my case at every opportunity. She was working with me to show the discrepancies in what had happened to me when I was first certified. She's been a partner in this and has gone through the wringer with me about my situation with Harrisburg's administration and executive individuals.

This treatment was not the first, not the only incident where we were somewhat persecuted because of our relationship. Well, you know, my wife is White, right? So that didn't go over well in places like Huntingdon, Pittsburgh, Greene.

YPM

Who gave you a hard time about your interracial marriage—correctional staff, or other inmates?

Freddie

The staff; I never had a problem with inmates. We always had problems with staff. Sometimes they wouldn't even call me for visits. They would tell me the pass got lost. They called the block and gave information, but the block didn't transfer it to me.

YPM

Weren't you enraged?

Freddie

We were relying on God. I mean, I'm not going to say I didn't have attitudes with staff, but I never acted out. If staff did something that I didn't like, I had gotten to the point where I was educated enough, sophisticated enough to put what I had to say down on paper. And I would write letters. I would put in complaints. I would talk to anybody that wanted to talk to me as the investigation went on. I would even go to court. Now granted, some of these responses didn't engender goodwill from staff and the prison, but they never had to worry about me being physical with any officers. I might talk to them in a rough way, but I never used profanity. I just leaned on dealing with them through the process. This gave me a way to vent my frustration, anger, and feelings of injustice. But you need to understand; I had to give my wife the strength and the hope that all she was doing—sticking with me, believing with me in God—wasn't in vain. That was my goal.

YPM

You wound up back at Graterford SCI, now called Phoenix SCI. You connected with Yokefellowship Prison Ministry, which is the ministry we're both involved in currently. How did you make that connection with YPM?

Freddie

I was involved in the church at Huntingdon SCI. Friends said, "Chaplain John Rush is starting a program called Yokefellowship. We can go down, fellowship, and talk about the Bible and stuff." But I was transferred from Huntingdon to Pittsburgh. I did get a chance to talk to John Rush a couple of times while at SCI Pittsburgh. When I went to SCI Somerset, a good friend named Victor told me we got to go to the Yokefellowship program. When I went, I was introduced to Fred and Mike, who were volunteers. The services were beautiful. We talked, we shared. Then we broke up into small groups and discussed the message and what we got out of it. After I had attended for four or five months, Fred gave up his time and allowed me to develop a message to give to church participants. That's when I began to believe that I had a mission within Yokefellowship.

We had services on the blocks, encouraging guys to come every week. If we didn't have 50 or 60 guys attending YPM at Somerset, we didn't have any. So we were always packed with guys coming to our services.

When I was at SCI Greene, I involved myself in church. Pastor Harris and I became really good friends. She allowed me to work for her in the chapel, develop talks, do some singing, and be a church assistant. I was reading the Bible on my own, studying with some people in the prison when we were out on the blocks. Then I got a transfer to SCI Houtzdale. My involvement became extensive because we had services for an hour and a half. I met different people that came in. Houtzdale was another place where we had a lot of people coming to our services. I earned a meritorious transfer back to Graterford in 2010.

My first mission was the church. A couple of friends of mine were worship leaders for a Yokefellowship program led by Pastor William Jones at Graterford. A year or so into my participation, I was asked to be a worship leader. We had some time when seven or eight guys took the opportunity to testify and talk about what they got out of what Pastor Jones had preached or taught. I told Susan, who was living in the Norristown area at the time, that if ever I got out of there, I would like to get in touch with Pastor Jones.

Low and behold, in 2012, the United States Supreme Court ruled that giving a juvenile the sentence that I received, life without the opportunity for parole, was unconstitutional. The court made the decision retroactive, so it applied to everybody sentenced before 2012. So I went down in November 2017 and got a new sentence of 48 years, time served. I was finally able to make it out on January 17, 2019.

YPM

Now you are the regional chairperson for the Delaware Valley Area Council of Yokefellowship Prison Ministry, and you're serving as a director-at-large on the state board. You're trying to give back. How did that happen? How did a man who remembers celebrating Christmas with his family twice and who spent most of his life without physical freedom become a person who wants to give back and wants to help others? How did God get you where you are today?

Freddie

When I was in prison, I got educated and believed I had a voice. I could restructure the things that I knew I had done in my life that were wrong. I was a selfish person. I spent years away from my sisters and brothers. I had three younger brothers die. Some of them never got to be 25. That made me think of myself as selfish because I couldn't be there and maybe help them live a different kind of life, to see life differently.

But when I look at it, I know I didn't have anything to offer if I would have been on the streets with them. I don't know if I would've done the same thing. Would I have been in the same predicament that they were? I wasn't educated. I didn't have a voice. I didn't even know what I could do. Could I do anything other than steal and take things from people? Maybe work an honest job here and there? But I didn't know how to hold a job down. So, I grew up in prison, and I discovered I had a different life to live in my growing up. I had a better life to live. I had a life that I was capable of living. I had a wife that I was committed to.

I had friends that had been in my life since the time I entered Graterford. I had friends that had stuck with me for years. Praise God. I thank God for all the years He gave me my friend, Linda. She died in October. This woman was a part of my life from 1972 until the day she died. She was there at the gate for me when I got out. She was a friend of my wife for over 30 years. The Yokefellowship program gave me an avenue. It taught me God would level the playing field. God will work things out. God will open doors for you.

God will make people forget that you ever did anything wrong. For me, it was a clear choice. You understand that I am now modeling what I know God calls us to do. That's to be unselfish, that's to be caring, that's to be social, and it's to be supportive. It is to give your last coat or shirt if you can do without it. Give it to the person who needs it. And that's where I'm at. Yokefellowship gave me this opportunity. Pastor Jones called me as soon as I got out.

I remember John Rush, the Eastern Regional YPM director, visiting our weekly Yokefellowship meeting in the chapel. Pastor William Jones, our long-time leader, told me he had gone to lunch with John Rush and had been offered the position as YPM Eastern Regional Director. Pastor Jones said he wanted me to work with him when I got out. We had done so much over the eight years at Graterford. It was an easy choice for me. It was like God extending the olive branch saying, "Here's what I got for you. Do you understand? I prepared you for this. I want you to take this and run as my ambassador and disciple to the people."

And that's where I'm at right now. I don't do everything perfectly. I don't think any of us do. But I believe God has given me the gift to recognize the needs of people. Some of these needs are based on my own experience. I know guys need places to live. Even though I didn't need a place to live, there were obstacles. I can now try and transpose that information to other situations. I realize that when people come home, they might run into obstacles with housing or other circumstances. I'm saying they might run into the obstacle of not having a proper ID.

They might run into obstacles relating to transportation, not having anyone to transport them to the places they need to go for medical care. So many other things, all wrapped up in this charity work that is Yokefellowship Prison Ministry. That is giving God's message.

YPM

Well, who's better qualified than you to speak to returning citizens. You have credibility, Freddie. God can use you because you gave yourself to God. You accepted Christ, and God is using you for something greater than yourself. It's an honor to interview you. Your transformation is a victory for the Kingdom of God. Thank you on behalf of all the rest of us who have been free during those 49 years while you were incarcerated in correctional institutions. You know what prison is. You know what physical prison is and what spiritual prison is. You know what it feels like to be physically free. But more than that, you know what it feels like to be spiritually free. "Therefore if anyone is in Christ, the old has passed away, behold the new has come. All this is from God, who through Christ reconciled us to himself and gave us the ministry of reconciliation." (2 Corinthians 5:17-18) You are a new creation.

Thank you, Freddie, for being the disciple that you are. Your life is a story of God's amazing grace.

John Freddie Nole
Chair, Delaware Valley Area Council, Yokefellowship Prison Ministry
Meeting at the Door
nolejohn346@yahoo.com

Biblical Reflection

Seventeen-year-old Freddie Nole pointed a plastic toy gun at an old man he and his friends were robbing, and that man ran after Freddie and his friends. The store owner had an aortic aneurysm and died the same day. Freddie hid from the police for seven months but received a life sentence after his arrest.

Life is a gift from God, and each life is connected to other lives. The man who died had family and friends who loved him. Contributing to the loss of another's life is a very serious offense, deserving severe consequences. Even so, reasonable people could question whether life imprisonment without parole was a just sentence for Freddie.

As a young boy and a teenager, Freddie knew that "we all have a sense of right and wrong," but he had been getting away with doing wrong. He had "...no problem taking risks to do things for my family and my neighborhood. Risk taking was a badge of honor." Freddie was not committed to the "Word of God" or the commands of God. So how did Freddie emerge from 49 years of incarceration with a love for God, a grateful heart, an optimistic spirit, and a passion for helping others?

While Paul was in prison, he wrote one of his letters to a dear Christian friend and a fellow worker named Philemon, a Roman citizen and Christian who had a house church in Colossae. Philemon owned a slave named Onesimus who had run away and made his way to where Paul was in prison. Onesimus ministered to Paul and became indispensable to him. Under Roman law, the punishment for a runaway slave was death. But Paul prevailed on Onesimus, the runaway slave, to return to Philemon despite the risk that he might be arrested and executed. Paul wrote the New Testament letter, Philemon, so that Onesimus could give the letter to his master when he returned.

In his prison letter, Paul asks not only that Philemon forgive Onesimus but that he accept Onesimus no longer as a slave but as a "true Christian brother!" Paul writes confidently, knowing that Philemon will do this. In verse 11, Paul plays with the name Onesimus which means useful. "Formerly, he was useless to you, but now he has become useful both to you and to me."

Freddie Nole thought of himself as a useless person, a selfish person. While he was in prison, three of his younger brothers died before they reached 25. He could not help them or his family. But one day, while sitting in a prison chapel service, Freddie heard God say these words just loud enough for him to make out, "Alright, I'm ready for you now. Now is the time I want you." Freddie came forward and accepted Jesus Christ as his Lord and Savior and was baptized. God kept sending people to minister to Freddie in prison as Onesimus had once ministered to Paul, and Freddie ministered to those incarcerated with him.

If Freddie had never received his physical freedom, his life in prison would have been useful, meaningful, and joyous because he had received his spiritual freedom. But now that he is physically free, his ministry has expanded. And as Onesimus, a runaway slave under a death sentence, became a brother to his one-time master Philemon, Freddie Nole has become a useful brother to his family, community, and Yokefellowship Prison Ministry.

Chapter 2
Keith Rodrigues

Keith Rodrigues was from a stable home in a Colorado town. Keith went to school, served in church, played sports, and learned a trade. But he came within a few feet, a few seconds of causing death and destruction to others and killing himself or causing his long-term incarceration. It was his addiction to drugs and alcohol that came ever so close to ushering Keith through the gates of Hell.

YPM

Where were you born and raised, Keith, and who was your family? Please describe the kind of life you had when you were young?

Keith

I was born in 1957 and raised in Pueblo, Colorado. My mother and father had 13 children. I have seven brothers and five sisters. We grew up in the Catholic church and went to a Catholic school for eight years until it closed. I was an altar boy. All of us got confirmed, I guess cause that's what people do at church.

YPM

Were you taking your faith seriously or just going through the motions?

Keith

As an altar boy, you had to get the wine and water ready. And back in the day, it was real wine. It wasn't grape juice. And I was drinking the wine. So I grew up as a Roman Catholic, but I was going through the motions.

I had really good parents. They taught us how to work. When we got our first paycheck, they'd take us to the credit union and open an account for us. Then we had to give my mom a little bit of money for food and the rest we could put away for clothes.

They taught us the right way. I had a good life as a child playing baseball and stuff. And then, in junior high, I started using alcohol and drugs. Our family would get together for Christmas. There was always alcohol, but it was not abused. The adults would have their drinks, and we kids would always have a little wine or beer; I guess they thought that was cute. I started hanging out and playing sports quite a bit. I met new people and got involved with marijuana. I continued smoking marijuana through high school.

After high school, I moved to Dallas, Texas, with my brother for three years. I started getting into alcohol and different kinds of speed and crack and acid. I was working and doing drugs.

As life went on, everything increased—the alcohol, the drugs, the experiments with different drugs. My alcoholism grew out of control there. My drug use kept growing when I moved back to Colorado, and I got hooked up with my old buddies and started getting into more trouble. I spent a weekend in jail and got arrested a couple of times. At this point, I'm addicted to drugs and alcohol. This is how life is now. The abnormal became normal.

YPM

You did not feel like addiction was a problem for you at that point. So what were you doing for a living?

Keith

I was doing cement work, the same thing I do today.

YPM

So you're getting into your addiction, but it's just how life is. It's all normal for you.

Keith

When I was in Texas, it was so bad that I wrecked the car and left the scene of the accident. I met a priest on the way back to the house, and I asked him to pray for me; he prayed for me, and he was trying to help me, but I wasn't ready for help.

YPM

So warning signs are emerging, but you're just not recognizing the signs.

Keith

I had wrecked a car in Colorado before I left, so I moved to different places, but my life did not change.

YPM

You spent a weekend in jail. Why?

Keith

I got caught drinking and driving.

YPM

So what came next in your life?

Keith

I continued on that path for quite a while and just survived. I got caught by the law a couple of more times in Colorado and spent a little more time in jail. And every time I got caught, I'd say, "Oh boy, I'm going to stop." And as soon as I got out, it was back to the same old routine, on that cycle, on that merry-go-round. I couldn't get off by myself. I was working in the precast yard, and then we built a 14-story high rise, and we finished that up, and my sister who had moved east came to visit us. Since I was laid off because we finished that building, she said, "Why don't you come out and help me move?"

Her husband was an HVAC man for the nuclear plants in Pennsylvania. So I said, "Sure." So I went out and helped them move.

Later we moved from Berwick, Pennsylvania, down to Exeter. And then I saw all the jobs out there, and I told my mom to send me my tools. So I've been in Pennsylvania since 1980. I continued my drinking and met guys who brought me to some of the local clubs, and we signed up to the clubs and found a good connection to get pot and crack and coke.

I had all kinds of guys offering me drugs. I'm back in the same old cycle. You can run away from home, but that doesn't change your life. So I started getting in trouble. I got caught driving under the influence and spent a couple of weekends in jail. And then I spent 90 days in Lancaster prison. I met some guys out here who knew a lot about drugs, and I grew some of the best marijuana in my basement. That was just crazy now that I think of it because if I ever got caught, my wife Deb would have gone to jail too.

YPM

So now you are married. Tell me about that?

Keith

I met my wife at a bar, and we went together for about eight months and then married.

YPM

And you're still married to Deb?

Keith

Yes, we are. We went through the fire together. I just praise the Lord that we're still together.

YPM

What were the charges when you went to Lancaster County Jail for three months?

Keith

The charges were driving under the influence and giving a false report. I said I was my brother because I already had several convictions. So I lost my license for three years, and I had to walk everywhere. Before I got married, my sister and her husband moved to Arizona. My addiction and alcoholism were very bad. I was homeless. I was sleeping in my truck.

After work, I'd steal a sandwich from Turkey Hill, and then I'd go to the club and get some alcohol in me, get some drugs in me. And then I would fall asleep at the barn near where we worked so I wouldn't be late for work. I was in that cycle for a while. After working for a while, I got a room and lived in a motel for a year. I got so far behind on rent because of my addiction and alcohol that I was evicted. Finally, the bar owner rented me a room above the bar. I was in my addiction pretty bad, but I paid him all the time, and he never kicked me out.

Shortly after I started living above his bar, I met my wife. And then we fell in love. We had our addictions together. We would meet at the bar. We both drank, and we both did drugs. She didn't do a lot of the pot. She did the coke and crack and heroin and everything else. There wasn't a drug out there we didn't do.

It got so bad that I washed my breakfast down with shots of tequila. I wasn't raised that way. It was crazy. I'd walk into the bar after work. I was timid, but after a few beers, I was just as wild as could be. And then it got worse, and we would drink as much as we could. You got known for drinking and drugs, and I got in a lot of trouble. We'd go to every party. Then one day, I asked my mother-in-law and my wife to go for breakfast at the club, and we did.

I washed my breakfast down with tequila, and then we took my mother-in-law home, and my wife and I went to another couple of places. And then, by lunchtime, we went to another place, and there were a couple of stools open at the bar with a guy sitting in between. By this time, we had done a couple of lines of coke, a bunch of pot, and a bunch of shots. And I asked the guy to move over, and he said he only moved over for White people. I was in no shape to be told nothing like that. So I threw my beer glass on the ground, and then they threw me out for disturbing the peace and public drunkenness.

Then somebody heard what the guy who would not move said, and they gave him a ticket for slander. But I wasn't satisfied with that. So I went to one of my Native American buddies, and we drank some more, which was about 3:00 or 4:00 in the afternoon. I dropped my wife off. I went home, and I got five of those one-gallon Prestone antifreeze containers. And I ran to the gas station, and I filled them up with gas. And I went back to the establishment that I got thrown out of. And I put one in the front seat with me. I had a little Chevy pickup truck at that time, a little five-speed, and I put four in the back seat. And I was probably about 15 feet from the doors into this fire company bar.

I poured a gallon of gas all over the front seat with me in it. And then I lit it on fire. And I drove into the building, but that wasn't God's plan for me. The pickup just bounced back off the doors, and the next thing I knew, I was outside the truck. The pickup windows were rolled up, and I was on the outside just smoking. The building never caught fire.

I was burned but not that bad. I was smoking; I was on the ground, and then I ran, and they caught me, and they took me to the hospital and handcuffed me to the bed and tended to my burns. Then they took me to the county prison. They gave me one phone call, so I called my wife, and she had already heard what had happened. So they kept me in the hospital unit for several weeks until I was healed up.

And that's when I met Reverend John Rush because he would come down to the hospital unit, and he'd always say, "Hey, I'm never in a Rush. How are you doing? What do you need? You need a Bible?" And I said, "Boy, I need a Bible." So that was the first time I met Reverend Rush. And so he brought me a Bible, and I started reading my Bible.

As I was getting better, I met a guy going to the same maximum-security unit, and we became pretty good buddies. He had been in and out of prison. He knew the ropes, so I stayed with him. When it was getting close to the time to go to maximum security, I was really scared. I'm figuring I'm going up there with all these crazy guys who have murdered, raped, and robbed. And then I thought about what I did, and I was just as bad as them. So they took me into maximum security, and I started doing my time there. I would go to Bible studies, and I started going to church.

YPM

Were you using drugs when you were in prison?

Keith

No.

YPM

So you're sober for the first time in a long time. How did you get through detox?

Keith

Just by the grace of God. God stepped in. I always quote Jeremiah 29:11-13. "'I know the plans I have for you,' declares the Lord, 'plans to prosper you and not to harm you, plans to give you hope and a future. Then you will call on me and come and pray to me, and I will listen to you. You will seek me and find me with all your heart.'" God says, "I will listen to you; if you look for me, you'll find me. If you seek me with all your heart." Well, I started trying to do that. I knew what I was supposed to do because I had grown up in that kind of family, and I had good parents. They taught me right from wrong. I just couldn't make the right life choices.

YPM

So at this point, you are feeling that you need God. You need an answer. When offered a Bible, you knew you needed a Bible. You're getting more serious about your spiritual journey. You say I need deliverance from this lifestyle, and only God can save me. You are in a huge mess. You are in maximum security.

Keith

I'm looking at facing murder charges, attempted murder, aggravated assault. They have everything on me. I'm looking at 20, 30, 40 years in prison, and I have no money. They tell me I need to go through all these programs, and the guys are saying, "You gotta go through these." These are the inmates telling me you got to go through these programs to make it look good for you, for the judge. So I started going to Bible studies. I met Reverend Rush, the head chaplain at the Berks County Prison, and the people from Yokefellowship Prison Ministry a few more times.

Before I went to prison, I would get paid on Friday. And sometimes, I would stop at the bar, and I wouldn't come home until all my money was gone. I was married, and my wife and I were fighting. It was just terrible. Sometimes I wouldn't even know where my truck was. Sometimes my truck was halfway in the driveway, and sometimes I didn't know where it was.

YPM

You are in prison and facing very serious charges. But you are sober and turning in a better direction. What about your spouse, Deb? Was she still drinking and using drugs?

Keith

Yes, she was. She was still doing her thing. I never had the chance to talk to her about the right way.

YPM

So you're forced into sobriety, and Deb was in the same old pattern at home. Was she able to visit you?

Keith

Yes, and I'd call her. She would be hammered, and she would be passed out. The only lifestyle we knew was drinking and drug abuse.

YPM

You're going to all the Bible studies and the programs to make it look good for the judge. And then what?

Keith

I have to get a lawyer, and I'm not sure exactly how it happened, but I ended up getting one of the best lawyers in Berks County. And at that point, my family got some money together to pay the attorney. I went to the preliminary hearing, and they read off the charges I am facing, including attempted murder, which scared me. So they took me back to prison, and I started figuring out what I was going to do, and then my mom came from Colorado with some money. It was one of the worst moments in my life when my mom came to one of the hearings and saw me in my prison outfit, all shackled up—what a terrible, terrible feeling.

YPM

I can't imagine.

Keith

It was just the most devastating, shameful feeling. After everything, your mom and dad did for you, this is what you did to them.

YPM

Terrible. But your mother was still there for you.

Keith

My mom's still around. My dad was still alive at this time. So we kept going on. The attorney was supposed to make a deal for me, but he found out my dad owned a tire shop and wanted more money. And I said, "No, you're not going to take my dad's tire shop from him." So he quit fighting for me. But I started going to all the programs, and I had a chance to go to the ADAPT program (Alcohol and Drug Abuse Prevention and Treatment Program). That was one of the hardest programs to get into when you're in maximum security. But I wasn't ready to change. So I went over there, and they gave me like three pages of rules. And I said, "I'm not following these rules." So I said, "You might as well take me back to maximum security where all I have to do is sleep and watch TV." So people thought I was crazy because I didn't want to go through that program. But I kept going to the Yokefellowship meetings—that's where I met a lot of good guys.

YPM

So Yokefellowship volunteers are visiting you in prison and leading Bible studies. You are physically in prison and a prison of your own making. You're going to Yokefellowship Bible studies and meeting Yokefellowship volunteers. You are seeking what is right. But there's a part of you that's still resisting—you're not going to follow three pages of rules. So what changes your thinking, what happens?

Keith

I couldn't understand how God could forgive me. They kept saying. God will forgive you. If you want this new life, come up for the altar call. So I went to like 13 altar calls. I wanted the blessing but not the God. And so I'd go up for the altar call, and I'd feel good for about an hour, and then after that, the old Keith was back. I just wasn't ready to change. So when I went to that ADAPT program, it was the same thing. I wanted the blessing to make the judges see that I was trying. I just wanted it to look good.

I wasn't ready to change, and I couldn't get past that hump. I was in maximum security for about 12 months. I was there for such a long time they had to reclassify me and send me to medium security. I continued going to Bible studies and going up for altar calls. But I wasn't ready to change. During this time, my wife would come and visit me. Sometimes I don't know how she got to visit me because she came in drunk, hammered like crazy. And then when I'd call her, she would still be drunk, and it was wearing on me.

I couldn't do anything for her, and I didn't do anything for her, and then I got another opportunity. One night I was in my cell in J block. And I started reading my Bible, and then I fell on my knees, and I asked God to forgive me my sins. This is about midnight. I said, "Lord, forgive me my sins." And I confessed all my sins, when I was a little boy stealing money from my mom's purse and my dad's change can, stealing candy bars from the store, all my dirty sexual sins as a young man and older man. I repented of every sin that I could remember, and I asked God; I said them out loud.

And I said, "Forgive me for these sins and the sins I don't remember." And I remember being on the floor in the cell crying like a baby in the fetal position. And that was the night that my life changed. You're all by yourself in the cell, and nobody else is there. It is only God and me.

YPM

You're praying out loud. Are you praying loud enough that other people can hear you?

Keith

I couldn't tell you. I was talking like I'm talking to you. I was talking out loud and with such emotion that it just wore me out. It was just a changing point because then the Lord sent the Holy Spirit upon me. And that night was the best night of sleep that I ever had. So I gave my life to God. I slept like a baby in my prison cell.

YPM

You had years of addiction and resistance to change. And it's difficult for you to believe that God could forgive you, but it turned that night. So what made you free that night as you prayed out loud? You were still physically in prison, but now you felt spiritually free?

Keith

It was that night of genuine repentance. Yeah, that night. And then I started seeking God instead of just seeking his blessing.

YPM

You were honestly and humbly pouring out your sins to God, and you believe that's how you got free of the addiction and the attitudes that were binding you?

Keith

I know that's how because I could feel the Holy Spirit on me. I'd never felt that before.

YPM

What did it feel like to "have the Holy Spirit come on you"?

Keith

It was just like a whole weight came off me. It was just different. I can't even explain it. A whole weight came off my shoulders. It was just like somebody pulled a truck off me.

YPM

When Jesus says, "For my yoke is easy, and my burden is light" (Matthew 11:30), maybe that's what He means?

Keith

Oh, man. I remember quoting that verse. I remember quoting that verse.

YPM

So now you're a new man. You've got the same outward circumstances, but you're a new person in Christ. What happens next?

Keith

Then I had a chance to go back to the ADAPT program, but this time I went back with the Lord, and I finished the program early, and I became a leader. I was allowed to go outside the prison for the work-release program during the day. I was going to get sentenced, but everything was moving very slowly. Finally, my court date was coming up, and my attorney said, "I need to meet you. I need more money." I said, "Nope, whatever I'm going to get, I'm going to get." And they worked out a deal where I had to spend two years in prison and have five-year state parole.

YPM

Say that again. How long did you spend in prison?

Keith

Two years. Then they gave me five-year state parole. So I got out the week before Christmas 1996.

YPM

You were facing attempted murder and all those other charges.

Keith

I was looking at the chance of getting 20 years. But Reverend Rush said, "With the nature of your crime you don't have a chance, buddy."

YPM

So what do you think? How did God do it? Do you think the judge concluded that you were not a bad person at heart but an addicted person who had made a good turn?

Keith

I can't explain how God did it. Before I was able to go to work release, I was working in the greenhouse yard, where there was more temptation. In prison, you have the addictive behavior where you are trading things. You start saving your coffee. Your coffee was like your drugs. Your dinner was like your drugs. You had the same drugged-out behavior in there as you did on the outside. You were using different items, coffee, food, laundry. Whoever was doing laundry, they can do your laundry four times a week instead of once a week, and you're trading favors instead of drugs.

But when I went to the work-release program, I worked in a greenhouse. I hadn't felt dirt for a year and a half. Before prison, I was in the dirt every day. So I just started throwing it in the air. I said, "Wow, isn't this great!" And then a construction company needed help, and by the grace of God, I got on that. I can't tell you how God did it, but these circumstances started happening. After that night in J block, I dedicated myself to the Lord, I changed.

I quit cussing. I would quit cussing for 30 seconds. And then I went to a minute and then two minutes and then five minutes and then 10 and then 20. That's how I quit cussing. And people could see the change in me. And then I read my Bible. I stayed in my room, and I read my Bible continuously, and they could see the change in me. And then I got out of all of those games, and I started living for the Lord. I wrote a prayer to the Lord, just thanking him. He could see I was genuinely changing. He was opening doors that could not be opened in any other way. When I was working for the construction outfit, I paid off all my fines, and I was able to send money home to my wife.

Then I met my pastor, Shelly Lee. He came in, doing Bible studies with Hillside Christian Church. We became friends. He was a good man. Then, they started a furlough program at Berks County Prison for the first time. I went to the classes, but the counselors and everybody said, "You're never going to get out of here on furlough because of the nature of your crime." But the judge signed my paper.

I don't know why he signed it. But the counselor came back and said, "You ain't going to believe this." The counselor who told me a month before that I would never see the outside came back and said, "The judge said, it's okay." Things like that happened, and I kept living for the Lord. I fasted. They give you a special dinner in prison for Thanksgiving and Christmas. Instead of having that special dinner, I fasted and spent my time in prayer. I prayed to God, "You've given me so much. I don't need this. I need to spend time with You."

YPM

How did fasting those special Thanksgiving and Christmas meals make you feel? How do you think that fasting helped you?

Keith

Nothing else in my whole life was satisfying me. I wanted the Lord to satisfy me!

YPM

You were changing. You said you gave up cussing. Some people might say, what's the problem with cussing? Why does that even matter? It's just how the world is these days. Why was it important for you to change the way you spoke?

Keith

Because it proved to the Lord that I'm living out His Word in my life, it says in James, how can sweet water and bitter water come out of the same mouth? (James 3:10-11)

YPM

You're becoming a new man. You're on the road of sanctification, not simply justification. You're becoming more like the person God created you to be, but what's happening with Deb? Are you growing apart because of this? Is she confused now?

Keith

She's still in her addiction, and I'm waiting for a green sheet to get out. And she says, "When you get your green sheet, I'll come to pick you up, but she was still in her active addiction because that's the only life we ever lived.

YPM

What effect were the changes in you having on Deb?

Keith

She couldn't believe my change was real. I had always used everything to manipulate her, so she thought I was using God to manipulate her. When I was in prison, Deb couldn't manage the house by herself, so a lady moved in to help Deb. But she took advantage of Deb. She was bigger than Deb, and she was more aggressive. She would take Deb to the bars, get Deb drunk, coked-up until she was in the blackout stages, and then take her home. She found where we had our credit cards, and she got Deb's PIN. She charged $5,000 on Deb's credit cards. She took our savings account down to nothing. She drained us financially. She threatened Deb physically. Deb couldn't get her out of the house. So we had this burden on us too.

It was getting time for me to get out. Deb was working the whole time and still in her addiction. But some of the guards there did not want you to get out because you're their 401(k). There were a few Christian guards who would bring you a scripture verse. But others would just laugh at you. They would tell me my green sheet was there, and then I'd get all excited, and they'd say, "I was just kidding." They loved playing those mind games with you. They would play games with urine tests. They would try to make you stumble. If I mess up, I'd have to go to the hole, which would be a new charge on me. And then I'd get some more time. They did that over and over to people.

YPM

But you were strong enough at that point not to fall for that temptation.

Keith

They almost had me one time. They threw my urine test away. I had to take another test without any water. And by the grace of God, I was able to take another test. There are so many unexplainable things that God moved that I cannot even explain. And then the day came to get out.

I called my mother-in-law, and I said, "Tell Deb to come to get me." And she said, "Well, Deb, can't come and get you. I'm going to come and get you. I'll tell you why later." I said, "No, tell me why now." She said, "I'll tell you why later." So we had an argument on the phone. I could feel the old Keith coming back up. Then she told me Deb was in rehab. So Joanie, my mother-in-law, came and picked me up and brought me home. Of all the people I knew before I went to prison, and I knew thousands, only one came to visit me. And not one person came over to ask Deb can they do anything for her. The only one who did come ripped us off and took all of our money.

YPM

You found out who your true friends were and who your true friends were not.

Keith

I was home alone that night. When I was in prison, I became friends with a real good man named Jackie Williams. He was from Reading Yokefellowship. He would come in so excited to preach about the Lord. He had also been delivered from a life of crime, and he gave us his testimony. I just really hit it off with him. I was sitting in the living room, it was about 8:30, and I had a choice—make dinner or go down to the bar and get a cheeseburger or call for prayer. Jackie Williams would always say, call me for prayer. That first night was such a battle. I called Jackie for prayer. I didn't go down to the bar. We prayed, and I made it through the first night.

Let me back up a little bit. When I was still in prison, I was able to get a weekend furlough. My wife came and got me on a Friday evening, and I had to be back Sunday evening, and I couldn't go out of the house. We were going to go to bed on Friday evening, and when we were lying down, my wife said, "I have something to tell you." And I said, "What?" She said, "I have been unfaithful to you." And I said, "Well, I forgive you because God forgave me." If it had been the old Keith in my addiction, it would have been a murder-suicide, and only the grace of God gave me that ability to give forgiveness. She heard it, and she accepted it that night. We just slept together. We did not get physical. We just went to sleep. She still needed to see that I was a man of my word and not the old Keith.

On one furlough, Shelly Lee, the pastor, baptized me, which changed the heck out of me. When I came up out of the water, I came up crying like a baby. So there was that night on the floor of my cell confessing my sins, and now my baptism was like another layer came off me, another weight. And when I came up out of the water, Deb was there, my mother-in-law and father-in-law were there. Our two best friends were there. I remember the pastor's wife singing. "Now I belong to Jesus, Jesus belongs to me," and I couldn't take it. I just broke down. And that was so special. That was August 10.

YPM
So, how did Deb wind up in rehab?

Keith
It was getting so bad, and her parents were talking to her too. After that lady had taken everything from us, her parents were helping out, and they put conditions on Deb. They said we want the best for you. She spent her 30 days in rehab. She came home, and she could see I was a changed man. After I got baptized, Pastor Shelly Lee told me, "When you get out, you can come to our church which is only five miles down the road."

The first Sunday was a battle. I got up, and I wanted to go to church. But the hardest thing for me to do was open the door and get in the truck. I drove to the church parking lot. The door on my truck felt like it weighed a hundred tons. I could hardly open the door. A voice in my head was saying, "They don't want you. They don't want no ex-con in there." I had a hundred reasons why I should not go in there. But I opened the door, went into the church, and sat in the back. The only reason I went in was that I knew that Jesus died on the cross for me. I couldn't tell you what was preached that day. I was so paranoid, believing everybody was looking at me. I remember I was supposed to give to the Lord when they passed the offering plate around; I gave $5.

One of the greatest things that helped me was that our neighbor was there. She was a little elderly lady; her name was Edie Pierce. She was a grandma. She had gray hair, and her health wasn't good, but she knew me before I went to prison. And when I got out, I would jump over the fence, and I'd go pray with her when I'd have my rough times. And God was sending her like an angel to me. So I would jump over a little two-foot fence, sit with her, and pray with her. And that was one of the best things that happened to me, having her as a neighbor. And I was able to help take care of her, feed her, and do many things for her.

God taught me and showed me a lot of things. The whole time I had this relationship with Edie, Pastor Shelly Lee was with me and helping me. We'd have communion with Edie. I kept going to church pretty regularly, and I'd asked Deb to go to church. But she said, "Nope, nope, nope." So I went to church for two and a half years by myself. And then Deb said, "I want what you have." She could see the peace of God in me.

YPM
Was Deb sober?

Keith
She had been working on it since I got out. By the time she said, "I want what you have," she was sober. So she came to church with me, and she got baptized, and her mom and dad were baptized. Then her best friend asked me to baptize her and her husband. I kept going to church. But I was so scared to give my testimony. I told God I didn't want to do that. I'm not going to do that. I heard so many people give their testimony in prison and out of prison.

Then it seemed that after they gave their testimony, they ended up back in prison, and that was the last thing I wanted to do. So I never gave my testimony. After a couple of years, Pastor Shelley asked me if I would say the communion prayer, and I said, "No." And the Holy Spirit said, "Yes, you will!" So I had to tell Pastor Shelly I would say the communion prayer. The leadership team watched me for a couple of years. Then they asked if I would be on the leadership team. I said, "Nope." But the Holy Spirit said, "Yes, you will!" So I told pastor Shelly, I'll be on the leadership team.

YPM

When you say, "They asked me to be an elder, and I said 'no,' but the Holy Spirit said 'yes,'" help me understand what you mean? So when the Holy Spirit says something to you, what do you hear?

Keith

It's a restless feeling. I feel like I am fighting him. I have no peace until I agree with the Holy Spirit. God took care of me, and now I'm saying "no." And I'm thinking, and I have a heavy weight on my shoulders. I want to move on, but the Holy Spirit wouldn't let me move on. His words were always in the back of my head.

YPM

So when the Holy Spirit fills you, the Holy Spirit is persistent. You knew it was the Holy Spirit when you knew you should do it, but you kept saying, "No, I can't." Remember how you said that the car door felt like so many tons? Was it Satan putting that weight on you, leading you to say no?

Keith

Right, but the Holy Spirit, He lifts a weight away from you, but He puts another kind of weight on you. He says, "You gotta do it my way, friend." He gives you that restless spirit to let you know when you're doing the best for the Lord. And when you're not doing the best for God, when you're doing something halfway right, He brings you all the way. That's when I fall on my knees and give genuine repentance to the Lord. There's no doubt. I know what the Holy Spirit says.

After I got out, I wanted to go back into Berks County Prison and give the guys what I had been given. So I went with Pastor Shelley and filled out all the paperwork. The first year they denied me because they had to do my background check. So the next year, we did it again. And they allowed me to go in. So I went in with Pastor Shelley Lee for about 14 years with the prison ministry. Some of those guys would try to play Pastor Shelly. He told them about God, and they were trying to play him and have him be a victim in their pity party. So when you come in from the outside and try to help them, the first thing they think is you don't know what it is like.

And then I said, "Well, let me tell you what I know. I sat in those chairs. I wore those uniforms. I would deal my French toast. I'd deal my turkey dinner." I said, "Let me tell you what I know." And so they would sit back and listen and not be able to think I did not know what it was like.

YPM

What did you say to the inmates when you told them what you knew?

Keith

I told them I lived my life. God always had his hand extended to me, and I was looking for everything else. I thought sex would satisfy me. I thought that alcohol would satisfy me. I thought a new car or money or drugs would satisfy me. But the only one who's satisfied me is Jesus. He said, "I am the way." So when you have the freedom to try all those other things, try me instead. And He never pulled His hand away from me. He just waited for me to grab it. And then He grabbed me, and that was the best thing and He never let go. And I have never let go since. It's been such a great thing, and I have such great men in my life. I'm so blessed. After we started living a different life, Deb had a couple of relapses, but I haven't, and it's only by the grace of God.

YPM

And Deb went through it all with you.

Keith

She went through the fire with me, but we're both living for the Lord now. Edie Pierce got worse, and she had relatives stealing all her money. So Edie asked if I would be her power of attorney. And I said, not without Pastor Shelly. So she transferred the power of attorney over to the two of us. We did everything for Edie. She could not see anymore, so we would feed her. Edie got sick with cancer and asked if we would stay with her. We helped her until she passed away.

God was refining me through this situation. I experienced God's goodness, his mercy. Pastor Shelly watched me grow and live my life and make the right choices. He was helping me. I had been going to church for about 10 years.

I was enjoying life because God was in my life. He was my life. And then my mother-in-law's best friend passed away. And we were all at the funeral home, and we'd been waiting for the minister for a long time, and my mother-in-law said, "Keith can lead the service. He does it at church."

The funeral director said, "What do you need?" I said, "Just give me a Bible." So he gave me a Bible, and I led the service. The Holy Spirit came upon me, and I did the service for her, and it went well. My neighbor was there, my neighbor's son was there, and he said, "You did such a great job." And then, when his mother passed away, her pastor was out of town, so I did that service.

Then another lady from Bolivia had a brain tumor, and she couldn't leave her house. Nobody from the big church where she attended would visit her. So I went and sat with her, and she told me her story. She asked me if I'd come back. So I went back, and I took communion to her. As she got sicker, I kept ministering to her and talking about the Lord.

Her family would come over and make food while I ministered to her, and they would listen, and when Clara passed away, they asked me to do her service. And then her sister Maria said, "Keith, will you continue to minister to us?" And I said, "Sure." So I got them Spanish-English Bibles, and we did Bible studies. I speak a little Spanish, and that helped. And because all these things were happening, they asked me to be an elder of the church. And I said, "No." But the Holy Spirit said, "Yes, you are!" So I told Pastor Shelly, I guess I'm going to be an elder of the church.

We have all these good men in church—lawyers, accountants, insurance men—and they wanted me, an ex-con. I couldn't get that through my head, but God said, "You do it; you need to do this." So I talked to Pastor Shelly and asked him how I could get ordained. He said, "Well, you've been doing pastoral work for the last couple of years." I said, "Well, I was just doing what God had put in my hands." And so he met with the board, and they ordained me on January 9, 2011. It's just been so unbelievable. I chose to be a drunk, and God chose me to be a pastor.

YPM
You got your freedom. You were on the floor of your prison cell and at the end of your rope, and you reached out for God's hand.

Keith
Yeah. I reached for the hand of God.

YPM

You confessed your sins and asked for forgiveness, and a weight was lifted. Then you were baptized, and another layer of sin and guilt was lifted, and you have stayed free. So you believe the way you have stayed free is by living your life for the Lord?

Keith

That's it, living your life with the Lord! He says, ".... apart from me, you can do nothing" in John 15:5.

YPM

Apart from God, we cannot maintain our freedom.

Keith

2 Corinthians 3:17 says, "Now the Lord is that Spirit: and where the Spirit of the Lord is, there is liberty." Liberty is freedom. I have to stay with the Holy Spirit. I need to have the Lord be a part of everything I do because He says, "Without me, you can do nothing." He's allowed me to exist. He's allowed me this freedom.

YPM

Here you are free and serving, and you could have spent decades in prison. You tried to drive your car into that bar and commit suicide and kill a bunch of other people. But instead of spending a lifetime in prison as an inmate, you have gone back to visit and to share what you know with inmates. You have witnessed to Edie and Clara and her family and so many others.

Keith

God has allowed me to go on the mission field in the Dominican Republic. We built a church five miles from the Haitian border. The first night we slept in an old dump. The following day, we got up and sang praise songs to God. I couldn't sing. I said, "Who am I to be here?" I cried again. I just cried like a baby. I said, "Who am I, Lord?" And so, I was able to go on about 15 mission trips. We were able to go down to Mississippi for Katrina relief. We made several trips down there. I go to the Crow Creek Indian reservation in South Dakota for a Native American church called Diamond Willows. We're going to go again this year and pour concrete for them. God has put such good men in my life.

YPM

You have stayed free by giving your life away. For example, you fasted instead of eating your Thanksgiving meal because you wanted God to be first in your life. You gave your life away when you found true freedom.

Keith

This is God's life, not mine. And that's why I say it's God's testimony, not mine. I keep my freedom because I'm doing this for God and not Keith. When I did it for Keith, I was killing myself, and now when I am doing it for God, I'm living.

YPM

It's been an honor to hear your story. Thank you very much for your time and for sharing your story. And please tell your wife Deb that we admire her for staying with you and for her victory.

Keith

All right. You got it.

Keith Rodrigues
Creator Craftsman Ministries
k04rod@ptd.net

Biblical Reflection

Jesus was traveling through Galilee with his 12 disciples and women who had been healed of various evil afflictions and illnesses like Mary called Magdalene; Joanna, the wife of Chuzra, Herod's manager; Susanna; and many other supporters. He was proclaiming the Kingdom of God, the way God wanted things to be, and the way, in God's time, things would be. (Luke 8:1-39) One day they sailed across the Sea of Galilee to the Gentile land of the Gerasenes.

As Jesus stepped on the shore, he was met by a crazy man, "a victim of demons," according to Luke. The man was naked and lived amongst the tombs in the cemetery. He experienced periodic convulsions. The authorities placed the crazy man under guard and bound him with chains and shackles. But he was out of his mind and would break the chains.

He screamed at Jesus, "What do you want with me, Jesus, Son of the Most High God? Don't torture me!" (Luke 8: 28b NIV) Jesus asked his name, and the reply was "Legion" because there were so many demons in him. Jesus gave the order, and the demons went from the man into the pigs, and the crazed pigs stampeded over the cliff into the water and drowned.

Word spread, and the people came to see what had happened and found the crazy man sitting at Jesus' feet, wearing clothes and making sense. Something miraculous had happened.

Keith Rodrigues would tell you he was no less crazy and possessed by demons than that crazy man who accosted Jesus. After doing his cement work each day, he would steal a sandwich from the Turkey Hill store to use all the money he had earned on drugs and alcohol. When Keith was drunk and high, he was offended by someone in a firehouse bar. So he turned his pickup truck and himself into a gasoline-soaked bomb. Keith was determined to destroy himself and the people in that bar as he crashed into the building. But God stopped that pickup truck and saved those lives.

And then, one night in a fetal position, weeping on the floor of a prison cell, Keith Rodrigues confessed every sin he could remember committing and every sin he committed but could not remember. And he gave his life to Christ and the Lord "sent the Holy Spirit upon me," and Keith "slept like a baby." And ever since, Keith has sat at the feet of Jesus, sober and in his right mind.

This prayer/poem written by Keith Rodrigues came out of the night he gave his life to God in his prison cell:

GOD'S LIFE IS IN ME

This life I am living is not my own.
It comes from the Grace of God who sits on His throne.

Each morning I wake up, I kneel down and pray.
And ask God to lead me thru this new day.

I thank Him and praise Him with all my heart and my soul.
I ask for His blessings of strength, guidance, and control.

You are in my mind, and my heart and my eyes can see.
That it is only thru You that I may be FREE!!!

Thank you, dear Lord, for putting peace in my heart.
For forgiving my sins and giving me a brand new start.

So at night, before I sleep, I kneel down and pray.
And thank God for bringing me thru another day.

So I lay down and drift off into my sleep.
I know my Savior is with me, and my heart is at peace.

So another night has come, and another day has gone.
So I sleep and wait for a new day if only my Father's will be done.

It is You who I live for and You that I need.
To strengthen and guide me, by your Blood, I'm FREE!!!

Chapter 3
Charity Sampsell

How does a well-known and respected small-town gal with a husband and children find herself as the centerpiece of a front-page scandal weeping in a prison cell? The answer is that small-town gals who are well known and respected with husbands and children are just as fallible, just as vulnerable when weakened by emotional pain, just as capable of giving in to sin as all the rest of us. What is most remarkable is the story of how the grace of God lifted and restored a sinner who was just about as low, as shamed, as powerless, and as done with God as a person can be.

YPM
Charity, how did you get started in life?

Charity
I'm 41 years old now, and I grew up in central Pennsylvania with my mom, dad, and younger brother. I've lived in this area since I was two years old. I have my roots here. School, church, family, and friends,

everything was grounded in this area, and that's just where we've always been.

YPM

What kind of a little girl were you, a tomboy or a girly girl?

Charity

I was a little of both. We grew up in the country, and as a little girl, I loved being outdoors. As I grew up into my high school years, I played field hockey and basketball and managed the boys' soccer and baseball teams. I was very much involved in church. I was involved in a youth ministry called "Campus Life." A Christian drama production group would go to various churches and perform, which I was active in for quite a few years. So sports and just being in that atmosphere were a big part of my life growing up. I also attended church camps and was surrounded by my friends most of the time. When I was 16, I started working and shopping a lot because that's what I wanted to do. So I was always very busy, whether outside or with friends or at church; I was always very social.

YPM

What kind of student were you? Did you like school?

Charity

When I was in elementary school, I got straight A's. When I was in high school (grades 7-12), the majority of the time, I was on the honor roll with A's and B's. I did get some lower grades as I got older and closer to graduating. I always wanted to get the perfect attendance award, and I never liked missing school. I enjoyed school. When I got older, my priorities started to change. I still wanted to do well, but I didn't put in the time to succeed that I did when I was younger.

YPM

Were you a middle-class family? Were there tragedies or difficult times in your childhood?

Charity

We were a middle-class family. My mom stayed at home with us until I was like 12. When I was 12, my dad lost his job. He had worked for a bakery in Williamsport, and they just shut down. So my mom started working. It didn't affect me that much. We lived out in the country. If we wanted to go somewhere, we would just ride our bikes where we could. I got my driver's license as soon as I turned 16. So I guess financially, my mom and dad went through a lot, but I never really knew how deep that went, from my perspective, life was pretty normal. We never went without, and I started working and bought a lot of things for myself.

YPM

Were you thinking about going to college or about going to work after school?

Charity

I always wanted to go to college. My mother worked at Bucknell University. Bucknell offered an opportunity. If an employee worked there five years full time, anybody in that family could go to college for free. But my mom had only worked a total of three years full time when I was a senior. I was unable to attend college after graduation. That was pretty disappointing for me because I did want to go to college. But, if I wanted to go, my parents said I had to wait two more years, and then I could. So after I graduated, I kept working. I was a manager at Wendy's, which was my first job. I worked there until I was 21, and that road led me down many other roads.

YPM

Tell me about some of those roads. What was your romantic road? Were you dating? Were you married?

Charity

I had boyfriends and dated different guys all through school. When I was growing up, I just wanted to be married. The thought of that was all I wanted. I remember from a religious standpoint that the year 2000 was coming, and everyone, everywhere, was preaching the world was going to be over. It put a fear in me that I would never get married. After I graduated high school, I started dating someone I had met through a friend. He was bad news. But I fell for everything that he said. He was not good or right for me. And I don't say this lightly because I don't like to say anything bad about people, but there was nothing good about him. Long story short, we dated, got engaged, and then married. I thought I could change him, and I thought that it could be great. But it was the complete opposite.

YPM

How old were you?

Charity

I was 19 years old; it was a year after high school. After we married, I got pregnant with my two boys. It was a time in my life when I did not seek wisdom or listen to any wisdom that I heard. It all happened so quickly.

YPM

How far apart in age were your boys?

Charity

My children are 11 months apart. They became my entire world.

YPM

So you're married with two little boys, 11 months apart. What happens next?

Charity

I left him. We were only married long enough for me to be pregnant twice. It was a really bad situation with lots of abuse and lots of cheating. And I didn't want my children anywhere near that type of life. And that's a type of life that I had never personally experienced before. I wanted my boys to experience a great life, not a crazy awful one. So I left with my two boys and became a single mom. I continued to work and took care of them myself for around three years. After about three years Ryan, a friend, and I started dating. He's been my husband for 15 years now. However, we were not always together through that time.

YPM

Tell me about Ryan.

Charity

In high school, I worked at Wendy's. Ryan had a girlfriend who worked at Wendy's when I was there. I met Ryan through her. He would visit his girlfriend, and we all became friends. As time passed, he and his girlfriend ended up getting married and then went through a divorce while my ex and I were going through our divorce. Through a phone call, one day, Ryan and I connected.

YPM

Did Ryan have children?

Charity

Yes, he had a little boy Tyler who is 18 now. Denzel is my oldest, and he's 20, and Dominic, my youngest, is 19. So they are all very close in age.

YPM

You said that you and Ryan were not together the whole 15 years. What happened?

Charity

I had separated from him a couple of months before I went to prison. We were not together.

YPM

Alright, so you're married to Ryan. How many years were there between the day you married him and when you went to prison?

Charity

Eight years.

YPM

You have the three little boys—Denzel, Dominic, and Tyler. Did Tyler stay with you, or was he mostly with his mom?

Charity

He was back and forth; he was actually with us more.

YPM

How old were the boys on your wedding day?

Charity

Denzel was 5. Dominic and Tyler were 4.

YPM

Are the three boys pretty good buddies?

Charity

They can be. The boys have all had lots of good times together. Denzel and Dominic have always been a little closer. They have a lot more in common. And they have a special bond as they have gone through different life seasons together. Overall they are good brothers and friends to each other.

YPM

So you're a single mom with two boys, and then you marry Ryan, and his son Tyler is with you quite a bit. So for eight years, you're together. What else were you working on at that time?

Charity

I went to college and became a dental hygienist. When I was in school, we got engaged, and I graduated a year after getting married. As soon as I graduated, I was offered a job. I liked being a hygienist and working in healthcare, and I liked only working four days a week. It was a good financial career for me, and it gave me the flexibility to be present as a mom for sporting events and school. So working and taking care of everybody was always important to me. Ryan and I also opened up a gym together in the latter part of those years.

YPM

So Ryan is very different from the first guy?

Charity

Ryan was very genuine in how he treated the boys and me. Ryan has always been amazing. He was very honest, dependable, hard-working, caring, and loving. He was very present and always provided. He was a helper, a coach, a teacher, and a committed husband.

YPM

How did you go from being a mom with these boys and wife to Ryan and a dental hygienist to a prison inmate? You had never been in trouble before. So this was a big shocker. Help us understand how that happened.

Charity

Let me back up a little. When Ryan and I were first dating, I had spent a lot of time in prayer because I didn't want to make any more relational mistakes. I prayed, "God, I really love this man. And I want to spend my life with him, but if this is not the best or not what you have for me, then I don't want to go down this road with him." And God was very clear in showing me—this is the way I have for you. So we got married, and it was good. And then it gradually changed. I think that both of us had a lot of growing up to do. We had never been put in situations that challenged us—if that makes sense. We were selfish and prideful and had issues to work on that we never had or even thought of before. We ended up fighting a lot. Sometimes blending families isn't easy. There were always those dynamics of trying to please everybody and trying not to play favorites. We had our challenges in parenting, and there were a lot of times that we just didn't compromise. We both just did it our way, which doesn't work.

As much as we wanted to be together and have some good times, we would work against each other. It wasn't just me, or it wasn't just him. It was both of us. And it just got worse and worse and worse—the fighting, the disappointments, the unmet expectations, the hurt feelings, the anger, the unforgiveness, the strife, and the heartache.

I would pray, "Please help me, Lord. Please help me because this isn't what marriage should be." I knew marriage was hard, but this was way too hard. As time went by and things got worse, I got to the point where I just felt so broken and hopeless. I've always been very independent. I've always taken care of myself and taken care of a lot of things. And in these moments, I was crying out to God, crying out, "I need You to help us! I need You to help me." And everything got worse. So in my desperation, I wanted my life to be good, I wanted all of us to feel loved—I remember quitting on God.

I walked away from God, and I said, "You know, I'm just going to do this on my own. I'll take care of myself because You don't care." And I just started to believe all those lies that God didn't care about me and that my family didn't care about me, and nobody cared about me. It was a very dark place—a gradual downward spiral.

YPM

You're in a spiritual struggle. You feel like God quit on you. So you quit on God. Am I putting words in your mouth, or is that fair to say?

Charity

That's correct. It was very spiritual for me because, in my heart and my mind, I always believed in God. I always believed God could do anything. I would cry out, "Why, why are You not helping me? Why are You not helping us?" But looking back, God was very much involved in our lives, and His heart was to help us. I just didn't know Him. I only knew about Him. So I didn't know how to connect all those dots. And I didn't know as much as I thought I knew in my immaturity and ignorance. There was a lot that I didn't know, and it was easy for me to believe the lies that He didn't care about us. I lived by what I saw rather than what I truly believed. What I thought I knew about God was wrong. God did care, and He did love me, but I didn't feel it or see it, so I didn't believe it.

YPM

So not only is there a break in your marriage, there's a break in your relationship with the Lord. Now you're alone, depending on your strength, your own devices. What happens next?

Charity

Sometimes there are just not enough words to describe what a person goes through. I was just at a really low point. And I was hurting during that time. I didn't reach out to anybody because I thought I could handle everything on my own. My son's friend had a rough life, so he spent a lot of time with our family. It was something else that I had put on my plate because I thought, "We'll take care of you because we're supposed to take care of people." My son's friend had a sister, and she began to come over and spend time with us as well. She was just as broken as I was, just at a younger age. I could somewhat connect with that because I knew how brokenness felt.

Nobody knew all the things I was going through, but it was so easy for me to recognize that in somebody else because I was walking that same path. I also had a problem with wanting to please and help everyone. She was around all of the time. In my attempt to help her, it was easier to be led down the wrong road because of where I was positioned spiritually and emotionally. Things went in the wrong direction, and we became sexual.

At that moment in my life, I didn't have anyone to turn to. I had dug myself into this big hole, and I had no idea how to get out. And this wrong direction only added to all of the hurt and the darkness that I was walking through already.

YPM

Let's get to this "way wrong relationship." How old was the young woman?

Charity

She was two weeks away from being 16. I was 35 at the time.

YPM

So the relationship is "way wrong." Did you know it was wrong as it was happening, or were you rationalizing? Was one part of you saying yes to the wrong, and the other part saying no? Were you out of sorts, or did it all seem right to you?

Charity

I'm trying to go back to that moment. I knew it was wrong. It was never right to me, never. It was wrong. I had gotten to a point where I thought that not one single person cared about me, not even God, and it was nice to be cared about. I always knew it was wrong, but it felt nice to be needed if that makes sense. I wasn't brought up that way. After it happened, I felt so stuck and paralyzed and remember thinking, "now what do I do?" So I lived numb and in a blur. It was like I was walking around dead.

YPM

Were you and Ryan physically separated or just emotionally separated?

Charity

We were physically separated. I had moved out, and my two children were with me.

YPM

So this "way wrong relationship" goes on. How is it discovered?

Charity

The girl had written me a note, and she asked me if I would write one back to her. And I said, okay. So I did, and her aunt found the note I had written. And then it got turned into the police, and that's when that whole ball started rolling.

YPM

Tell us about that ball and how it rolled. What did you hear next? Who did you hear it from first?

Charity

She told me what happened with her aunt. And then I think it was a week or two later the police called me in for questioning.

YPM

So you didn't get an attorney. You just went in and told them everything they wanted to know?

Charity

I didn't know how any of this worked. I didn't know what to do, and at this point, I had still not told anyone about what happened, so I was trying to figure it out on my own. I remember watching TV, and they would always read you your rights. That didn't happen to me. It was a very casual conversation at the police station. I remember the police knew that my children's biological dad lived in another state. And they used that as leverage to get me to talk. They said, "You're going to lose your kids," and all this stuff because the police had questioned everyone before me, so they knew a lot about my life before I had even stepped foot in the police station. I didn't know what to do. So I just talked to them for about an hour and a half. Terrified to lose my children, I started answering their questions and telling them what had happened. My victim and I had sexual intercourse, which I told them. I never hired a lawyer because I didn't know I needed one. After that day, maybe a month later, I ended up in jail. I had hired a lawyer, but obviously, I had said so much, and there was not much a lawyer could do.

YPM

You have given up your constitutional right not to incriminate yourself. You've told the truth to the police. You gave law enforcement what they wanted, and now you're behind bars. Is this big news in the community?

Charity

It was "ginormous" news in the community. It's a small country town, and we were very well known by everyone. Ryan and I owned our own business. The boys excelled in sports. So we were always everywhere with everyone. We were all very popular. So when everybody found out, their mouths just hit the floor. I bet there wasn't one person in town that didn't know what happened.

YPM

There's a separation in your marriage, and there's a separation in your relationship with the Lord. And now you're behind bars, and you're publicly humiliated. How did you deal with those blows, the physical imprisonment, and the emotional pain and shame? How did you cope? How did you manage when the doors locked behind you? How were you doing on the inside?

Charity

Before I got arrested, I was angry at God because I felt like He had let me down. Now being behind bars, I was really angry at God. Before I got arrested, I was praying, "Please make a way, just stop this, don't let this go in the direction that I fear, I don't want to go to jail!" You know, praying quick prayers and hoping that God would intervene and just shut it all down. So when that didn't happen, it just took me further in my emotions—more hurt and more anger. And I was in shock. I remember the very first night when they put me in the cell and shut the door, I thought, I will wake up, and this is going to be a dream.

I would cry all day and all night, all day, all night. And I know in those moments, I know that He carried me because I can't even describe in words what it was like because it was so bad. It was awful. I was in shock that my life had gotten to this point, and in the beginning, I was so mad. I remember my mom came in to see me one of the first weekends of my jail time, and she said, "Just run to God." I said, "No, I will not." If He thought I was done with Him before, I'm really done with Him now.

It was just total despair. You can't describe it. I would just cry; I didn't open my eyes for days because they were swollen shut from crying. That was probably the first two and a half months that I felt that way.

YPM

It is understandable during those two and a half months if you are thinking about yourself. You have committed a crime and are imprisoned, and there's publicity. What were your thoughts about your mom and dad, your brother, your boys, Ryan—was that crossing your mind at that time? Or were you in such shock and survival mode that you blocked that out? Were those kinds of thoughts already churning inside you?

Charity

I thought about my children 24/7. I had never been away from them at all, not for a moment. The only time I was away from them would be when they would spend the night at my mom's or a friend's house.

So they were my whole world. And being a mom, I'm the one who was supposed to protect them the most in this life. And I ended up separated from them and hurting them. And that was a really big load to bear. Some days I don't know how I bore it. That was the worst part of this whole journey. That was the worst part, letting them down and hurting them and my family as well. In the beginning, I blamed Ryan too and said, "If you would've just been there for me more and loved me better, we wouldn't be where we are." I had a lot of anger and resentment towards him.

My brother cried a lot when I was arrested. I knew that he was one of my biggest supporters. My mom was very embarrassed and very humiliated. And we already didn't have the best relationship at the time. My dad, my dad's great. He was there every second, every step of the way. So I would talk to him all the time, and he would come to visit. So there were different levels of emotions concerning everybody at that time, but it wasn't all about me. I couldn't believe any of us were walking through this mess because of me.

YPM
How does the legal process continue?

Charity
The first lawyer we hired hoped that everything would get dismissed because they found loopholes and little spots where they thought things would change. But I wasn't going to lie. I wasn't going to do that. So we ended up firing him, and then we hired somebody else, and it was a huge battle against me.

So it was never an easy process. They wanted to throw the book at me as hard as they could. So it always felt like it was an uphill battle. There was a lot of going back and forth with the new lawyer and many delayed court appearances for whatever reason. I was in county prison 15 months before I got sentenced. It was exhausting. It was harder because I would be in the news or the newspaper when I was going through those months when I was in county prison. And other inmates and other people in trouble were sent home with two months in jail or four months in prison for the same charges as me. And there I was going nowhere.

As I continued to sit in county prison, it was difficult as days turned to weeks and months and then a year. And the D.A. is still talking about giving me a lot of jail time. And I didn't understand why. Nothing is happening to all these other inmates. So it was very hard and very exhausting. But through that time, I had come back to the Lord, and I had been surrendered to Him. In these very tough moments, I was trying to stay hopeful and full of faith that when I did go to sentencing, I was going to get to go home.

YPM

Take us back to that first two and a half months. You were in shock. You were separated from God, separated from your boys, separated from your husband. How did you come back to the Lord? What happened in that year? What was your spiritual journey in prison during that year?

Charity

Well, my mom had mailed me some books, and she had sent me a Bible. I knew that I wasn't gonna make it without Jesus. So despite my attempt to do it on my own, I finally surrendered and said, "Fine, Lord, let's just do this." He was always a part of my life. There were times in the past I would drift away, but I always came back. So I knew that He was real, and I knew that He was with me and in me. I knew it would be a really smart decision to humble myself and run back to Him. And that's what I did because I knew even in my anger, I wasn't going to make it without Him, and I wanted to get home as soon as I could. So I said, "All right, we'll do this. We'll do this your way." And once I made that decision, I dove in. I grew up in church, and I had a relationship with Him. But it was different this time. There was much more urgency, and it became much more real. There was no other option for me, and there was nowhere else to try and turn. I had run out of options, and I'm just going to say it like that because He was the only one I truly had.

YPM

You say you humbled yourself. How did you humble yourself?

Charity

Instead of throwing my hands up at him and saying, "I don't need You," I said, "I do need You, and I need You to help me." It was me surrendering to Him and letting Him be a part of my life. It was letting Him back into my heart, into the places of me that needed His love and healing and touch the most. Our relationship was never on that deep a level before. The Lord had spoken to my heart eight months before, and He said, "I want to help you. I want your time. I want your affection." And I said, "Nope, I'm good." So now it was me running back to Him and saying I was sorry. It was letting Him love me and letting Him begin to work. And I gave Him my attention. I think that would be one of the biggest things next to my heart. I gave Him my attention.

YPM

We are in a time when sexual offenses are treated very seriously. Tell me about your relationship with your brother and parents and your family when you were in prison. What was your thought process? What was your attitude toward the person that you'd hurt? How were you working that out? Were you talking to God about that?

Charity

My intention was never to hurt anyone. That's not how my story was portrayed to the public. As you said, sexual offenses are treated on a different level. I remember praying that everyone who was involved, in some way, would be healed and that those that didn't know Jesus would find Him. I began to lean on my family for support and guidance, and we walked and talked through many things. In regards to the victim, I prayed that she would be okay. God knows everything, and He knows the ins and outs of everything that happened. I prayed that everybody would be OK, and I left it there. I didn't revisit it. I didn't go back to it. I just left it in God's hands and moved on. I didn't wrestle with the victim aspect of things. I was always so focused on my children, focused on my family, focused on God, and focused on coming home.

YPM

So would you say that the single most challenging thing for you was your separation from the boys, or was there something even more difficult than that?

Charity

No, no, it was them, it was them.

YPM

Did they come to visit you in prison?

Charity

They did, yes. My oldest didn't want to come a lot when I was in county prison, but he did. My youngest did want to, but it still wasn't a lot. They did not visit me in state prison; it would have been too hard. It was so far away geographically, and some significant time had passed, and they were so tired of me being gone. It would have been way too hard on all of us. But yes, being away from them was the absolute worst. That was the worst part of the whole thing.

YPM

What grades were they in at school?

Charity

They were in middle school when I was arrested, and everybody in town knew about it, so all their buddies knew.

YPM

So you're finally coming to the sentencing. Did you accept a plea bargain?

Charity

The sentencing day arrives, and I'm anticipating I can finally go home! And no, that doesn't happen at all! I accepted a plea deal of 2 to 10 years. At sentencing, I had already been in jail for 15 months. And while that time did count, I had more months to serve now in state prison. Those few months turned into two years, and I served a minimum of three and a half years. No one tells you at sentencing or prior of all the state programming and classes you have to take there. For sexual offenders, it takes a year and a half or two years to complete those courses. So I got sentenced to two years. I'd already been in prison for 15 months. But because you have to go through all the classes even to be considered for parole, my time just kept getting longer and longer and longer. And that was another hard thing for me. I never knew when I would get to leave because it's such a long, drawn-out process. I never knew when I would come home, which was horrific for me. I never had a physical date on the calendar.

YPM

So you didn't have a release date, and you're in state prison now. Was that when you first connected with Yokefellowship Prison Ministry?

Charity

When I first got arrested, I was in county prison for 10 months—an hour away from where I lived because they don't have a women's prison in my county. They did not have Yokefellowship there. But later, when I was taken to Snyder County Prison, a prison closer to my home, to attend court, I was able to connect with Yokefellowship there. YPM was also available in state prison.

YPM

What was the impact of Yokefellowship Prison Ministry on you? In Matthew 25, Jesus says when we visit those in prison, it is as though we visit Him. How did those Yokefellowship visits impact you?

Charity

The big impact on me initially was just the fact that they cared. I was very well known, I was very popular and had a lot of friends. But when I got in trouble, they all left. Everybody turned their back on me like they didn't know me; that was a hard pill to swallow. So my first experience with Yokefellowship was "Wow, these ladies are here, and they don't know me, but they accept me, and they support me, and they care about me." It was huge to know that they were there to help me, and they didn't even know what I had done, and they didn't even care. It was pretty awesome. I had never experienced that unconditional love before outside of the family.

YPM

So the heaviest burdens for you were separation from your boys and not knowing when you would get out. Did you ever come to any kind of peace with either of those difficulties or was there no peace until you had the boys in your arms and you were free?

Charity

There was always a part of me that had a huge belief in the greatness of God. And He walked me through that. So I started to see just how amazing He was and how great His love was for me. So in that process, He showed me in His Word the future that He had for my kids and me. So I walked in that. I was reading the Bible and praying and listening to church on TV. Spiritually, I knew that my relationship with my children would be better than when I left them. Faith began to rise in my heart even though I missed my sons. My daily walk had switched gears, and I knew that everything would be okay. I was still crying if I couldn't get them on the phone or if I couldn't be with them, but there was peace in me. I knew that everything was going to be okay.

Part of my journey with God was just trusting Him and trusting His Word, trusting that all His Word would come to pass and His promises over our lives were going to be true. It got easier. I went through a lot of disappointments, thinking maybe this month will be the month I go home, maybe this month? I've always believed in miracles. So that was a huge part of my prison walk. Maybe I'll get a miracle this week? God can do anything in a day. I was very intentional about trusting Him. I went through many disappointments, but He always picked me back up and kept me going. And there were times where He would tell me. You need to get up. And I listened. I just finally got over myself and knew that He knows best. So I trusted Him. I just trusted Him. It wasn't always easy, but He got us through. I knew His restoration for our relationships and the time we lost would be fulfilled!

YPM

You spent a lot of time incarcerated and got to know many other women inmates. What did you learn about those women, and what advice might you give to people who want to reach out to inmates or be helpful to inmates? Who were those women? They're all different. They're all individuals, but what did you learn about your fellow prisoners?

Charity

There were many women prisoners who never even knew that Christians existed. One woman said, "I didn't even know people like you even existed, people that just cared and would pray with you and would listen." So there was a majority of women who had never been exposed to someone else that loved the Lord, someone who belonged to Him. Most women want to be respected, and I don't always like to use that word because I think it gets thrown around the wrong way a lot. But I'll give you one example.

When I was in state prison, I would go down to the day room, where everyone could gather, from 8:00 in the morning till 11:30 in the morning. And I would watch TBN and the Hillsong channel. I would watch Christian worship and preaching every morning. And one day the other women had the TV on, but nobody was watching it. So I changed the channel. And one girl got cocky. She said, "I was watching that, and you just can't come down here and change the TV." I said, "I apologize, I'm sorry. I didn't think anybody was watching it. We can turn it back." And she said, "No, it's okay. I'm alright." I knew that they weren't watching TV. She just wanted me to respect her and ask her if I could change the channel even though she didn't care one way or the other. I think a lot of those women, they've just never been given that ounce of respect. She just wanted to be valued enough to be acknowledged.

Going forward, I was always very mindful of approaching everyone with respect. "Are you watching that," or "Are you using that?" They just want to be recognized. I think that so many of them have never experienced people asking, "How are you doing?" Or "What can I do for you?" So in my example, when I was ready to change the channel, she changed her tone and said, "Oh no, no, no. You can watch it." I was thinking, okay, you just really wanted to be asked. You wanted to be acknowledged. I think many of those women have just never been noticed or had anybody genuinely care about them, even in small ways.

YPM

Tell me if you think I'm right. So people come in from outside, and noticing inmates, caring about them, and listening to them is very powerful, is that fair to say?

Charity

Oh yeah, because I think they grow up in places where they don't matter to anyone, or they matter for the wrong reasons. I tried to be very intentional in my approach. Not one person the whole time I was gone ever gave me a hard time. And in those places, everybody knows what you're in prison for. It's easy for other inmates to treat people with my offense in a bad way. But I had God's favor everywhere I went, and even the ladies that would cause the most trouble would ask me if I needed anything. I think they've never been cared about, which explains why they seek attention and do whatever they need to do to get it.

YPM

You've traced how you became free spiritually, how you got reconnected with the Lord, but how did you get free physically? How did you get out of prison?

Charity

When my minimum was up and I was able to see parole, I wasn't done with my sexual offenders class, resulting in a parole denial. I had to wait until that was completed, and then I had to go through the whole parole process again, which took another six or seven months after my minimum. After seeing parole for the second time, I waited three more months for them to give me their decision. I got paroled. But another thing that they don't tell you is that when you have a sex offense with minors, you can't live with minors. Even though I was paroled and able to leave prison, I couldn't come home and be with my children, which of course, was another blow. So that prolonged my being released even more because my children lived with my mom and dad. And I had to find another place to live.

I tried a couple of other home plans but got denied. I finally ended up going to a center in Williamsport. My two years minimum turned into three and a half years. Then my children ended up moving back home to Ryan's, which allowed me to move in with my mom and dad. It took almost a year to be released after I saw parole the second time and to get home.

YPM

You're living with your folks, and the boys are with Ryan. What did it feel like being free from prison but still being separated from your boys?

Charity

It was not easy. I trusted God that He was going to bring us all together. I could go to church and see my children there, but I couldn't even wave to them and say hello. It was awful. It was pure torture to be home finally, and yet I couldn't even smile at them because no contact was allowed. But God gave me the strength to go through every day to make it until we could be together. I wouldn't have lasted without

Him, for sure. It was just a daily surrender to Him and trusting Him and believing Him, and letting Him carry me on the days where it was just so hard.

YPM

Where are you today? How did you get to where you are today? You're back with Ryan, and the boys are with you. How long did it take from the time you got out and were living with your folks until you and Ryan and the boys are reunited?

Charity

I had been in prison for about two years, and God and I had worked through a lot of stuff. He had healed me, He had grown me, and He had strengthened me miraculously on the inside. I got to the point in my prayer life where I was asking, "All right, Lord, what happens when I leave? What does my life look like? Am I married? Am I not married? What's the plan?" As I reflect, so much of my disappointment and hurt stemmed from the fact that I had obeyed God and everything failed. "God, you told me to marry Ryan. And I wanted to, you know, I wanted to, and I obeyed you. So I don't understand that all this devastation and destruction happened and that hurt." It was a spiritual hurt because I did what God told me to do. I felt so lost and confused as we had started the divorce process right after I got arrested.

I was glad when the Lord told me to marry Ryan. I just didn't understand why or how it could end the way it ended. And that was hard. So one day, at around my two-year mark in prison, God told me, "You've only been divorced one time." My whole terror at the process of going through another divorce was never realized. He showed me that we were still going to be married and that had always been the plan. I thought, "Oh my gosh, there's no way." I hadn't talked to Ryan the whole time I was gone. So I said, "Okay, Lord, if that's still the plan and has always been the plan, You will have to work on it!"

I listened, and I obeyed. I knew that Ryan and I were going to be back together. As time went on, Ryan would send divorce stuff into the jail, but I would just throw it away. I wouldn't even look at it. I didn't tell anybody what God had said to me concerning our marriage because I knew what everybody's response would be. I was walking on my faith journey, and I didn't need anybody to detour me from that. So when I got home to my parents' house, a half year from when God spoke to me, Ryan agreed to meet me, and I told him, I said, "You know we're going to be together." And I told him I loved him. It was the first time we had talked in almost four years. Ryan said we need to sign these legal papers preparing for divorce. And we did sign the legal papers, but I knew we would be signing different ones in the future. I had complete confidence that God's Word would come to pass in our lives. And I told him, I said, "We're going to be together." And that was in the fall, and by March of the following year, Ryan and the boys and I were all living together again. God made it all happen pretty quickly. So within a year of my getting out, I was completely reunited with all my family. Ryan and I never divorced. The paperwork was stopped at the courthouse. I was only ever divorced one time—just like God told me!!

YPM
So how are you? You got free. You got reunited.

Charity
I'm great! I lean completely on the Lord for everything. When I was in prison, it was Him and me for hours and hours and hours a day. It's the same now. I practice the presence of the Lord all the time. I spend as much time as I can with Him during the day. And I stay in the Word. I feed myself spiritually every day. I just let Him lead me. My pride was a

really big wall in my life, and it was a wall that He tore down probably about halfway through my imprisonment. How do I say this? I don't ever do any part of my life without Him. I keep Him at the center of everything that I do. I stay connected with people who care, love, and support me.

Two of my closest friends are the Yokefellowship ladies I met through the ministry in county jail. I'm very intentional about my relationships and what I allow in. God showed me who He was, and He never let go. I listened.

YPM

So you're back with your husband and with your boys, in the same church, in the same community. You went through an embarrassing, challenging, agonizing number of years, but you're restored. I think that many times people in your situation would move, they would go somewhere they are not known for a fresh start. So how has it been for you to live in the place where what happened is so well known?

Charity

It's really good. It's really good. I know that I don't ever have to feel shame, and I don't ever have to feel humiliated because Jesus carried all of that for me. So I don't ever need to pick that back up. He carried all of that, and it says so in his Word. God showed me that I don't ever have to feel condemned because Jesus carried all of that for me on the cross. So I live with Him, and I know who I am in Christ. I never have my head down. I am full of hope, and I'm full of joy. And I know that it's only going to keep getting better because He's so good to us that way. And his Word is true. So when I came back into the community, I was excited to live. I was excited to have my life back.

For a person like me to walk-through the places I walked through in prison, everything else is really easy. I've never once struggled with living my life within the community. And everybody's so happy for us everywhere we go. Everyone's always hugging us and "loving on us" and just saying how happy they are and they're proud of us. And even in the church, everybody had their arms open wide. So I know that God is taking care of us, and I trust Him to do that. I just believe what He says, and that's how I live my life, and that's where I stay.

We all make mistakes and fall, and it is what it is. But my life is to glorify God. And I know He's going to use my life in a big way and not just with what I went through but what my family went through. So there's a joy that He's going to continue to restore. And I think of all the people that we will be able to help. And there's no shame in that. There's no shame in our story of bringing glory to God, healing others along the way, and living an abundant and full life together as a family.

YPM

Thank you, Charity. That's the gospel story. That's amazing grace, and it's beautiful to hear, and I know your story is going to help other people who've been down very low to know that God can reach us wherever we fall, wherever we go,

Charity

People have asked me, do you have regrets? And I say, "I wish that none of the bad would have happened." But looking at who I am today, looking at Ryan and me, and where our children are, I can't be sad about that. I can't have regrets about that. I'm thankful that God does work all things for good. And He's not done. I know for the rest of our life, He'll be working! And that's what I'm going to focus on!

YPM

Thank you, Charity. It's been an honor to be part of such a meaningful conversation. I appreciate your honesty and your willingness to be so humbly transparent. That kind of truth is powerful. Jesus is the way and the truth, and His truth leads people to God. Your truth is going to help others. Thank you.

Charity Sampsell
Power for Freedom Ministries
charityanne1014@gmail.com

Biblical Reflection

Jesus was teaching in a courtyard of the Jerusalem Temple. The religious scholars and Pharisees tried to trap Jesus into contradicting the Law to bring charges against him. They placed a trembling woman before him. She was guilty, without a doubt, caught in the act of adultery. They said, "In the Law, Moses commanded us to stone such a woman. Now what do you say? "(John 8:5 NIV) They continued to badger Jesus verbally. He bent down and wrote something in the dirt with his finger. He told them that whoever was not a sinner should throw the first stone.

Imagine the dread in that panic-stricken, humiliated woman as she anticipated what it would feel like as the stones broke her bones and tore open her skin? What if she had children? She would have been thinking about them and what would happen to them. But then, beginning with the oldest, the scholars and Pharisees walked away. Jesus asked her where her accusers had gone. He asked her who was left to condemn her, and she affirmed that they all had gone. He told her He would not condemn her either and that she should stop sinning starting now.

Who knows what led that woman to sin? What we do know is that Jesus saved her life and her soul. So what prompted Charity Sampsell, or what may lead any of us to sin? The miracle is how God restores us and saves us. Charity remembers a time in her life when "....I did not seek wisdom or listen to any wisdom that I heard." Charity remembers "quitting on God." She says, ".... I lived numb and in a blur; it was like I was walking around dead." But then Charity tore down her "big wall of pride," and she confessed, "I do need you, and I need you to help me. It was me surrendering to Him and letting Him be a part of my life. It was letting Him back into my heart, into the places of me that needed His love and healing and touch the most."

Today Charity lives forgiven and free in the same town where it all happened. She attends the same church, her family restored, and she has served on the board of directors of Yokefellowship Prison Ministry, doing her best to help inmates and returned citizens find the grace she did.

Like a woman caught in adultery, she has a testimony, "God showed me that I don't ever have to feel condemned because Jesus carried all of that for me on the cross. So I live with Him, and I know who I am in Christ."

Chapter 4
Zachery Brooks and Tamir Hodges

Zachery and Tamir are intelligent, physically vital, personable men with evident leadership ability. They worked hard. They achieved. They had money, the respect of their peers, and the attention of beautiful women. They were making their money illegally but were justifying drug dealing by helping their families, friends, and neighborhoods. Yet, despite all they had, "they did not feel right," they were not "making any progress." Zachery was a Christian, and Tamir was a Muslim. God put Zachery and Tamir in a prison cell together to lead them into a deep relationship with the "One" who is "....the way, and the truth and the life."

YPM

Tamir, please tell me about your early life. Where were you born, where were you raised, who was your family?

Tamir

My mother and my father were married in West Philadelphia. My father had a military background. He was stern and strict in certain areas, and his drug use enhanced that intensity. He had an abusive relationship with my mother. So I was around domestic violence growing up. I can remember it very vividly. My mom tried to do the best she could to shelter and protect me.

My uncle and aunt would try to protect my mother and fight my father. My uncle, a drug dealer, actually shot my dad six times. He tried to kill him. He was trying to protect his family. My uncle was very well known in the neighborhood.

Drugs were already incorporated into my youth. I could see my uncle doing drugs. I thought it was cool. My father and my mother broke up. My mom was a single parent raising two kids. We struggled. My father's side of the family is mostly Muslim. My mother is a Christian, but some on her side were Muslim. The people I was around, my peers, were Muslim.

I already knew what I wanted to be. I didn't know any better. My mother was in three or four different relationships with infidelities and domestic violence. So I think I know where all the anger in me came from.

I had a real bad temper growing up, and a lot of it came from what was going on at home. My mother did her best. She sent me to the best school she could. When I turned 12, she sent me to a military school called Scotland School for Veterans Children. She sent me there, and I met some cool people. It was a life-changing scenario to get me out of the inner city and around some positive, influential people and football. I played receiver and cornerback. I got recruited and scouted. I went to Thaddeus Stevens College of Technology in Lancaster. But I started being around Philadelphia and into the people that my mother didn't want me around. I started getting around my Muslim cousins, and they were all into the streets.

It was not just with the drugs they were selling. I was trying to live the life they were living. I was a promising junior college football player during the day, and at night I was selling weed and cocaine. I started to get engaged with weapons.

I did not know who God had intended for me to be. I got kicked out of school twice. I got into two fights at school because of my temper, and the dean kicked me out. But the football and track coaches pleaded my case, and they got me back on the team and back in school. I got kicked out again for selling drugs. They found drugs in my room. I was ashamed to go home. I went back home for three months, and my mom was so disappointed. She said, "I worked two or three jobs to help you get to where I thought you should be. And you were going in the direction that I was hoping. Now you come right back to ground zero." But I didn't hear those cries. I was thinking, "Oh, are you now?" And I went back out on the streets. They showed me the ins and outs of the game, teaching me how to manipulate and structure drug dealing. I don't want to sound too big for my britches, but I was learning how to live in a drug or crime organization, learning what you gotta do if someone disrespects you or what to do if someone doesn't have the money to pay for the drugs.

It was a whole new terminology that I knew but not in depth. My cousin helped me, so I got interested. I loved it. I loved the group, the glitz and glam that came with it, the women liking you, the guys respecting you, and all those things that come with that lifestyle. The devil always shows the good but never the bad. They say the devil will always show you your potential but not the whole picture. So I didn't see my future very clearly.

It's hard to make money with people on the streets who are not on the same page as you. It's hard to get on the same page with people in the streets because people have different intentions. My cousin's intention was to "look fly" more than get rich. This is the guy who taught me everything. He wanted the money but just to blow it. I didn't want that. I was 21. I got locked up and was in and out of county jail.

YPM

You said your cousin wanted to "look fly." What does that mean?

Tamir

"Fly" means he wanted all the name-brand things. He was willing to walk around with $500 shoes, $300 jeans, expensive shirts—but he would only have $10 in his pocket.

YPM

So if you "look fly," the girls like you? Is that why you would want to "look fly?"

Tamir

Oh, absolutely. No one wants to admit that, but most things you do are for females. The "bad boy" image or the "I'm rich" image impresses people.

Zachery

I want to touch on what Tamir is saying. I came from poverty, so when I first got some nice stuff, I never looked back. That was one of the reasons I was living that life.

Tamir

It was the same for me. Having a single-parent mom and having siblings, you don't have much, and when you see your mother's girlfriends and what they have. And in the neighborhood, you see people wearing Michael Jordan sneakers they bought at the store. But I am wearing my worn-out Champions, and I'm getting teased.

My mother would say, "If we get the sneakers you want, we can't pay the cable bill; we can't pay the light bill. We might have $75 a month to pay for groceries instead of $150. We can't get you what you want just so you can feel accepted by your peers." I couldn't have these things on a regular basis. When you're born into poverty, it's crazy. My mom would send me strategically over to a girlfriend's or friend's house because we couldn't afford food. She told me there were times we didn't have money, and I had to sleep at my aunt's house. Mom would be working overnight and just be hungry, but she would send me somewhere else for a couple days so I could eat. Our pride was hurt.

I said, "Mom, but we have grandmom." But she said, "Your grandmother is a very strong woman; she doesn't know our situation. That's not how I was raised. I was raised to get out on my own and do it the right way." So I am glad Zach touched on this. I made bad choices but underlying some of those choices was poverty.

I remember after I started making money going into McDonald's and buying maybe 15 people something to eat, and it wasn't just getting fries. I bought everybody's food because it felt good. I can remember going to bed at night and being so hungry my head hurt. I would drink water. I was tired of eating bread. I wanted food, but my mother could not afford food. That's how it was for an inner-city kid with a single parent. It was very difficult at times, and that drove me.

YPM
What about your early life, Zachery?

Zachery
I grew up in North Philly in a section called the "Badlands." There was a lot of heroin, a lot of murders, violence, robberies, selling drugs. We didn't know we were poor because everybody was poor. I thought this was normal until I saw people outside the neighborhood or somebody with money. I thought, "Wow, they don't have food stamps!"

My grandma had 12 kids, so we had a big family, too, and we're very family-oriented. My family was all in one house at one point. We had family gatherings, cookouts, eating and drinking together, and parties all the time. It was fun growing up.

It was the 1980s and 90s, and crack cocaine was running rampant. My mom was in the streets for a little while dealing with drug addiction. But then she wound up meeting the Lord, and she was delivered from all that. There was a lot of crazy stuff going on during that time, but my mom always made sure we went to school with someone. She made sure we had something to eat before we went to bed. It was a hard time, just like Tamir said. We had to eat syrup sandwiches and mayonnaise sandwiches. Sometimes we had to borrow food from a neighbor. I have one big brother and two sisters—one older sister and one younger sister.

My mom started going to a Mennonite church. She was in the streets, and they asked her to go to church, but she did not want to go with them. And then she went with them, and it changed her life. Now the Mennonites were such good people. When I met them, I said, "Man, these are some real good people." They used to come around our neighborhood and pick us up to take us to church, and people thought they were the Feds, the F.B.I.

YPM

Were these Mennonites White people?

Zachery

Yeah, and we were not used to seeing that. But the Mennonites were White and nice. They had a church on Sixth Street. So they would pick us up, and we would go to church on Sundays and Bible study on Tuesday and Thursday. And they did this all the time. And these people helped me look at people differently. They took us outside of the neighborhood. They took us to Lancaster County. There were pigs, and we went camping out in the woods and had campfires and stuff like that.

It was so different. I saw more than just North Philly. When they came into our lives, we went out there for the weekend and stayed with them, which opened up my view to a different world. All I knew was the neighborhood and dealing with the people there. I looked at different races in a new way. They were White, but they weren't racist. These people showed me that they genuinely loved people. So I changed my outlook on how I looked at the world. They exposed us to something different.

My little sister and I went to that church as I grew up, and my mom went there. But then my mom started going somewhere else. As I grew up, my mom did the best that she could with food and school— everything we needed. But once I got to high school, things started to change. I had no money, and people would come to school with nice clothes, too. I was wearing the hand-me-downs that people gave to me. It frustrated me. I'm in my mid-teens and thinking, "I don't want to keep wearing this stuff. My mom is trying to do everything. She can work, but she can't get me a pair of Jordans—they cost $200! I'm seeing a guy on a corner, and he has the CD and jewelry. And I'm like, "Man, I

want some of that. I want some of that money so I can get what I need."
So I started hustling. I started being a "lookout" for drug dealers to let
them know cops were coming. I was 14. I got $50 a day from the drug
dealers.

Tamir

There is something I want to make clear. What Zack went through and
what I went through getting into drug dealing were different. It's like
someone getting rich quickly compared to someone who worked for
everything. Zach started as a "lookout." They gave him more things to
handle when he showed he could handle things. It was different for
me. My older cousin gave me things and showed me things. "This is
what you do." So I was put in a position to be more successful quickly.
Even in the underworld, if you work your way up from the low level—
which is a lookout—you gain a lot of insight. I didn't have that insight.
My cousin would say, "I'm gonna give you an ounce. And this is what
you need for an ounce, and this is what you have got to have from the
deal." So that is how I learned. But Zach had to appreciate every dollar
because he worked up from the bottom.

Zachery

I was working on a block that had heroin on it. They were probably
making $16,000 a day. I made $50 a day by looking out for them and
letting them know when the cops were coming. Then they gave me my
shift. It was just like a job. There was a 12:00 to 8:00 shift, 4:00 to 12:00
shift and a 12:00 to 8:00 shift.

YPM

When you saw the police, how would you signal? Would you whistle,
would you wave your hand? How would you tell the other guys? Did
you have a system?

Zachery

The way we acknowledged the cops were to say "one time"; if it was two cops, you say "two times." So I would ride my bike around the neighborhood every 15 minutes to see if the cops were watching the block. I would let them know if there was a suspicious car, and they would shut down the block. We would shut down for a little bit and then reopen.

I started making a couple of dollars. I hustled out in West Philly. I was doing this at 15 years old. Then I went to a block at Fourth and Berks, and the dealers gave me a shift. On my first day, I made $400 in about three hours. I wound up catching the case (getting caught) because the cops were sitting right down the street, but I didn't care. I'm going to make all this money. So they had me on juvenile house arrest. And once I got off that, I kept hustling because I had to make money. I was hustling all around the city, everywhere. I wound up catching another juvenile case. But I was still going to school. I started getting really good grades. I used to get A's and B's at school even while I was in the streets and smoking weed and getting high.

I was popping Xanax pills like crazy. I was drinking syrup and liquor. At 15, I would do this and go to school. I'd be high on weed and shooting dice in the back of the school. I caught another case when I was 17, about to turn 18. My mother sent my little brother and me out to Indiana because things were getting hectic. She said, "I want you to go out there and see if you and your brother might change. Maybe the setting will help you and change my wallet too?"

I worked a little bit, but then I started selling drugs. I was going to sell weed out there. I started acting crazy. And then I came back to Philly. As soon as I came back, I was selling drugs again. I caught three cases real quick and got locked up for a year. When I came out after that, I started getting money. I stopped getting high, stopped smoking weed, stopped popping pills. I had been lying to myself. Nobody I knew that made money got high. My friend had a block, so I jumped in with him, and we got it together. We had a run for about a year.

YPM

Tell me if I have this right. You two are young men who grew up in similar circumstances. You don't even know you're poor at first. You're just living the way life is lived in your neighborhood. Tamir, when you went to Lancaster, you saw a different world. But you are not questioning life in your neighborhood or yourself and what you are doing. You are trying to get some money to have the things you want to help your family and friends. You're not feeling guilty. You are not feeling shame. You're trying to make it in life. This is how life presents itself. This is the way you get ahead. You are both active in the drug scene. But you are not looking into your soul and your heart. You're not reflecting on yourself. You're just living life. Is that fair to say?

Zachery

I was just living in the way that my neighborhood presented itself. Selling drugs is the only way I know. I don't have doctors living around me. I don't know any politicians. I know drugs. And this is what I see—this is my model, how you make money. I don't have a guilty conscience because this is what you do; this is how you make money.

YPM

Sometimes when a person hits a low point in their life, they change. But you two weren't at a low point. You were trying to make it in life. You didn't think too much about it. You "caught a case," Zachery, and you had to do juvenile detention at home. That's just what you do. That's normal. You were living the way that you saw other people live. You weren't thinking beyond that. You were young guys, and you were not thoughtfully considering the decisions you were making.

Tamir

That's true. We didn't know. My uncle was my idol. He had five or six different cars. I saw him around countless women. As Zach said, doctors, lawyers, politicians, and musicians just weren't around. You had people in the neighborhood who would say, "Don't do this," and I would think, "Yeah, that's what you say." But every day, I saw my uncle with the jewelry and the women, and they loved him. I wanted what he had. Do you know what I mean? You don't think nothing of it. You just think, "Oh well, this is what it's going to be."

YPM

So at some point, when they put you in prison for a longer time, did that start you thinking? Zachery, when you started to get in more significant trouble with the law, and you got convicted, did that get you thinking?

Zachery

When I got my first 5-10 year sentence, I already had two years in prison waiting for trial, and they had "pre-release," so I thought I can do another 18 months and be back on the street and get money.

YPM

So your attitude was, "I'm just in here till I get out. And then I can start making money again?"

Zachery

I had five years, and then I got another five years from another case while on probation. So then I got a third case, and the judge put them together for 10-20 years. And I started thinking, "Boy, this ain't a joke. I've got to do 10 years. That's a long time."

YPM

So now you start getting serious about life. Tell me about that.

Zachery

I grew up going to church. So I started praying. I started praying one day. This might sound crazy, but I grew up in truth, and the truth was always in me. When I was selling drugs, I would go into a house and watch a sermon on TV, or I would listen to a sermon, and then I would go back to selling drugs. I didn't know why I was doing that. I asked God to help me get out of the situation. I started going to church services in prison. I needed God to help me. And let me add this before I got locked up, I started feeling empty.

Before I went into prison, I was making a lot of money. I was reflecting, so I told my homies, "I can do anything I want, I can go anywhere I want, but it doesn't feel like I'm making any progress." And I prayed, "God, help me get out of the situation," because I was already in too deep. People relied on me so that their families could eat. I could not just leave because I got these people depending on me. So I prayed that God would help me get out of the situation. But then I got locked up.

I used to be embarrassed to go to church. I didn't want people to see me with the Bible because I was a thug, a street dude. So I used to go to church and act like I was on my cell phone, but I listened to the message. So then, after a while, I just kept going, and the Lord just got hold of me. And that's when I started going to church and reading the Bible, trying to learn how to read the Bible. And I just went from there.

YPM

So Tamir, Zachary was going to church. Were you going to Muslim services? Were you going to the mosque? Where were you in your faith?

Did your faith help you make sense of life? Was your faith sincere, or was it an image you were putting on?

Tamir

Well, it's crazy. My mother was a Christian. But my name was Kareem Abu Zaire. My whole name was Muslim. My uncle named me, and he and my older cousin were Muslims. And they were helping our family out financially. But my mom said I could not be a Muslim. So then, when I was 15, I started hanging out with my cousins and kids who were Muslim. I would come back from military school and hang around these guys, and we were carrying guns. We had a problem with a dude who lived two houses down from us.

I was in a transition. My mom was a Christian, and her mother was a Christian. I don't mean a religious Christian. I mean the spirit of Christ living in her; she was just different. But my father's brother was a Muslim. His name was Abu. He told my father, "You bring him to me." My uncle started teaching me the Quran, how to read and how to pray. And then he said, "I want you to go to your father and tell him what you learned." So I went to my dad, and I told my dad what I had learned.

My dad wasn't a Christian. He said, "If you feel comfortable doing that, I want you to do whatever's going to make you better as a man because the route you're going will get you lost. If you ain't going to be with Christ, maybe the Muslims are going to get you to God? Abu's the one that's going to make you better because my brother once had a drug addiction." My father's brother was big in the streets. He came home from a federal penitentiary in Texas. He was Muslim, and it changed his whole life around.

I became a Muslim when I was about 16 or 17 years old. My uncle had good intentions. But it's hard to pull me away from my friends, my peers, and they're Muslim, but they were trying to get retaliation. We were shooting. I was doing a lot of bad stuff. I thought, "Dang, this is going to come back and bite me in the butt." There's a lot of dumb stuff done. You know what I mean? Because I'm running around with the wrong crowd. My uncle was teaching me how to pray, how to handle myself, how to dress, how to look like a Muslim, how you conduct yourself as a Muslim. So no, it wasn't a jail thing. I was Muslim. I took my Shahada.

But the streets were too hard for me to resist. Abu told me to do the right thing. He would say, "We got to go pray." I'd say, "I need to go to the basketball court to tell my homies. Give me five minutes, and I'll run down the street." I would get lost on purpose. He couldn't find me. Later on, he asked, "Why are you doing this? Couldn't you take five minutes to pray?" And I wouldn't do it. Cause I didn't want to.

YPM

So you two guys were alike. Zachary, you would listen to a sermon and then go back out and sell drugs. You went to church. You were listening but not practicing. Tamir, you were a Muslim. The Muslims don't teach you to sell drugs. They're against drugs. So you're both living a double life. You're both getting fed something better, but you're not digesting. Your friends pull you. You're drawn by the lifestyle you're living. So how did you first get into prison for any length of time? And when did you first get serious about changing?

Tamir

My first case came when I was 18. I was running with these guys at night. It was my cousins, and we were getting into drama. We're riding around trying to kill someone who killed one of my cousin's best friends. I'm living a lifestyle where I want to be this tough killer.

My older cousin went to jail for it. But I got exonerated. They couldn't find the evidence to pin it on me. Then when I went back to school after selling cocaine and weed, I got kicked out, and I did a couple of months in county jail. I was catching cases that eventually would catch up to me when I got my bigger cases.

I think a lot of guys in the gang, I think even entertainers feel the same way when they get a lot of money. They just don't know why they feel so empty. I got a beautiful girl. I got beautiful women. I got this money. I'm doing all these things. And I just didn't feel right. I just felt like something wasn't right. Zach said the same thing.

It was me and my girlfriend living in an apartment. And my cousin was living with me because he was living in a shelter in Lancaster. His mother was an addict, and he said, "Cousin, I don't want to live in a shelter; I'm tired of getting teased." So I gave him all my clothes. I gave him everything, and he lived with me.

The cops had a warrant for my arrest because someone wore a wire on me. They recorded phone calls. They had videotapes. So they came to the apartment. It was my girlfriend and me. They didn't have a search warrant; they only had a body warrant. They were going to book us because there were drugs in plain sight. I said, "I will give you verbal confirmation for you to search my house if you don't charge her with the crime." So he called his supervisor. He hung the phone up and said, "I will not charge the girl." And I said, "There are 14 ounces of cocaine in my book bag." And they said, "Oh, we didn't have you on that level." It's crazy. It's like Zach said. For Zach and me, there was this very similar strong bond with the people we were helping. I was helping my mom pay bills. I was taking care of my little cousin from the shelter. I was helping my girlfriend and her family out because their mother was struggling with alcohol addiction. I had a lot on my plate. And it just came to me. So they let her go, and they locked me up. And all the little cases that I was catching, I wasn't attending to.

Zachery

As Tamir said, we get into the streets a lot of times; it ain't because we are bad people. It's because we want to make a life. You want to make life better for yourself. So we take the outlet, and we use it to help people out, help people that come home from jail. I used to give wardrobes. Someone would come home from jail. I'd make sure they were right. I'd make sure they had a couple of dollars. I'd make sure they can take kids to do this or that. So you ain't just making money and blowing it. You make money and are helping people. You know you are getting money from people tormented by their addiction, but you use the money to help people. Right?

YPM

Selling illegal drugs is wrong and hurts people, but you are doing good things for other people. We all have some mixed-up thinking. You were pushing drugs, but you are trying to do some good and make it in life. There sometimes comes the point in a person's life when they figure out that their intentions might've been good but that their behavior was wrong. They were feeling empty but for a good reason. So now you're both in prison. How long a sentence did you each get?

Tamir

We got locked up at the same time. We both got about 10 years. Zach had 5 or 10 at the time. I had 7 to 14 years, but that became 10 to 20. I asked my lawyer what had happened? He said they're not playing that way with you since you openly admitted to these charges.

YPM

You're trying to do good. But the lifestyle is leaving you feeling empty. You had a significant income, but now you're in prison for a long time. And you realize something's not right here. You need to figure this out. So how did God get in your life to the point where you figured life out? How did you figure out what the emptiness was? You have both learned something about what makes a person fulfilled and happy. You started living out a new truth. How did you learn to live that truth?

Zachery

I had stopped praying, but God got hold of me. I kept going to church. And then, I started to understand how to read the Bible. I learned how to read the Bible by listening to sermons that go verse by verse. When I first read the Bible, it was like a foreign language. I started getting deeper. And I had a Muslim cellie, and we got into a little debate. And I was just a babe in Christ.

He called one of his friends over who was more knowledgeable. He started questioning me, and I couldn't answer the questions. I thought this was never going to happen to me again. I thought I'm going to learn this book! I'm going to learn about the history of this book. I am not going to be caught like that and not be able to defend my faith! So I started reading apologetics and understanding my faith. And the more I learned, the closer I got to God. The more I learned the Bible, the more I prayed to the Lord. My relationship with Him was deeper and more intimate.

He opened up my eyes, and I became a leader in prison. When I met Tamir, I admired him because he was dedicated to his Muslim religion. I used to be around Christians that were not as dedicated. So I thought, man, if Tamir put that dedication to the Kingdom of God, it would be crazy. He would tell me about his daughter and stuff, and I knew

Christianity was the right way. I thought Tamir couldn't go home and teach his daughter Islam because he would lead her the wrong way.

The Holy Spirit spoke to me and said, "Don't speak to Tamir about the Bible, don't debate about the Bible, only speak to Tamir about love because the love of God is stronger than anything." I studied Islam a little bit because I just studied every religion, trying to have a basic knowledge. I understood that you cannot have a personal relationship like you can with Jesus. I was talking about God's love; how does God love you? How do you love God? How do you love people? Because I know love is a relationship. So how can you experience the love of God the way you're supposed to? So we would talk about different things like homosexuality. Tamir said, "I can't love them." And I said, "But the guy is still lonely. The guy still needs love."

YPM

So when you said God opened your eyes to see things differently when God taught you the truth, what did you see? What was different in the way you thought?

Zachery

When I was younger, I never used to listen. But when God opened my eyes, I started seeing things the way my mom taught me. I realized she was right. I started seeing how life was. I was looking at reality.

Tamir

The way you were living was fantasy. That was a lie. I was glad that you got to see clearly, to see what life is really about. That opened Zach up. And he opened my eyes that way, so I started seeing what life was about too.

YPM

Tamir, you were a dedicated Muslim. You had a cellmate in Zach you respected, and you know he respected you. So how did you start seeing the truth about life?

Tamir

I was a dedicated Muslim. I was teaching classes. I thought every Muslim should have insight into the religion and want to be the right person. I was running the Ramadan program. I had a lot on my shoulders in the Muslim prison community.

I was in the honor block and got into some trouble. So I was moved into Zach's cell. When I knew it was him, I was glad. When I got to the cell, he was in a class. But when he came back, he was so mad because he had the cell to himself. He said, "You're my man, but I've been in this cell alone, and there ain't nothing like having a cell to yourself!" And he ain't lying, there ain't nothing like it.

So it was all right. I knew that Zach was a Christian. But I did not know how passionate he was or how strong his mind was. I'm still Muslim. I was not a strict but a very diligent Muslim. I loved it. I loved reading. I loved the fact that I learned another language. I loved getting up early. I loved being disciplined.

So that discipline and the religion of Islam catapulted me into trying to be the best Muslim I could be. I told you about my mom's brother who had all this money and shot my father. He was Muslim. He named me. So I gotta do this. I'm following in his footsteps. This is what I wanted. But Zach is right. We never argued about what someone said or what Allah said.

Zach would stick to the love narrative. Zach always treated me with love. Some cellies you like and some you don't. There's always a point where cellies need to believe in each other. But since we had a relationship before and Zach was a sincere Christian, and I was a dedicated Muslim, it made it very easy. It was a very cohesive relationship.

If one of us had some food, the other had it too. We wouldn't even ask. It could be my last one, but if you were hungry, then you got it. All right, cool. That kind of relationship helped me. Plus, I knew Zach before he was a Christian when we were selling in the streets. I knew him smoking cigarettes in the yard. I knew him trying to cut his hair, and he had this bald spot, and I said, "Yo, what's up with the bald spot?" He could have said anything, but I remember how humble and sincere he was. Seeing a guy who was once addicted to heroin and crack kicking the habit was impressive. Just because I wasn't addicted doesn't mean he was wild, and I wasn't. Zach had his ways, but I had my ways about me.

I was trying to live for Allah, trying to live the right way. Zach kept loving me, and I think this was important for me at the time, but I didn't see it. I'm still Muslim. I prayed every morning. I fasted when I needed to fast. I gave my brothers the last food I had. I would do the best I could. I would be the best I could be. But I know it helped that he never pushed Christianity on me if that makes any sense. He never made it uncomfortable. We were cool. The only thing I hated, he's a reader. So he would read at six, seven o'clock in the morning with the lights on while I was trying to sleep.

But that was his thing because he loved to learn. He said, "Bro if you ain't got information, you ain't got enough." As I got older and more mature, I could see what he was saying. The pivotal point for change in my life came after Zach and I were separated. Because the prison population was overcrowded, some of us were transferred, and Zach went to York County Prison in Pennsylvania, and I went to prison down in Virginia.

I'm a Muslim, and I'm hanging around these guys, but I'm still doing no good. I was portraying an image. And this older Muslim said to me, "You're not cut like that." I was so upset. My pride was hurt. I was 24. I thought, "Who are you to talk to me like that?" The whole night I couldn't wait to see him. He said, "What I see in you I don't see in everybody else; you have a heart." It caught me by surprise. "I wanted you to ponder on that all night, and I wanted you to get upset. You've got a heart. If you're going to be a Muslim, be a Muslim! Stop trying to have one foot in and one foot out. If you influence these younger brothers who look up to you, influence them the right way into the Islamic state of mind. So then another thing, I hear you say you're a killer. Who told you that? They lied to you. You're a good dude. You're a good brother." He cared about me. And when he said that it took a toll on me emotionally. Maybe he's right? And I start looking at life differently. I'm like, hey, you know, maybe shooting people and selling drugs and womanizing ain't all that it's made out to be.

Because I knew that if I kept my same ways, I would end up back in jail even if I was a Muslim. But back to Zach and me being cellies, Zach's love for me and the way that God spoke to him made it water-tight. But my transformation from Islam to Christianity wasn't solidified when I shared a cell with Zach. I think Zach's relationship with Christ was better because I wasn't just a jailhouse Muslim. My faith was serious. For God to come into my life the way He did and Zach to see it firsthand, I think it made his relationship with Christ stronger.

YPM

So you're both sincere. You're both practicing your faith. You've both got good hearts. So how do you get free? How did you get out of physical prison and spiritual prison? Tamir, you became a Christian. I am interested to hear the climax of that story. But, Zach, why don't you start? You're good buddies who share everything, but then you split up and get released. How have you been able to stay free?

Zachery

When I was in prison, I decided I was not going back to jail! I used my time to learn. I took a course in HVAC—heating, ventilation, air conditioning—and business education, where I learned how to type. I learned interview skills. I learned how to do a resume. I learned about entrepreneurship. I learned about marketing. I learned about business management. I learned how to invest in the stock market. I learned different things, and these tools helped me when I got out. I can interview because I know how to speak. I can fill out an application because I've learned these skills in prison.

When I got out, my goal was to be in the ministry because that's what God called me to do. So I started looking for a church to make my church home. I started going to churches throughout the city of Philadelphia. Every week I would go to a different church to see where God might use me. I wound up going to a church that my cousin attended.

And one day, the pastor gave an invitation to become a member. And I asked him, "If I become a member here, there ain't no set of rules that I got to follow? Because I don't want to be all religious but not real." He said, "You come in as you are." So I became a member of New Canaan Baptist Church. I wanted to serve, so I asked the pastor, "Y'all need help with anything?" He said we need somebody to clean the church. So I cleaned the church every week for a year. I was doing whatever needed to be done. I was cleaning the bathrooms. I was cleaning the pastor's office. I was cleaning the sanctuary. I was cleaning the kitchen. I was mopping. I was sweeping outside the church.

Then the pastor said, "Man, I want you to teach a Bible study." Then I taught different classes for new members. Then the pastor said, "You need to become a minister." I'm in ministry classes right now. I preached my initial sermon on April the 18th, and I will be officially licensed as a minister.

I have stayed out of prison. I have stayed free by staying connected to the Body of Christ, by staying connected to the church. That's what's keeping me free on the outside. If I stay connected to the Body, I will keep my sanity, and that will keep me focused.

YPM

What about you, Tamir?

Tamir

There was a young woman I was very fond of who came back into my life. She said, "I know you're Muslim, but I'm not going to be with a man who worships two Gods. I want you to be a Christian man." She was not the first woman to tell me that. But from her, it didn't hit the same. I was lost for words. It caught me off guard. So I went to my good Christian brother, Antwan. Zach and I know him very well. I told him what had happened. He said, "Pray about it." He asked, "Can you pray to God?" I said, "Nah." He said, "Can you pray to Christ?" I said, "I don't know, can I?" He said, "You sure can."

He said, "You can pray to God by walking. You ain't gotta be in no ceremony." He said, "I don't shame Muslims, but I'm just telling you a lot of that stuff is hyperbole. God loves us and wants us to stay spiritually clean. He had to send His Son. That's the story, but I don't want to get too deep into that." I said, "Okay," and I prayed. I kept praying, but I stopped offering Salat, an Islamic prayer. This had a domino effect because I was very influential in the Muslim prison community.

It took a bad turn, and a lot of relationships that I had went sour. It made me feel uncomfortable. But I just kept praying. And I started going to Bible studies and allowing God's call in my life. My brother told me that if you go for God, it will be cool for women, but if you ain't doing it for God, it's no good. I said, "God may have used her, but He doesn't want her to be the end-all and be-all." He said, "Right, God knew who He had to bring into your life to get you to change your life. This was probably God's final chance to save your life. Just imagine that you have a chance to save your life. If you become a Christian, it doesn't mean you won't die, but it means you will live forever spiritually. Can you say the same thing about Islam?" I said, "No."

He said, "You answered your question. God may have used her, but only God can determine how you live and if you live forever. I was open. I was on the ushering board with Zach every Sunday down in the chapel. I wasn't doing this for a woman. I was doing this for my life, for my spirit. I started to engulf myself with it, and it became a whole different thing. He groomed me to lead Bible studies to teach people so that I could teach myself. He said, "If I give someone a fish, they eat for one day; but if I teach you how to fish, you have something to eat forever. I can tell you what the Lord said, but I will show you how to read the Bible. I can show you how to use a Concordance to help you grow spiritually. Then you'll never go spiritually broke." That's what he said; that's how I got it.

I didn't waste my 10 years in jail. I got my CAD, Computer Architectural Design Services, my barber's license, and Zach and I got our HVAC certificates. I went to Career Link. I learned to do interviews and resumes.

There's no reason why I should go back. I think God has given me all these things. I learned how to be job-ready.

I stayed attached to God through prayer. I understand that you're in a storm, or you've just come out of a storm, or you're about to go into a storm. Once you understand that you are always in a spiritual battle, it keeps you from reverting. I know what I'm up against. I know that I need Christ to win. If I'm broke, it doesn't mean I go back to selling drugs. I have to be patient. God has something better for me. Or if my wife and I don't get along, it doesn't mean I go behind her back and cheat. It means we've got some growing to do.

And I understand that God's understanding is far beyond ours. The way it feels His process is going now doesn't mean it's going to be this way all the time. And I don't feel empty like I did when I was selling drugs. I have four kids. I am married. I have a great job. God has afforded me things that I never thought I would have. That's why I'm free and how I stay free. My friendship with Zach was what God intended. Zach and I didn't know that all this was going to happen in 2015. That's how you know God exists.

YPM

So the major reason you turned from Islam to Christianity was the belief about life after death?

Tamir

Absolutely. In Islam, there are certain things you look forward to, but there is no relationship.

YPM

In prison, there is a strong fellowship among Muslims. They are very dedicated. They support one another. So how should someone in

Christian ministry reach out to a person in Islam if they're open to it, understanding you can't force anybody? If you were talking to another inmate that's a practicing Muslim, and he says to you, "Why shouldn't I just stay with Islam? What's the difference, Tamir? Why can't I just be a Muslim and be with God?" What would you say to him?

Tamir

I would tell him that he's been misinformed. But for me to challenge a Muslim would be different because I know my approach. I was a Muslim. But for someone coming in from the outside, like Zach said, it's different. I remember when a volunteer named Mary Clouser asked me this. She said to me, "Tamir, how do you reach the Muslims?" I said, "You've got to be patient. Keep doing what you're doing. You'll leave the flock to chase that one. You'll get one. You know what I mean? I can't say what is going to change him." Zach said he read about Islam, but knowing it in depth is kind of hard. I can say that what changed me was how Zach was with me. He never changed. The Muslims are very open if they see that you're consistent. Eventually, that is going to get them. That's going to spark their interest.

YPM

So we go with what the Holy Spirit told Zachary. Love Muslims. Don't be arguing about the Bible. Thank you for that, Zachery. Virginia Smith told me about you. How do you know her?

Zachery

I used to go every Thursday to Yokefellowship when they came in for Bible study. So I know Virginia and Mary and Liz and Don.

Tamir

I went too.

YPM

What can you say, Zach, about Yokefellowship Prison Ministry and the impact it had on you?

Zachery

I loved your Yokefellowship because of the conversation. It wasn't just somebody teaching you the Bible. Everybody got to discuss the Bible. We grew close. I got to understand how you think and what you were going through. And that changed the whole dynamic of Bible study. It wasn't just somebody giving you information. We connected on a different level. I use the Yokefellowship method when I lead Bible study now. I try to get people to interact and speak about how Scripture impacts their lives.

Instead of just giving you historical factual information, we allow the Holy Spirit to speak to each of us to build one another up. Yokefellowship was one of my favorite Bible studies; I went there for five years. That's how I built relationships with Don, Mary, and Virginia. They were the consistent people that came in all the time. And I have built relationships with them outside of the prison ministry. I'm close with them. They're my friends.

YPM

So Tamir, do you agree about Yokefellowship?

Tamir

Absolutely. A lot of brothers were going there to have an outlet. I remember one brother who was mentally disturbed, and he would have outbursts of words. I would get frustrated. Why is he mad? And Zach said, "Let him speak. That means a lot to him. There are probably other places where he's trying to speak, and people look at him like he's crazy. We might not understand what he's saying, but for him to get it out is good for him, and he's not hurting nobody; he's just talking."

And when I heard that, I thought, Zach's a little more mature than I am. And he gets it. But that platform that Ms. Virginia and Ms. Mary, and Mr. Don brought was good for us. They were the same. They loved us every day. They came in with a good positive attitude. So you can tell they were just good people.

So if someone didn't understand the spiritual side, they could still see these are good people. They showed love for us even if they did not know us. They hug you. They give you a handshake, and Don, man, I love him! He's some good dude. He's the best and his wife, Mary. I loved it. I looked forward to it. Their company was very well appreciated, but their love—their spiritual love—was very positive.

YPM

Guys, I learned a lot. Thank you very much. I appreciate meeting you on Zoom. I hope we can meet in person someday.

Tamir

Man, I'm glad they brought us up to you.

Zachery

We are looking forward to hearing from you.

Zachery Brooks
Executive Minister, New Kingdom Church, Philadelphia
zbrooksphl@gmail.com

Tamir Hodges
Active Eight Church
tamir.hodges84@gmail.com

Biblical Reflection

Until they were caught, convicted, and incarcerated, Zachery and Tamir seemed to have it all, but they each sensed they were missing something. A man came to Jesus one day who seemed to have it all as well, but he also felt he was missing something (Luke 18:18-25). This man was a leader among his people. He is described in various translations as a ruler, a judge, or a local official. Luke reports that he was very rich. He was the kind of man that people would respect and who would likely attract the favorable attention of women. Like Zachery and Tamir, this rich ruler thought of himself as a good person.

In response to Jesus, he claimed he had always kept all the commandments. Jesus knew better. Jesus knew what Paul would soon write in Romans 3:23, that all people have sinned. To emphasize this point, when the rich ruler calls Jesus "good teacher," Jesus replies, "Why do you call me good? No one is good except God alone." Because they were generous in helping family, friends, and neighbors, Zachery and Tamir rationalized their sin and thought of themselves as "good people."

Jesus could see into the soul of the rich ruler. So he told him if you want eternal life, if you want what you are missing, "You still lack one thing. Sell everything you have and give it to the poor, and you will have treasure in heaven. Then come follow me." (Luke 18:22) This made the rich ruler very sad. It is difficult to obey Jesus, seek the Kingdom of God first and trust that God will provide everything else you need. But that is the decision Zachery and Tamir have made.

For Tamir, it has meant following Jesus and turning his back on the status of the drug dealers' cars, clothes, and women and living a simpler life. For Zachery, it has meant being a church custodian, cleaning toilets, and preparing for ordained ministry. Both men have found what they were missing.

Chapter 5
Lewis Lee

Lewis Lee was not pressured into joining a gang when he was moving into a new community; he wanted to join the neighborhood gang. It was the way to be accepted. The gang "protected" the neighborhood. Lewis felt no pressure beyond peer pressure when he was invited to use drugs; he wanted to use drugs. Those two decisions stunted his emotional, moral and spiritual growth. When his brother killed a rival gang member in a street battle, Lewis felt nothing but "victory." When his partner in an attempted robbery killed a man, 15-year-old Lewis felt no compassion or remorse. When Lewis was sentenced to a term of life without parole, he did not cry or comprehend the gravity of what he had done or what he faced. He was numb.

But when Lewis Lee finally got sober and fully kept his promise to follow Jesus Christ as his leader and as the one who gave him forgiveness, Lewis grew emotionally, morally, and spiritually. Lewis was not numb anymore. Lewis was free.

YPM
Please tell me about your start in life?

Lewis

I was born in 1959. I had three older brothers, but only one lived with me because my two oldest brothers had a different father, and I grew up in what I thought was a very good, loving home. Later on, I came to understand that there were addiction issues. My mother and father were both alcoholics. My father was a very heavy gambler. However, even in that environment, it was a loving family. I was not physically or sexually abused or anything else in that way, shape, or form. My mother and father always provided for me and my brother. We never went without, but as I said, later on in life, I understood that there were addiction issues. So that caused some problems. But for the most part, it was a loving family. The family did not cause the downfall in my life. I grew up in West Philly, around 41st and Lancaster.

YPM

What about your religious life as a family?

Lewis

I was sent to Sunday school as a little child, but it wasn't something that was done every Sunday. I can never remember going to church with my mother, father, and brother at the same time. So church with my family was not a part of my life growing up. My aunts and uncles were very close, and we were a close-knit family. At the age of about nine years old, my family moved to the southwest part of the city, to a better neighborhood, a bigger house. I was maybe in the fifth grade when we moved. And that's where my life took a downward turn. When I moved into that neighborhood, I became involved in street gangs.

YPM

Tell me how 9-year-old Lewis got involved in a street gang. What happened?

Lewis

That's something that you did. You come into the neighborhood, you hang out with guys, and the guys that you hang out with are part of a gang, and you just joined the gang out of fellowship. You know, just being a part of the guys. You've heard stories about people being pressured to join gangs. I didn't experience that. I joined the gang because I was new to the neighborhood. This is what was presented to me, and I just became a part of the gang.

I was not a good student in school. I didn't like school. I went because I had to. And when I didn't have to go, I didn't. I started smoking cigarettes. I started smoking marijuana. Then somebody introduced pills. I started taking pills, and you just go up the drug chain. One thing I didn't do was I didn't gravitate toward alcohol. For some reason, I just didn't like the taste of it. So I didn't. I was not an alcoholic. I didn't drink alcohol, but I did every drug that was presented to me, and that became a part of my life.

YPM

So you're in a gang because you're a new guy in the neighborhood, and that gets you involved with some addiction issues with drugs. Did you guys play basketball, or were you doing vandalism? What else was the gang doing?

Lewis

Well, the gang was protecting the neighborhood. And at times, there would be gang fights with other gangs. And that was just the life that we lived. But mostly, it was a close-knit neighborhood. You stayed in your neighborhood because you really couldn't just travel the city. Because at that time in the early 70s, gang warfare in Philadelphia was very popular and very dangerous. So you couldn't travel the city because people would ask where you were from, and you just didn't have the freedom to do that. So a lot of my life was spent in my neighborhood, protecting the neighborhood, and we just hung out and did things that kids did—a little bit of vandalism and those types of things, you know, house parties with girls at that time was pretty popular. So we went to house parties on the weekends and drank and got high. And at times, there were some violent gang fights. For fun and recreation, we played basketball, football, and stick ball.

YPM

There were violent gang fights? Help me understand what that means. What's a violent gang fight look like? Are you swinging fists or something else? When you were 9 years old, you weren't in a gang fight, were you?

Lewis

Well, sure. Sometimes gangs would come together, and the young guys would fight the younger guys. And then the guys in the middle ages would fight the guys their age. Or maybe I might've gone up into another neighborhood that we were having a gang war with. And then I would try to find somebody and do bodily harm to them and vice versa. My brother Chris was also a member of the gang, and he was about a year and a half older than me. Sometimes we fought with baseball bats, clubs, sometimes with guns. These were the weapons of the war.

YPM

So it's serious business.

Lewis

Right. Very serious. If you were to look back at news clippings from the late 60s to the mid-70s, you would see that gang war violence in Philadelphia was common. You're talking about numbers of dead like what is happening now. Looking back on it, it's just unbelievable that the mindset of so many people was killing each other over areas of the neighborhood that nobody owned. It wasn't like you were trying to rob my house. You didn't live here, so now I'm going to try to do bodily harm to you.

YPM

Did you ever think about what made that happen? What possessed all those guys to live that way?

Lewis

What was that gaining for people? Was it a sense of manhood? I don't know. What was the motivation? That became just the way you lived, and you didn't think much about it.

I look at it now from a spiritual perspective. Without God in a person's life, your life is subject to anything; the devil gets in there, and you are subject to anything. Now you have gangs called the Bloods and the Crips in the country. They are doing the same thing that I did growing up—protecting the neighborhoods, claiming the neighborhood, and saying, "If you don't live in this neighborhood, you shouldn't come here. And if you do come here, we are going to do bodily harm to you."

YPM

So what's the next stage? Are you still living at home with your mother, father, and brother?

Lewis

Yeah. I'm still living at home with my mother, my father, and my brother. I think that my youngest brother was born in 1972. But in 1973, I witnessed my older brother, Christopher, kill somebody in a gang fight. I saw him shoot the person. I saw the person drop to the ground and die right in front of me. And at that time, I had to be 11 or 12 years old. So my brother Chris was sent to prison in 1974 for killing a young man during a gang fight.

YPM

So when you're 11 years old, you see your brother kill someone. How did you process it? What did you feel when you saw that happen?

Lewis

Nothing but victory. There was no remorse, no shame. And that's because there was no God in my life. And that was it. It was him or me, him or my friends. I didn't have nightmares about it or anything. So in 1974, my brother was sentenced to 5 to 20 years and was sent upstate. That same year the gang violence pretty much died out—kind of made peace with a lot of the enemies in the neighborhood. And then, once that happened, I got very heavily into drugs. And then I started a life of crime. I started burglarizing houses, snatching pocketbooks, and those types of things to get money so that I could support my drug habit.

YPM

Now take me back to your brother. How old was he when he committed that murder?

Lewis

Christopher had probably been about 17 years old, somewhere around there. He pled guilty to third-degree murder.

YPM

So now your brother's in prison, what's happening with you?

Lewis

Well, at that time, I'm still supposed to be going to school, but I'm not going to school. I'm just running the streets, just hanging out, getting high, robbing, burglarizing. Sometimes we might get in a car with a couple of guys, and we'd go out into Delaware County and snatch pocketbooks, anything I could do to get money so I could support my drug habit.

YPM

I understand. So how long does that go on? You must've gotten arrested at some point.

Lewis

In the summer of 1973, my mother sent me to the store to get some groceries, and I decided to steal the groceries so I could keep the money so that I could buy drugs. I went into the supermarket, put the groceries in a shopping bag, and tried to walk out the door. And the security guard stopped me at the door. Of course, I hadn't paid for the food. That was my introduction to the police. I was taken to the police station. They called my father, he came to the police station and saw me locked up and told them to take me away.

I was heartbroken to hear him say that. Because I was a juvenile, they took me down to the youth study center. That's where all juveniles went in Philadelphia. So I went down there. I went before a judge and was adjudicated and was put on probation. I wasn't put in the juvenile placement or anything like that. I was put on probation. So I had a probation officer monitoring me, and because I wasn't going to school and the probation officer found out, he brought me back to court. And in January of 1974, I was given a juvenile placement, and I was sent to Glen Mills.

I stayed there about four months, and then there was an incident that happened at Glen Mills, with the residents up there, and a lot of us were sent back to court. The courts released me to another juvenile placement center, but this was not like Glen Mills, where I had to live there. I was living at home and had to report there every day. This juvenile center was way out in the northeast part of the city. I had to take a train or bus to go to this place during the summer of 1974. And so I went maybe three or four times, and I said, "No, I'm not doing this every day because it's summertime. Everybody's out of school. I'm being sent all the way out here, and I'm missing all of the fun." So I stopped going.

YPM
And as a result?

Lewis
My probation officer sent me back to court. So I was back before the judge and given another juvenile placement by the end of the summer of 1974. I was sent to Cornwells Heights Juvenile Center for a 90-day evaluation, and at this place, I had to live.

My counselor at the time was retiring, so he gave me a favorable recommendation after my 90 days. And I was released and sent to attend a private school in center city. At that time, the drug of choice on the streets that I was involved with was speed, methamphetamine, in a powder form. At that time, everybody was snorting it, and it was the type of drug not to bring you down but keep you up. Well, when I came out in about November 1974, the first night, I was hanging out with some friends, and we were in a bar.

And so the guys said, "Let's go somewhere." I'm like, "Well, where are we going?" "Come on, come on!" So we left the bar and went into this abandoned house. So I'm thinking to myself, what in the world is going on here? So we go into the house, and now all of a sudden they pull out needles, and they are now taking this powdered drug that's in a cellophane bag, and they put water in there, and they mix it up, and they draw this out into a needle. And now they are injecting this in their arms. And this is the first time I'd ever seen this happen. And I'm, at that time, 14 years old. And it just blew my mind to see them doing this.

Then they asked me if I wanted some, and I said, "Oh no, that's just a little too much for me." We went back to the bar to hang out for a little while. Then they said, "Come on." So we went into the bathroom in the bar, and they're doing this again. And they asked me, did I want some? And I said, "Yes." So I put my arm out, and he put the needle in my arm, and after that, I was hooked instantly.

YPM
Really.

Lewis
Yes! After that, the drug just took over my life. In November of 1974, that drug took over my life. And that's all I lived for every day, to shoot that drug into my body. I was already living a life of crime; now, I was doing everything I could do to get money. Then in March of 1975, one night, a friend and I decided we were going to rob a drugstore. We figured we can get money, and we can get drugs, and we can go sell the drugs. And when I look back on that, it just really goes to show how a youthful mind really doesn't think.

I know what money looks like, but I didn't know what drugs look like. I didn't know what pharmaceutical drugs looked like. So how can I steal and sell drugs? But that was our thought. We were going to go in there, and we're going to get these drugs, sell them, and we're also going to have money. So we drove out to a drugstore in Delaware County and attempted to rob a drugstore. And unfortunately, it didn't go as planned, and somebody got killed and lost their life. And that person who got killed happened to be the chief of police of Glenolden.

YPM

So it's you and one other person, and you're both about 14 years old?

Lewis

At that time, I'm 15, and he would have been 17.

YPM

And you two guys had a gun or guns?

Lewis

He had a gun; I had a gun.

YPM

And this chief of police just happened to be in the store?

Lewis

We came up to the store, the store was closed 'cause we got there late. We had called to find out what time the store closed; the store closed at 10 o'clock. So we sat. We looked into the store, and we saw two people. We decided to wait for them to come out of the store. And then we would take them back to the store. That was the plan. We went to the back of the store and hid until they came out. Two people who came out of the store were walking down the street and were getting ready to get into a car. So we came from behind the building, and I approached the person who was getting in on the passenger side.

My co-defendant approached the person who was getting in the driver's side. When I got to the person who was getting in the passenger side, they were already seated in the car. So I had my gun in my hand. I pointed it at him, and I told him to get out of the car. And as he was getting out of the car, he reached into his jacket and drew a gun from under his jacket. And the first instinct that came to me was to run. And I ran, and he started shooting after me. He didn't hit me. I was apprehended. I was taken back to the scene of the crime and told somebody had been killed. I was taken to the police station, and then I found out that the chief of police had been killed. These two men that we thought were a customer and the owner of the place turned out to be two officers who were off duty and in plain clothes.

YPM

Wow. So it was your buddy who shot the officer?

Lewis

Yes, my co-defendant is the one who killed the chief of police.

YPM

So the drug took over your life. That's what you lived for, I hear you. Now you're in huge trouble. You know how the law works; whether or not you pull the trigger, you are responsible. What are you feeling now? Now you haven't stolen a bag of groceries. Now the chief of police is dead. So what are you feeling? What are you thinking?

Lewis

Well, the crazy thing is that when I look back on it, I did not understand the ramifications of my actions. I did not understand what serious trouble I was in. I can't even say that I was remorseful at that time for the person who had lost his life. I just didn't feel anything, and I didn't realize how bad a situation my life was in. I was too young to know. And when this crime happened, and I was in prison, the Delaware County police departments got together, and they started looking at other crimes from that county perpetrated by young African Americans. And I was given two more cases. One of them I did do was a home invasion.

They found my fingerprints in that house. So I was charged with that, but then there was another drugstore out there that had been robbed, but I didn't do that one, but still, they charged me. I'm 15 years old. I have a homicide case, a home invasion, and a robbery of another drugstore on top of my head. And I just don't understand. And I can't even comprehend how serious this situation is.

YPM

So what happens next?

Lewis

I started going to trial in the case for the drugstore that I was charged with during that trial; the owner of the place was asked by my lawyer, "Well, how did he come to identify me?" And he said that it was by mugshots. As soon as he said that, my lawyer asked for a mistrial. I was granted a mistrial, and they didn't retry me within a certain amount of time, so eventually, that case was thrown out, which was good because I didn't do it. So I beat that case. In the case of the home invasion, I was found guilty of that because my fingerprints were in the place, and I was given a sentence of 5 to 10 years. I pled guilty to second-degree murder for the homicide robbery. I pled guilty on the bad advice of my lawyer, receiving a life sentence for that at the age of 16. I'm in the county, I got a life sentence, and I have a 5- to 10-year sentence running consecutive to the life sentence.

YPM

A life term and another along with that. So what happens? Where do you go then?

Lewis

I'm in the county jail because of my age. I'm separated from everybody. I'm not out in the general population. The first month or so, my co-defendant and I were in the hole, and then he turned 18. So he was put in the general population. I was still a juvenile, and they had opened up a new wing in the prison where they were receiving inmates. When new inmates first came in, they would be housed there, get processed, and then be put into the general population. And that's where I was sent to live. So I lived there for about a year and a half until 1976. Then I was sent to the state prison at Camp Hill.

YPM

So tell me about that first year and a half in prison. How was it hitting you emotionally? You're addicted to drugs. The general population was another bunch of guys. Were you happy? Were you scared? What were you feeling?

Lewis

I wasn't feeling anything because, at the time, I was separated from everybody else in the prison. I wasn't in the general population. It was a good experience when I look back on it. I thank God for how He orchestrated that because I was in an isolated place. I was put in a cell on the block where new inmates were processed. I stayed on that block. I ate on that block. I lived on that block. And the good thing is that I got to know the staff on that block, the counselors and everybody like that, because I was a child and I got to know them, and I became very good friends with a lot of the staff there. So it was a good experience. It wasn't a bad experience how that worked out for me.

YPM

Did you cry? Were you lonely? Were you frustrated being locked away?

Lewis

No, I wasn't. I mean, it's strange. It kind of worked out to my advantage to be placed on that block at that time. Because at that time, what happened was that I had access to the telephone. So I would be calling home, calling friends on the streets, and different things like that. And so, during this process, I was calling one of my friends on the street, and I could never catch him at home. One day I called, and his sister answered the phone, I asked, "Is Michael home?" So he gets on the telephone. And I hear giggling in the background.

So I asked him, "Well, who's that?" He said, "Well, that's my sister." I said, "I'll talk to you later; put her on the telephone." So he puts her on the telephone, and we start talking, and as kids, we just hit it off right. Then we became very good friends, and she's still a friend and a very integral part of my life. But it started back then when I was maybe 16 or 17 years old. And so she started to visit me at the prison, and it saved me. And like I said, being the only person on that block, I had the run of the block. I could receive telephone calls. The guards loved me because I helped at nighttime when they had maybe a load of prisoners come in. I was able to help them process the prisoners and different things like that. Strange as it is, I never was depressed or anything like that as a result of the situation that I was in.

YPM

What happens now? You're getting older.

Lewis

I'm getting older. I'm done with the initial stages in the courts. So now I get sent upstate to start my time. And so, at 17, I got sent to Camp

Hill State Prison. My friends from the neighborhood I grew up with are there. My brother is still in. My co-defendant is there, serving his sentence.

To go there, it's just like a homecoming. All of the fellows are there, and I just immersed myself in prison life. And I started going to school because I didn't have my GED or hadn't graduated from school or anything like that. So I started going to school and got my GED. Then I started taking college courses, working towards my associate's degree in business management. But at the same time, in prison, it was just like being on the streets because drugs were there. And so that became a part of my life—drugs in prison—and also messing with homosexuals because there were no women in prison, but there were men in prison who thought they were women. I became involved in that. And so it was drugs and messing with homosexuals and gambling and just living every day.

YPM

See if I have this right; it wasn't so bad. It's hard for me to comprehend, but somehow, it wasn't so bad for you. You weren't thinking, oh, I could be getting an education. I could be married and have kids. You weren't sitting around missing what you didn't have. You were back in the gang.

Lewis

Right. I learned to adapt to the life before me, and that was prison life. Don't get me wrong. I was still appealing my case. I was still hoping that something would happen there. But even then, I still didn't know the magnitude of what a life sentence meant. I came to be a member of an organization in prison called the "lifers." All the men who had life sentences were part of the organization, and the goal of the organization was to change laws and find better ways of living together. I was involved in that, but even then, you could not have told me that I would spend 40 years of my life in prison because it just wouldn't work out for me. If I had been able to see that, there's no telling what I might've done, but I couldn't see it. So what I did was just live life the best I could. The things that I did were always to please the flesh because there was no God in my life.

YPM

How did you get from a place in life where your goal was to please the flesh to the time you began to become the man you are today? What happened? How did that work out?

Lewis

The young lady that I met when I was in the county jail was a Christian. She was brought up in the Christian faith. Her mother was a pastor. When she came into my life, she wasn't following Christ. But in 1983, she was still a part of my life, and she rededicated her life to the Lord. That's when she introduced me to Jesus. She told me about this man named Jesus who died for me. This was the first time that I'd ever heard anything like that. When I look back over my life, and the times I went to church, I don't have any recollection of anything being said about me being a sinner or anything like that. So this was new for me, but it struck a chord. And so, in 1983, I decided to surrender my life to Jesus.

YPM

What was her first name?

Lewis

Her name was Karin.

YPM

And was Karin married, or was she single?

Lewis :

At the time, she was single.

YPM

In 1983 how old were you, and how old was she?

Lewis

She's a year older than me. I was 24.

YPM

When Karin introduced you to Jesus, did she do it on the telephone, visit you, or write a letter?

Lewis

She was coming to visit me when I got upstate—maybe once a month, maybe every other month, something like that.

YPM

Did you have to talk behind glass?

Lewis

No, they were contact visits.

YPM

What would she tell you about Jesus? What did she say?

Lewis

She told me that He died for my sins, that He loved me and that I needed Him. I can't remember exactly, but I knew that she presented Jesus to me as a savior and someone I needed in my life. Because like I said, when Karin was first involved in my life, she wasn't following what she knew. So when she got her life right, she knew what I needed in my life, and that's when she started talking to me about Jesus.

YPM

Help me see if I have the correct picture of Karin. She isn't just talking about Jesus. He's not just in her head anymore. He's in her life.

Lewis

Right, right. Karin has come back to Jesus.

YPM

Jesus is living in her. And then you see the change in her. I'm assuming she's got a certain peace or joy about her. Are you going back to your cell and thinking about it? What was your thought process?

Lewis

The thought that I had was that if I wanted to keep her in my life, I needed to get to "know this Jesus." That was the thought. So me getting to know Jesus was a two-edged sword because I needed Him, but then if I wanted to keep her, I needed to keep Jesus. When she shifted from who she used to be to now following the Lord, I knew that for me to keep her in my life, I had to get to know God.

YPM

Well, that's honest. At first, you wanted to keep Karin, but to keep her, you needed to know about Jesus. When did it change? When did it become "wanting Jesus" more than wanting Karin? Did that surprise you when it happened?

Lewis

That happened later. When I surrendered my life to Jesus, Karin was still a part of my life, but then she left my life. So now she's not in my life, but Jesus is. At the time I surrendered my life, I was going to church, and that's where I became familiar with Yokefellowship Bible study because that was one of the Bible studies.

YPM

Was it a true surrender when you surrendered your life to Jesus or was it going through the motions to impress Karin?

Lewis

No, it was a true surrender because not only did I pull away from the world, I stopped getting high. I stopped gambling. I stopped messing with homosexuals and everything. I turned away from that life. And one of the good things is that because of who I was at that time, I wasn't pressured. I wasn't persecuted by my friends because now I'm not living that life. They respected me because of who I was. I know that's a hard decision for some men to make in prison, to turn away from the world. And now, all of a sudden, you live for the Lord. Peer pressure sometimes keeps men from making that decision, but I didn't have that. So I was able to turn away. I was able to start going to church. Karin sent me a Bible. I was going to church, and I was still respected by my friends.

YPM

So for the first time in your life, you are living for something other than your pleasure. You are feeling good. Up until you surrendered to Jesus, if I hear you correctly, you lived for the moment, you lived for money, you lived for drugs, you lived for the gang. You didn't think much about deeper things, life and death, and responsibility and guilt. It just wasn't part of your life. And now, all of a sudden, Jesus is in it. So are you thinking back over your life and what's happened and reevaluating? Does life look different to you now?

Lewis

Well, no, I can't say that I went back and started processing things or anything like that. I just moved forward in terms of living a good life. That's what I did, because like I said, I went to church, I went to Bible studies, and now I'm moving in a godly way, and that's what's happening in my life. I had a job in prison; I was going to school. So I'm living a wholesome life. I still have friends, I wasn't abandoned by my friends, but I'm just living. My mindset is different, but I never sat down and started reflecting on life or anything like that.

YPM

Is it fair to say that this is the happiest you've ever been in your life?

Lewis

Oh yeah, yeah. I'm happy. I'm at peace because I'm not being driven by my flesh. The flesh is a taskmaster that needs to be fed. So I'm at peace. I'm at peace because I'm not gambling. I'm not chasing those things. I was at peace for the first time in my life, and I didn't understand it.

YPM

Now you become a different person during a life term in prison. Talk to me more about how life looks to you. Go back to the Yokefellowship Prison Ministry; how did you get connected with Yokefellowship?

Lewis

Yokefellowship just came. It was good. They were one of the Bible studies that I attended. I think they came in on Tuesday nights. It was a good group of men. I can sense genuine love, genuine concern for us as prisoners. And it was just a good experience. I had a very good experience with the men from Yokefellowship. That was the only Bible study at that time that I can recall that I attended. I don't even know if there were any other Bible studies that made an impression on me back in

1983. But I remember the brothers from Yokefellowship and how we would go over to the chapel at night and break into little groups.

I don't think he was a pastor, but there was one gentleman from the Yokefellowship group who knew the Word. He knew the Word! The other men were laid back—real layman type—but he knew the Word. I just wish I remembered who he was because I would like to see the man and let him know what has happened in my life. I can't remember his name, but I had a very good experience that was more powerful than the church service at the time. Because in the church service at the time, the chaplain left a lot to be desired.

YPM

You didn't go to school much when you were a kid. Could you read the Bible for yourself?

Lewis

Yeah, I can read. I can read and write.

YPM

Were you doing a lot of Bible reading at the time?

Lewis

I was doing a lot of Bible reading, and I was doing a lot of Bible courses, the little Mailbox Club Bible courses through the mail. I got involved in them, and that's how I learned a lot about the Bible, the Bible stories, and different things, doing those types of Bible courses. But my walking with the Lord only lasted for about six months.

YPM

What happened?

Lewis

One day out of the blue, somebody offered me some reefer, and I took it. I smoked a joint, and I was off on the dark path again. And I went back into the world. I went right back into the world, and I stayed in the world for about seven years. Yeah, I went right back at it. And then, in 1989, I sensed the Lord speaking to me in a way that I knew was God because I started getting the thought that "there's a better way to live, there's a better way to live." This was the recurring thought that I was hearing, "There's a better way to live." And so 1990 is when I rededicated my life to the Lord, and I've been with Him ever since.

YPM

So you had seven more years in the wilderness. And now you've rededicated your life to the Lord. Are you finally realizing that this life sentence will be for a long time, that you're not getting out of there anytime soon?

Lewis

No, in 1990, it still hadn't hit me in that respect because I still had some appeals in the courts, and there was still some hope. And I knew about the commutation of sentences and those types of things. It had never looked like "this is where I'm going to be for the rest of my life." So I was growing at that time, I was growing in the Lord, and I was active in the church. So that wasn't an issue. I reconciled that later on because I filed for commutation twice. After the second time being turned down, I had a conversation with the Lord, and I said, "Okay, Lord, I know You are the only one that can get me out of here." I said, "If you don't want me out, then I'm where You want me." And I knew that God had the ability to keep me in peace. If this is where my life was going to be. I was mature enough at that time that I was able to have that talk with God. God is in control, and if He wants me out, He's going to get me out. If He doesn't want me out, this is where He wants me to be, and I can be at peace because I'm in the will of God, even though I'm in prison.

YPM

How were you using your life as a follower of Christ? I know you were active in church but were you helping other men in prison?

Lewis

In 1990, when I gave my life back to the Lord, we had just come out of the riot. I don't know if you remember the major riot at Camp Hill in 1989. In 1990 the prison was locked down for a year or so. At that time, we had developed a little fellowship with brothers who were still in prison, and when the church opened up, we used to go to church together. We started fellowshipping together. And when jobs started opening up again, I had a very good job in prison.

I had worked in what they called the furniture factory. But when the prison opened back up, that job was no longer available. Matter of fact, it moved outside of the fence. My supervisor, who liked me and wanted me to work with him, wanted me to come outside the fence and work. So he put me in to get an outside clearance. And I prayed earnestly and believed God that He was gonna open up the door and give me favor, give me an outside clearance. But I didn't get it. And when that didn't happen, I went to work in the chapel as the chapel clerk. And that's where my life became immersed in the things of God because now I'm in the chapel seven days a week. And that's where God just used me. I became very good friends with the chaplains. The chaplains started a leadership group. And I became a part of the leadership group of men in the church, and our job was to help the chaplains on Sundays do the services, to perform the services. And as a result of that, I started teaching Bible studies in the chapel. I was given access to councilmen and different things like that. And that's how I got to know a lot of the volunteers who came in.

YPM

Did you ever do any mentoring of younger men?

Lewis

Yes, I had the opportunity to do that, to mentor men. I've done that since I have been at Camp Hill and Mahanoy Prison. I left Camp Hill in 1999 and was sent to Mahanoy Prison, and the blessing about going there was that Chaplain Nelson Zeiset was there. I met him when he was a volunteer at Camp Hill. He used to teach Bible studies. So when I got to Mahanoy, it was like a homecoming to see him. He knew my character. And the first thing he asked me to do was usher. And I said, sure. So I was an usher in the church. And then he started a leadership team in the church, and he asked me, and I became a part of the church leadership at that prison.

YPM

How many years had you been in prison altogether by then?

Lewis

Well, that would have been from 1975 to 1999, so 25 years.

YPM

Twenty-five years, and you did a total of 44 years. How did that long stretch work? How did that go for you?

Lewis

Once I turned my life over to the Lord, it's been a beautiful journey. Just serving the Lord God has blessed me in so many ways, the fellowship of people from the outside, people coming in doing Bible studies, people coming in doing church services. It's just been one blessing on top of another.

YPM

So when "you're living for the flesh," you don't feel happy, you don't feel sad, you're just existing; but when you're "living for the Lord" even when you are in prison for decades, you look at it as a blessed time. Is that fair to say?

Lewis

Yes, yes, yes. That's about it. But that's not everybody's experience. It's a matter of perspective. Do you believe that God is in control, even in situations that are not the best? Is God in control? And if God is in control, then everything is okay. Now there is still an enemy. I battle daily with the flesh. I have to deny the flesh every day. I have to pick up my cross and follow the Lord. It's just a different mindset. It's just a different feeling because now I'm living for the Lord. So I know when I do right that God is there with me. God is protecting me. God is loving me. And it's just a beautiful way of living life.

YPM

So if you had stayed in prison until you died, you still wouldn't have been an unhappy man, leading a meaningless life from your point of view. Instead, you would say, the Lord is in control, and I'm doing what God has sent me to do?

Lewis

Sure. Because this is what I understand is the reality of the life we're living. I left behind a lot of good brothers. There are men I know who love the Lord just as much as I do, but the reality is that, unfortunately, some of them will be in prison when the Lord comes back. Not every believer will be out of prison when Jesus comes back. That's just the nature of this life. But it doesn't make a difference where you are physically; it's where you are spiritually. That's what's important. Because there are people outside, as I'm sure you know, who are in prison, they don't have spiritual freedom, but their bodies are free. They can do whatever they want, but they don't have true freedom. So if you don't have spiritual freedom, physical freedom means nothing.

YPM

Exactly, that's the theme of *Get Free and Stay Free*. Each chapter in this book is about people who have lost their freedom, lost their spiritual freedom, or never had it. And then they lose their physical freedom, and they go to prison. But that's not the end of the story. Each story is about a person that not only gets back their physical freedom but their spiritual freedom. They get free, and they stay free on both levels.

Spiritually, you're a man of peace. You've made the transition, whether you're in a physical prison or not. In Philippians 1:21 (NIV), Paul says, "For me to live is Christ and to die is gain." Paul did not know whether it was better to die and be with the Lord or live and serve Him. You're saying I'm at peace, I am free, whether I am in prison or walking on the street. But after 44 years in prison, you finally did get physical freedom. How did that come about?

Lewis

In 2012 the United States Supreme Court came down with a ruling that said it is unconstitutional to sentence juveniles to mandatory life sentences without parole. That ruling opened up the door for every juvenile who was sentenced to life to be resentenced.

YPM

The Supreme court said it was unconstitutional in 2012, but it still took you several years to get out, didn't it?

Lewis

Yes, because, unfortunately, Pennsylvania disagreed with that decision. So we had to wait for another decision from the United States Supreme Court before Pennsylvania would begin the re-sentencing process. I was re-sentenced to 30 years to life in 2018. Other juveniles who got re-sentenced would immediately be eligible for parole if they were over their minimum. If they had a home plan that was approved, most guys were out of prison in three months. When I went to see the parole board, it took about two months for their decision, and the parole board granted me parole. However, they set a date for my release 18 months in the future. So, in essence, they gave me a hit in disguise.

That was a blow because it was unexpected. It had happened to nobody else. So immediately, my lawyer investigated the situation because we just found it to be very strange. So my lawyer looked into the situation. She contacted somebody who told her that the reason was to appease the other officer who was there when the police chief was killed, which made no sense since I was still getting out. So I had to endure another 18 months in prison. And then, in January of 2020, when I was supposed to get out, I didn't get out because my paperwork was messed up. I got out on February 5, 2020.

YPM

So you got out, and now along with your spiritual freedom comes physical freedom. If you had to choose between the two kinds of freedom if you could choose to be either spiritually free or physically free, which would you choose?

Lewis

Well, I'm going to choose spiritual freedom. I'm gonna choose spiritual freedom over physical freedom.

YPM

Why?

Lewis

Because spiritual freedom entails eternal life, physical freedom entails just maybe 70 years of life. And then it's hell. Spiritual freedom entails eternal life.

YPM

But right now, you have physical and spiritual freedom. How's that going for you?

Lewis

It's going great. One thing I understand about God is that, as the Bible says, God orders our steps, and God has orchestrated my life. The life that I'm living now is what God has already ordained for me. And so I'm walking in my purpose, in what God has called me to do. And I have just had tremendous freedom. God has blessed me. You gotta realize when I went to jail at 15, I had not seen or done virtually anything. And in the time I've been out—maybe 14 months that I've been out—I've just done so much because of what God has allowed and blessed me to do. I took my first plane ride. I went out to Phoenix to visit my family.

And that was an amazing feeling because I'd never been anywhere before I went to prison. I never left Philadelphia. I flew to Phoenix and was out there for five days with my family. And that was just tremendous. And then, just living, you know, I started a ministry online called Men of Purpose. We meet every Saturday morning on Zoom. And I started that because when I came out, it's always been in my heart to do ministry because my passion is linking the church out here with the church on the inside, because I believe and feel that there is a gap between the church on the outside and the church inside. The church outside knows that people inside need the gospel and are willing to send missionaries, so to speak, into the prison, but there is still a disconnect.

You know, there's a stigma attached to those inside, even though they're now born again. And so there's a disconnect. So a part of my passion is bridging that gap because I know for me, the relationships that I was able to establish with the men and women in Christ have helped me in my transition out here. And I was able to establish those relationships because, in both prisons, I got a chance to meet a lot of volunteers one-on-one and just interact with them in ways that other men didn't have an opportunity. So I was able to build relationships so that when I came out, there were many men and women in Christ who were all in the stands, cheering for me and had been rooting for me and have been praying for me, and have been there for me.

So that is what has undergirded me in my walk, the Body of Christ, and also my desire to serve the Lord. So when I came out, I intended to go to church and start and build a prison ministry. Well, what happened? I got out, and there's a pandemic, and prison visiting is shut down along with churches. But I didn't allow that to deter me because I sensed God saying, "There's something else that you could do." And so that's why we meet every Saturday morning. And there are a lot of brothers who have been in prison, and there are pastors who come to this meeting every Saturday morning for that fellowship because, in prison, there's a unique fellowship amongst the brothers. So when you get out here, if there are no churches, a lot of men have lost that fellowship; they don't know how to find it. And so that's why I started the" Men of Purpose" ministry. And it's been a blessing,

YPM

As a man who once lived his life for the flesh, living for the moment, living for material things, who became a man who lives for spiritual things, what do you believe is the best way to lead people to the truth that you learned? What's the best way for all those young people, wherever they are, to learn to center their lives on the spirit and not the flesh?

Lewis

I believe the Lord will open up the door for me to speak to the youth. My message to the youth is simple: stop and think because that's something I didn't do. I never stopped and thought about my crimes and actions. So my message to the youth is just stop for a moment and think because every decision you make has a consequence that the enemy uses. The consequences are not always immediate. We think that everything is okay, but we know from a biblical perspective that the Bible says whatever a man sows, he will reap. So when you sow to the flesh, even as a young person, if you sow to the flesh, you will reap even if the reaping isn't immediate.

So my message to the youth is just stop and think about the decisions that you make. If you start smoking cigarettes, think about the consequences because there are consequences to smoking. We see the warning on the pack, but because we don't see immediate consequences like cancer, we think that everything is okay. But if you sow to the flesh, you will reap. So stop and think about sex. Your body says you want to have sex. What does that do to your life when you're 15 years old and now you have unwanted children, children born to children, now you are a 15-year-old father. What does that do? That sets you on a whole different course because now you have to take care of a child.

If you pick up a gun and you say, "I'm going to rob a store," have you thought this whole process out? What are you going to do when the owner doesn't want to give up the money? What are you going to do? Are you going to leave? Those things aren't thought through.

YPM

The mission of Yokefellowship Prison Ministry is to connect at-risk youth, inmates, returned citizens (former inmates) to Christ for salvation and changed lives. That's why we are here, to help yoke people to Christ so that their life will change and their eternal destinies will change. And you're certainly an example of that change.

Lewis

Well, thank you. God has tremendously blessed me. God is using me. I am just so excited every day about the possibilities that are there. I know that as I give my life to Him, I am being used by Him. God has good things for my life. And I'm excited.

I've tried to connect with all of the volunteers who knew me on the inside. I think I've connected with all of them. They know that I'm out. I haven't seen them all yet, but they know that I'm out. I wanted them to see the answer to their prayers because I know so many of them have been praying for me for 30 years.

YPM

I know that volunteers who visit prisons will be encouraged to hear how important it is for people from the outside to visit on the inside. Unfortunately, we've been shut out of the prisons because of the pandemic, and it breaks my heart. But we're coming back.

Lewis

Oh yeah, I can't wait for prisons to open because I'm going back when I get permission to do that.

YPM

Good for you. You have 44 years of credibility. That's a powerful tool to use. We need to get more people like you that are on the right path to go into the prisons and institutions and help inmates.

Lewis

That's why I have to go back. And that's why I will be going back. Inmates have to see it and hear it. I don't plan on going alone. I plan on taking the Men of Purpose Ministry back because those men came out of incarceration. And now they're out here, and they're living for the Lord, and they're making a difference in this world. And so the brothers and sisters need to see us. So I'm sure. Without a shadow of a doubt, I know I'm going to get approval to go back in.

Lewis Jerome Lee
Men of Purpose International
The Church of Christian Compassion
lee4jesus23@gmail.com

Biblical Reflection

We all have a choice to make. We can choose to seek the God who created us or attempt to find our purpose by chasing only the things this world offers. We can choose to be led by our flesh or by the Spirit. The choice we make will define our lives. Lewis Lee spent the first half of his life being led by the flesh. His life was marked by violence, addiction, ingratitude, and a lack of empathy. He was numb. But then he came to faith in Jesus Christ, and his life changed. 2 Corinthians 5:17 puts it this way, "Therefore, if anyone is in Christ, the new creation has come. The old has gone, the new is here." (NIV)

Lewis remembers how profoundly different his old life was from his new life. "I'm at peace because I'm not being driven by my flesh. The flesh is a taskmaster that needs to be fed. So I'm at peace. I'm at peace because I'm not gambling. I'm not chasing those things. I was at peace for the first time in my life, and I didn't understand it." Lewis is not naive; he knows how difficult and unfair life can be. "Do you believe that God is in control, even in situations that are not the best? Is God in control? And if God is in control, then everything is okay. Now there is still an enemy. I battle daily with the flesh. I have to deny the flesh every day. I have to pick up my cross and follow the Lord. It's just a different mindset."

Those who have not spent time in prison can only imagine what it feels like to be locked up for a day behind steel and concrete. Spending 44 years incarcerated, asking permission, being told when to wait, when to go, and what to do is incomprehensible. Yet, even so, God can redeem a man in that "valley of the shadow of death" and lead him to life and send him out to serve.

There is something much worse than spending 44 years in prison, and Lewis Lee knows what it is. He would give up his physical freedom and go back to prison rather than lose his spiritual freedom. Why?

"Because spiritual freedom entails eternal life. Physical freedom entails just maybe 70 years of life. And then it's hell. Spiritual freedom entails eternal life."

Chapter 6
Jeff Galitzky

Not everyone who spends time as an inmate wants to go back into prison to minister with inmates after they are released. Not everyone incarcerated gets a lifer as a cellmate who helps them make it through. Not everyone who gets out of prison has no problem "walking off"—completing years of parole. Not everyone gets through imprisonment without any racial issues. Not everyone who serves in Christian prison ministry begins life as a Jew.

YPM
Jeff, please begin by telling me how you started life. Where were you born? Who was your family? What kind of kid were you?

Jeff
I grew up in the Catskills in New York. I'm Jewish; both my parents were Jewish. I went to Hebrew school. I was bar mitzvahed.

YPM
Did you have brothers and sisters?

Jeff

I had a brother and a sister. I was the baby of the family. I was about five or six years old when my brother went into the service. My brother and sister wanted to get out of the house. My brother's way out was going into the service. And my sister got stuck at home until she was finally married. That was her way out.

YPM

Would you say you had a happy life as a kid?

Jeff

Life was difficult; I wouldn't say a happy life. It was all right. My parents weren't abusive or anything like that. My father didn't know how to show love to his children. He was a working man. He grew up in New York City and carried laundry bags when he was 12 years old for a quarter a day. He was born in Russia, and they moved to New York. I fought a lot with my dad. I got along well with my mother. I love my mother.

YPM

Did you like school? Were you good at school?

Jeff

I was average. I didn't excel or anything. I liked shop. I remember I went to wood shop, metal shop and got a little automotive stuff. And I liked tinkering when I got older.

YPM

So you get through childhood and get to your teenage years, and what happens for you?

Jeff

Well, I started driving and started getting into trouble. I got a lot of traffic tickets—speeding, bald tires, no exhaust, bad exhausts, a bunch of different stuff. And I was working; it seemed like back then for next to nothing. I just had an attitude. It seemed like the world owed me. And next thing you know, I started getting into trouble with the law. I started smoking cigarettes when I was 13. When I was 15, I started smoking reefer, and trouble just kind of progressed. And right after I graduated, we broke into the high school, and I got caught. Instead of going to prison right then and there, I was sent out to Pennsylvania. I knew a guy who was a Jewish man who had a relationship with the Mennonites in Pennsylvania. I don't know if it was an established program, but he was trying to get it set up. He was taking wayward kids and sticking them in these Amish families. They were Beachy Amish.

YPM

Was that old order Amish?

Jeff

They're the ones that drove with the black cars with black painted bumpers. I lived with them for about six months, and it was all about Jesus. They had Bible study, prayer and praise, revival meetings, church on Sunday, devotions every morning. I mean, you name it.

YPM

Were you angry that you were with the Beachy Amish, or were you enjoying it?

Jeff

Well, it was on a farm. I was on a dairy farm, one of the top dairy farms in Pennsylvania. It was called Dunwood Farms. I was out there for about six months, and I enjoyed that time. It was different. It was a different life. I eventually accepted Jesus, but I did it with my head and not my heart.

I felt the Holy Spirit urge me to do it. But I didn't have my heart into it. Eventually, I left. I wanted to do what I wanted to do. I knew what was best. So I left there. I didn't have a lot of Bible knowledge or anything. I learned stuff while I was with the people in the church during devotions, but I wasn't studying the Bible, and I didn't have a lot of Bible knowledge.

YPM
You said you grew up Jewish. Was your family active in the synagogue?

Jeff
We were Reform Jews. I can remember having bacon and eggs and bagels on Sunday. They made sure that I went to the temple all the time until I was bar mitzvahed. We went to weddings and funerals, but other than that, we didn't do that together.

So when I left the Amish, I wanted to do what I wanted to do. I spent the next 18 years doing what I felt was right for me. And that ended with me in prison.

I started out selling reefer. I sold pot for about 13 years. When that kind of dried up, I started selling cocaine. Then one of the guys I sold to got busted, and he set me up to sell to some undercover officers. That was pretty much the beginning of the end. So that's what got me into prison.

I knew I was going. There was no doubt about it; I just didn't know for how long. I didn't have any money, so I ended up with a legal aid lawyer, and he was kind of worthless. A couple of days before I went to court, I started cracking open a Bible again. The day before court,

I read my Bible, and I was scared. I was reading things that weren't making a lot of sense. But I said, "You know, Lord, I've done my life my way for the last 18 years, and this is what it got me. So now, can we do it Your way?"

So I go into court. I had bought a carton of cigarettes, and I had my pockets full. I had maybe nine packs of cigarettes packed into my pockets. You can't take open packs into prison. So I go to court, and the next thing I know, the judge is rattling off some numbers, and I see my lawyer adding things up.

So that's how I ended up with 7 to 20. When I saw my attorney writing 7 to 20 down on paper, my knees got weak. Remember the commercial with the Indian when he had one teardrop running down the side of his face. That was me. They took me into Lancaster County Prison, and I just started reading my Bible. I was in the county for 20 days, and I read every day—10, 12 hours a day. That's all that I did, pretty much. I came out to eat. I didn't hang out on the block. I didn't play cards. I just read my Bible. I remember when I got upstate, which was 20 days later, I was a wreck. I was actually into Exodus part way. I was partway through Exodus, and I was borrowing somebody else's Bible because mine didn't make it for some reason.

I was reading the parting of the Red Sea. And I can remember as I'm reading that I felt I was with the multitudes crossing the Red Sea on dry ground, and tears were just flowing down my face. I had to push the Bible out of my way because it wasn't mine, and I didn't want to get tears on all of his pages. It was quite an experience. So I just kept reading, and I signed up for pretty much every Bible study I could when I got into the upstate prison. And I started signing up for whatever correspondence studies I could. That's what I did. I went to work, read my Bible, and then worked out with weights.

Now when I went to prison, I was still smoking. And this actually kind of goes into another story cause I quit smoking in 1996 in prison. I had all these Christians pointing fingers at me, which is kind of funny. They're saying, "Don't you know the scriptures? Don't you know, your body is the temple of the Lord?" "I know," I said, "Yeah, I know all those scriptures, but when God is ready to deal with me, I'll quit smoking. You know, you're not the Holy Spirit. So when He lets me know it's time, it'll be time."

And I guess God got tired of me saying that because he hooked me right up. It was March 16, 1995. I went into prison on September 3, 1993. I had been living about two years with Lew—Lewis Lee—in a cell at this point. And they moved the furniture factory. They refinished it and made it into a dormitory. They opened that up, and we were the first group to go down there. And so it was Lew and me in a cubicle. And then we had two other Christian brothers join us. I was in the cube. It was 7:30 at night. There was nobody else there. The cube that we were in was a group room attached to the wall on the left-hand side. There was an aisle behind us and then to the right, another 10 or 20 cubes, just down the aisle. I'm lying in my bunk, and I'm smoking a cigarette.

And all of a sudden, I heard this voice, and it was an audible voice. And it said, "Why are you mocking me?" And I look around, and I look at all the beds in front of me, and there's nobody there and I kind of blow it off, and I keep on smoking and I hear it again. And it says, "Why are you making a fool out of me?" And I look under my bed. I look under the other three beds in the cube, and there's nobody there.

And I blow that off and keep on smoking. And all of a sudden, it comes again and says, "Why are you making a fool out of my name?" And I jumped up and looked over the wall behind me. There was a smart alec guy that was in the dorm, his name was Tom, and I expected to see him squatting behind the wall, and I looked, and there was nobody there. And I put my cigarette out. I said, "Okay, Lord, so you got this." I said, "Nah, I'm good for tonight. I don't see me smoking, but come tomorrow morning, I know me, and I'm going to want a cigarette, and you're going to have to do something about that." So I went through the rest of the night. I didn't smoke, and I didn't even have the desire. I told Lew about this and the other guys in the cube. And they were just kind of blown away. And next morning, I got up, and right away, I had that first instinct. I thought, "I want a cigarette." And as soon as that thought came into my head, I heard this, "How could you do that to me?" And I thought, "Oh, my goodness. Is that how you're going to play?"

So every time I thought I wanted a cigarette, I heard this voice, and it would say, "How can you do that to me?" And after about two days, I was pretty much scared. I didn't smoke anymore. Wow, now that was the only time, I've heard the audible voice of the Lord. It was plain as day. That was March 16, 1996, at 7:30 p.m. I still have the datebook from prison. And I have not had a cigarette since. I started walking fast for about a month or so after that and then started jogging. I went from 200 pounds and a 38-inch waist down to 159 pounds and a 32-and-a-half-inch waist.

I started lifting in 1994, which was amazing because I had back surgery in 1991. Two years before I went in, I had a final laminectomy on L5 S1. And I was babying my back because I thought I needed to. And when I got in there, I started doing things. I couldn't believe that I was squatting weight. I would put 150, 200 pounds up on my shoulders to squat. And if you'd have told me before I went to prison that I'd be doing that, I would have told you that you were out of your mind. So I ran for about four years straight. I ran a lot. So between studying the Word and the work I was doing in prison—which wasn't much—and running, that pretty much occupied all my time. Prison will keep you or kill you. It depends on what you do with it. I saw it destroy some guys.

YPM

"Prison will keep you or kill you." Is that what you said?

Jeff

Yes.

YPM

You say prison can destroy you. Tell me about somebody who was "destroyed."

Jeff

I've seen guys destroyed emotionally. I got sent in April of 1997 to another institution. They were opening Laurel Highlands, which had been Somerset State Hospital, and they needed workers out there. I didn't volunteer for it, but I got sent there. It was a geriatric prison. Some people had diabetes, people that had illnesses would go out there. And I saw a lot of people that just kind of gave up on life because they just couldn't handle it emotionally. If you've already got a disease, and you give up, it'll kill you. And I've seen that. I've seen other guys give up even before I got transferred. If you couldn't handle it emotionally and all you did was mope and whine and cry about the fact you're there and your time and what you have to do, it can destroy you. You can either do your time, or your time will do you.

YPM

You're in a different place. You're working, you've given up cigarettes, you're working out, you're reading the Bible.

Jeff

I chose to do my time, and God restored my lungs after I quit smoking. I was jogging 40 plus miles a week.

YPM

In the prison yard?

Jeff

Absolutely. I've jogged in place, in my cell, for two hours straight. With a pair of headphones on, I just put my mind somewhere else. When I came back to Camp Hill in 1998, they had some races, and I did a mile in 5:53. I was not a runner before, and I was jogging, but I sprinted at the very end. And I mean, that was all I had. There was nothing left. I couldn't have given you another 20 yards. I continued jogging, and when I was on pre-release, I jogged when I was at the center. I wanted to do the Harrisburg Marathon. In 2000 I ended up doing a little over a half-marathon, but I tore my meniscus, and that was pretty much the end of my jogging. I never got back into it.

YPM

Before I forget it, you referenced a roommate, Lewis Lee, who is in another chapter in this book, *Get Free and Stay Free.* You are White and Jewish and grew up in Catskills. Lewis Lee is Black and grew up in the city. What was it like where you grew up?

Jeff

When I was growing up, I didn't have any friends because there were no kids that lived near us. My mom was my only friend until I got into school. There was a 13-acre cornfield on the one side of us, a couple of small bungalows on the other side, and there were 87 acres of field and woods behind us.

YPM

Tell me about the relationship between a White kid from the Catskills who grew up out in the middle of nowhere and Lewis Lee, a Black kid from the city who grew up in gangs. You felt isolated. When you went to prison, you were crying and feeling it emotionally. You turned to the Lord. Lewis will tell you that when he went to prison, it seemed more normal. That's what you did in his neighborhood. You got in a gang, you got some time, you did your time, and you came out. You guys seem so different.

Jeff

Lew and I were on the same block. He had single-cell status because he was a lifer, and he enjoyed writing.

YPM

You were sentenced to 7 to 20 years, and he's a lifer. So what brought you together?

Jeff

We hung out outside. We played cards together. Lew was my pinochle partner for years. We lifted weights together in the yard. We had Bible studies out in the day room, and we were talking one day about possibly "celling up" together. And he says I got single-cell status and all that. And I said we couldn't just do it on our own. We had to request it from the block sergeant. We had to put an application to the unit manager, and he had to approve it. And the fact that he was Black and I was White, they didn't usually do that. And the unit manager approved it. We might've even prayed about it beforehand. I can't remember, but it was approved. And Lewis was life-changing for me. And let me clarify how. When an inmate has life, in his mind, in his world, he's never getting out. Life in Pennsylvania means life, not like Florida and some other states.

So when you have numbers, no matter how many numbers, there's always an end to it, at least. So Lewis encouraged me a lot. He got me through my time a lot. And he knows it. I've shared it with him. It gives you a different perspective on doing time when you do it with a lifer. We studied together. We memorized. I still have the composition book. We must've memorized a hundred scriptures. We would pick five scriptures every week, work on memorizing them, and test each other. We did Bible studies together. It was a time of growing close to the Lord. We had some really good fellowship together. He was my pinochle partner for five years. I talked to him the other day, and I said, "We gotta get a game together." I haven't played in 21 years. Life changes your perspective on things. When I got out, God opened a lot of doors for me.

YPM

How many years had you served in prison when you got out?

Jeff

Six years and four months. I got released to a halfway house. I went to Cameron Street in Harrisburg. I could see where God showed me favor in many things that happened when I was in a halfway house. I put in a home plan for my former mother-in-law's house. She was okay with it, but her husband didn't want it. He had some guns in the house that he didn't want to get rid of or take out of the house. So that got turned down.

I'm four months into the halfway house, and I've been working since the week after I got there. I got there on a Monday. The following Monday, I had a job. I had my home plan turned down, and almost every weekend, the place would clear out cause everybody was getting furloughs or going home to their plan. So I was stuck at the center and didn't get to go anywhere—my last eight months in prison. I was on "community detail," where we would go out and work. One of the places we did work was at Fairview Township. We painted the township building and cut many trees down for them.

All these guys are getting furloughs, and I'm just sitting there. So I started looking for an apartment. Other guys were looking, and they couldn't find anything. I called three numbers, and one number called me back. I told them a little bit about myself. They wanted to meet me. I went up, and it was an older couple. I was talking to the husband and wife. As it turns out, their son had gotten in trouble, and he was in prison in Johnstown. He was in state prison out there. He'd gotten out, and somebody gave him a chance, and they turned around and said, "So because of that, we're willing to give you a chance." I said "Okay." So I go back and start submitting my paperwork. And my counselor wasn't there at the time. He was having issues with his home life. There was some stuff going on. He was off for a few days. It was probably for the best because God was orchestrating this, and I didn't know it. I submitted all this paperwork to the counselor at the halfway house, who wasn't my counselor. They have to approve your paperwork. Then they have to go to the place you're going to be staying at, do a walk-through, and make sure everything's okay.

He got my paperwork. He did a walk-through, and by Wednesday, approved it. You have to have a phone because if there's no phone in the place, you can't go there or get a furlough. As crazy as it is with the phone companies, I called them on Wednesday, and I had a phone by Friday. I put in for a weekend furlough, and it was approved. So I spent my first weekend in my apartment.

I came back to the halfway house, and of course, they gave me a breathalyzer, and I had to pee in a cup. The following week I went to work. I stayed in the halfway house. The next week, I put in for another furlough. The next weekend I get called into the director's office, and he says, "Kid, you got your place, right?" "Yeah." "So you got a phone, right? I need your bed. Get out."

"What do you mean get out?" And he said, "I need you to pack your stuff, get out." I'm like, "Well, I can't just get out. It doesn't work that way. You know, there's state rules of the halfway house." "Oh yeah," he said. "Okay. So tell you what, normally you can be out for six days and you have to spend one day in the halfway house. It's called a six in one." Now what he did for me was, he gave me that six and one and then told me that I had to come in for three hours each week.

So I would come in each week and sit in the halfway house for three hours and then go back to my apartment. Now I wasn't allowed to be there since I wasn't living in the halfway house. I wasn't even allowed to use the weights and work out or anything like that. So the monitors would be there to keep an eye on me most of the time. They knew my situation, and they didn't want me to sit there twiddling my thumbs for three hours. So a lot of times, after 15 or 20 minutes, they'd say, "Let's go down the hall. We'll sign you out." That went on until the end of my time at the halfway house. After that, I was on parole. I walked off 13 years of parole.

I didn't have any issues. I had seven parole officers; they loved me because I was easy. They didn't have to worry about me. The last guy I had for four or five years. He used to find me on a roof. I did commercial HVAC and refrigeration. So he'd find me on some roof. Every year I would have to fill out a parole plan stating how I was and what I was doing. He had the thing filled out for me. Then he would call me and say, "So what roof are you on today?" Around September, he'd show up in the parking lot and call me and say he was here. I would go down and sign the parole plan, and off he'd go. That would be the only time

I would see him. Since he was out of Chambersburg, every time I was up that way, I'd stop in and say hello or give it to him voluntarily just because I was in the neighborhood.

God opened different doors for me. I was involved in other prison things. For example, I knew there was a ministry called Second Chance Ministries. They used to come in with volunteers, and they would count laps and pray with the inmates during the runathon. So I was on parole, and I was out one year—you've gotta be out a year before you can go back to the prison. So I put in paperwork to go in with Second Chance Ministries for the runathon, and it got denied. But then the lady in activities took the paperwork and went to the superintendent and said, "Look, I'd like him to come in," and she got it approved. So I went in and did the runathon with the guys I was running with the year before.

They also did a runathon banquet, and I got to go back in for that. So I went in for seven runathons and seven banquets. There was another amazing thing, and it was a God thing. A deputy called me from prison and said, "You know, every year, you seem to have somebody fighting for you to get you approved to come in. Why don't you fill out the paperwork to get your picture at the gate to be a volunteer?"

So I got approved and had my picture at the front gate of Camp Hill, and I went in as a volunteer with Yokefellowship Prison Ministry. But pride comes before a fall, and I did something very stupid. I had that ID with me before I turned it into the prison. I took a picture of that ID. And a buddy of mine who I was ministering did something stupid and went back to prison. I sent him a copy of this picture and said, "Look at the doors God is opening for me." That was just a big no-no.

I was involved in another program at Camp Hill, helping inmates reintegrate into society. Plus, God had opened the door to allow me to be on Lewis Lee's approved list as his spiritual advisor. And I was able to go into the prison he was in, Mahanoy SCI, and visit him. And it wouldn't cost him a visit because spiritual advisor visits don't count against you. I brought my wife up with me a couple of times. I went into the vending machines and bought him some stuff, and it was my way of pouring back into his life, blessing him, and giving back to him. I sent Lewis money. If there were something extra or something special that he needed or wanted, he'd call me and say, "Hey, if you got it, I want to buy this tablet, or I need a new TV. Can you send me $75?" I'd send it. No problem, no questions asked because of the effect and the impact he had on my life. I couldn't turn my back on Lew. He was my friend. He was my brother. That's what got me through my time.

YPM

When you went to Camp Hill, you met Lewis, right? Was that before the riot or after the riot?

Jeff

I arrived in 1993. The riot was in 1989.

YPM

Lewis talks about how he came to the Lord and then backslid for seven years. He went back to the world, and then he came back to Lord and stayed. Where was he in his spiritual journey when you were with him?

Jeff

He was in the Lord fully.

YPM

When the Supreme Court ruling came down and Lewis finally got released, you must have been elated. Did you have a party with him? Did you feel like you got out yourself? How did that feel for you?

Jeff

When he went to court to apply for his first court date, I was there. When he told me he was getting out, it was kind of funny because he knew about the motorcycle club and everything else. That's also part of where I was going with some of the other stuff. I've been with the CMA since 2003.

YPM

CMA stands for Christian Motorcycle Association, correct?

Jeff

Correct, and our chapter has done prison ministry for years. And that was another door that opened when I was going to the other prisons. There were six or eight of us that would go in. We had our praise and worship team, and we'd go in and do a complete service. Lewis was in Mahanoy SCI at the time, and we were going in, and I was visiting with him in the chapel.

So Lewis knew about the motorcycle club. I told him where it was and the meeting time. It was February of last year. I'm in the meeting, and my secretary says, "Well, Jeff, why don't you sit over here?" And I sat down. I turned around and looked to my left. I saw this black guy sitting there, and I didn't pay any mind. And then I turned around, and it was Lewis sitting next to me, and it just floored me.

YPM

Wow. So what did you guys do?

Jeff

We hugged, I bought breakfast, and we hung out, and we talked. I found out where Lewis was staying. A couple of weeks later, we met at a fast-food restaurant because I was going there to do work. And so he was there. I knew he always wanted to get into ministry, and he wanted to start something. In prison, there was a group of guys called "Men of Purpose," and I'm sure, I'm sure he talked about it. And he always wanted to try to get the brothers back together or try to contact most of them.

They do the Zoom thing on Saturdays, and when I can, I log in and join them. If I'm free, when they plan something, like a movie night or a Chinese buffet here in Mechanicsburg, I join them. My wife and I went over and hung out with everybody. I got off the phone with Lew yesterday. I've got an old boat. I told him we'll try to plan for August, and we'll go down to the marina. I'll get down there nice and early in the morning so we can get one of the barbecue areas. We'll have the guys all come down and spend the entire day and evening down there. And we'll just do some tubing, and anybody who wants can try water skiing. We'll just have some good fellowship and have a good time together.

YPM

Jeff, in the world we live in, race is a big issue. We're trying to unpack racial issues that go back hundreds of years, and it's not easy. So here you are, a guy who grew up in the Catskills in a Jewish family. You get in trouble and go to prison. You're White. On the outside, you're in the majority. But now you're in prison at Camp Hill, and you're in the minority racially. And then you room and with a black guy, and you have an excellent relationship. What does race mean in prison? How did you guys deal with the racial tension? How did you respond to the racial environment that was there?

Jeff

Believe it or not, it wasn't a factor. I had more problems growing up as a child. I was pretty much picked on and beat up my entire life for being Jewish. Guys on the street called me, "JJ, Jeff the Jew." I can remember in school, four or five guys would throw me into one of the corners and say we'll be down the hallway or something, and just start something on me. And that happened multiple times a week. So I was probably the least prejudiced person. I know the Jews have been persecuted for their entire existence. So when I got into prison, it didn't matter whether you were Black or White. If somebody was an idiot, they were an idiot. It didn't matter what the color was. So there's some White idiots, some Black idiots, you got to try to overlook it and just "love on people."

YPM

So it's like Martin Luther King said, your prison experience was not about Black and White. You were looking for people who cared about "the content of your character and not the color of your skin." So race wasn't an issue for you?

Jeff

No. Now there are many guys that, because they couldn't belong to anything else, many Black guys would grab hold of the Muslim thing. And it was because it was easy. After all, it gave them certain perks and certain advantages. A lot of guys weren't true Muslims. There's a lot of guys who try to grab hold of the Christian card and use it as a benefit. A lot of guys, when they walk out of prison, the first thing they do is they throw their Bible down, and they walk away. There were guys that had a change and had their hearts changed, whether Muslim or Christian. These people were real, and their experiences were real.

Camp Hill itself was a very protected prison because they put gates up everywhere after the riot, and you could only go so far without a gate that you had to walk through. So if you were into homosexual activity, you would find a way to make that happen. Whether you allow it or not, it went on, but it only went on with the people that wanted it. Guys weren't getting raped in Camp Hill. It wasn't like other prisons. I don't know if I want to say I was lucky to be there.

YPM

This book is about people that the Yokefellowship Prison Ministry has impacted. John Rush, a former executive director, gave me your name. Tell me about your experience with Yokefellowship when you were an inmate.

Jeff

Yokefellowship came on Thursday nights at Camp Hill. I always looked forward to them coming in. Larry Lingle was one of the main people. I've been to his church a bunch of times since I've been out. One time I was at a party for him. Yokefellowship was just a bunch of guys that loved the Lord. They would come in, and they just "loved on you." We would learn and study scripture. It was really good. They were a great group and so when I got out, I went in with them.

I went back into the prison a couple of times before I lost my clearance. I lost everything. I came off Lew's list. I wasn't his spiritual advisor anymore. I wasn't allowed to go in with a motorcycle group to minister in prison anymore. I wasn't allowed to go in with Yokefellowship anymore.

I put in clean clearance checks for seven years to go back in with the motorcycle group. And it was always denied. I wrote letters. I had written letters to Lew. I tried to get a meeting with him. I talked to counselors. I spoke with some of the pastors in the prisons, and nothing. I couldn't get anything to happen. And one day, the prison coordinator, which is my job now, was lining up the prisons, and he called me and said, "What are you doing this Sunday?" "I'm going to church. Like I normally do." He said, "No, you're not." He said, "You're going in this Sunday. They approved you to go in." I said, "Are you sure?" He said, "Yeah, that was my question. I was so concerned when I saw your name. I called the institution to make sure." And he said that I was approved. So it took seven years for God to put it back together again and get me back in the prison. Prior, I was only in a couple of months in a couple of institutions. After seven years, we were going into seven or eight institutions. Nice!

YPM

Tell me this, Jeff. I go to visit in prison as a volunteer, but it's not the same as a guy like you who's been there going back in. I understand the hesitancy to let former inmates back in, but it seems to me that if you can find a person that has been in, has gotten their freedom and stayed free, and has made the kind of life decisions you have, a healthy person with a good heart, that is powerful. Returned citizens going back in to visit have a credibility others do not.

Jeff

I felt that way when I was on campus.

YPM

I assume that when a guy like you comes in, the inmates see somebody in the flesh who's gotten free, who's made it, that prison didn't demolish. Somebody who didn't just do their time but grew. What does it do for the inmates when a person like you goes in and ministers to them?

Jeff

I know it touches them. I can only speak from a personal experience that I had. When I was in Camp Hill, a guy named Tom Elhodge came in, and I talked with him. I listened to him. It was money laundering. He did federal time, which isn't the same. He told his story, and it moved me. I thought, wow, that's phenomenal. It gave me hope and knowledge that change could happen, that you can grow. You can be something, make something of your life. So when I got out, all I wanted to do was go back in. It's kind of funny because a lot of other guys don't want anything to do with it. They get out, they want to put it as far behind them as possible, and they don't want to be going back in. I feel like that would be turning my back and abandoning everybody.

So when our motorcycle group would go into the prisons, the worship leader would usually introduce guys to give testimonies. When I gave my testimony, she'd introduce me, and I'd walk up and get the mic and thank them. I would tell them how glad I was to be there. Then I said, "Forget, my name is Jeff Galitzky. My number is CE1300." And all of a sudden, their eyes would get wide. That is my inmate number. And I had everybody's attention. "I wore the same color browns that you wear, the same state shoes that you're wearing. I did the same things that you do. I sat where you sit." It makes an impact just because we're on the same level.

And then I could just talk to them one-on-one. I told inmates there's hope after prison; there's life beyond prison. It's all about the decisions you make. When I left prison, I made a conscious decision that nothing I was going to do would bring me back. I can't control you or anybody else that gets in my circle. I can't control anybody else, but I sure can control myself. So with God's help, that was a promise. I made that decision. I made that promise. I was not going to bring myself back to prison.

YPM

That's advice for inmates. What advice would you give to volunteers who care about people in prison? Jesus said, when you visit somebody in prison, you are visiting Him. What counsel would you give to people in prison ministries who take the time to consistently be a presence in correctional institutions?

Jeff

All the inmates appreciate their hearts and their love. It is a little different than a guy like me. It's a different story. They're still giving you their time. They're still showing their love.

YPM

What advice would you give volunteers to be more effective? What should their goal be? What should their attitude be?

Jeff

Just keep on loving them. That's all you can do. Show you care. The volunteers are not going to have the same story I have, but they have a story. They have a story about how God changed them. Their life somehow changed. Their story may not have been dramatic but don't be discouraged. Just keep plugging away. Eventually, guys see the love. They see the commitment, and all you can do is just let God do His thing.

YPM

Jeff, it's been wonderful talking to you. I heard about you through Lewis Lee, and now I understand how you and Lewis connected.

Jeff

I enjoy being around him. Unfortunately, we don't get to hang out with him being in Philly. It was funny; I said this to him the other day.

There's different etiquette when you share a cell. One day Lewis hollered at me. I was brushing my teeth in the cell, and I spit my toothpaste out in the sink. I'm sure that's how you brush your teeth, right?

He hollered at me because he washed his clothes in the sink. He said, "You don't do that. You spit that in the toilet." I didn't grow up spitting my toothpaste in the toilet, but that's a cellie etiquette type thing. I called him up, and I asked him if he remembers, and he didn't remember specifically hollering at me for that. He said, "Well, that's just, that's just cellie etiquette." I said, "But what do you think about that now?" because I'm sure he's not spitting toothpaste in the toilet.

YPM

When I talk to Lewis again, I will ask him about toothpaste in the toilet. Jeff, have a great day. It's been good getting to know you,

Jeff

You do the same. God bless. Thank you. Have a great day.

Jeffrey Galitzky

Christian Motorcyclists Association, Tribe of David, Harrisburg, Pennsylvania

Jesus Ministries (Agape Farm), Shirleysburg, Pennsylvania

Crossroads Community Church, Mechanicsburg, Pennsylvania

jefgal93@gmail.com

Biblical Reflection

After Joseph forgave his brothers who had sold him into slavery in Egypt, a sin that led to him receiving a prison sentence, he brought his father Jacob and his brothers and their families to Egypt to save them from starvation. The Pharaoh had put Joseph in charge of the entire country because of his ability to interpret dreams and wisdom. Joseph was a returned citizen who got free and stayed free and became highly successful.

Over many generations, the population of the Israelites had exploded, and their numbers threatened the Egyptians. And now there was a new Pharaoh who did not remember Joseph. So the Egyptians devised a plan to crush the Israelites by forcing them into slave labor. But as the Israelite population grew, they were increasingly feared and hated by their Egyptian masters. They were persecuted until they were eventually led out of Egypt by Moses.

As a Jew, Jeff Galitzky was familiar with the historical persecution of the Jews and his own experience of persecution. In school, he was called "JJ"—Jeff the Jew—and some of his peers tormented him. As a young man, he gave his head to Christ but not his heart and then spent 18 years living life his way. When he was facing trial on charges of selling marijuana and cocaine, he knew he was lost and prayed, "You know, Lord, I've done my life my way for the last 18 years, and this is what it got me. So now, can we do it Your way?"

Sentenced to 7 to 20 years in prison, he spent his next 20 days in a county jail where he came out of his cell to eat but otherwise stayed there reading the Bible 10 to 12 hours a day for each of those 20 days. Then, transferred to a state institution, he was reading in Exodus about how God had saved the Jews when the Red Sea was blocking the path to freedom in front of them, and Pharaoh's army was closing fast behind them. "I was reading the parting of the Red Sea. And I can remember as I'm reading that I felt I was with the multitudes crossing the Red Sea on dry ground, and tears were just flowing down my face. I actually had to push the Bible out of my way because it wasn't mine, and I didn't want to get tears on all of his pages."

Jeff Galitzky was in that Israelite multitude. When you are facing a sea of 7 to 20 years in prison, and the enemy is your stubborn pride gaining fast behind you, you are in that multitude. You and I are in that multitude too. We all have seas in front of us which are too broad and deep for us to cross, and our greatest enemy, our tendency to be slaves to sin, is behind us and quickly gaining ground. So when we read in the Bible about how God made it possible for those helpless people to cross the sea on dry ground and escape their enemy, we better push the "Good Book" away, or we too will get tears all over the story.

Chapter 7
Jack Schrader

Most people interviewed for this book have had circumstances in their lives that increased the odds they might make poor decisions. For example, parents struggling with drugs or alcohol or poverty, gangs introducing violence or drug use, sexual or other abuse at home, poor schooling, the lack of a religious center, and the absence of good role models can contribute to a person making bad choices. But Jack Schrader was different. He had an idyllic young life. Except for some typical college behavior, he seemed to be on a clear path to an idyllic older life, but the road Jack was traveling on his life's journey collapsed.

YPM

Jack, we try to get to know a person from the inside out and understand their story. So please start with your childhood. Could you tell me where you came from and who your family was as you were growing up?

Jack

I was born in Williamsport, Pennsylvania, to John Robert Schrader, Jr., and Beverly Jane Schrader. I grew up on Loyalsock Creek in the country and enjoyed life as a kid. In elementary school, I went to a three-room schoolhouse. The first and second grades were in one room, the third and fourth were in one room, and the fifth and sixth were in one room; it was a really neat experience. We would go out and build forts at recess. There were two big things when you got into the fifth and sixth grades if you were good. First, you got to ring the bell for recess for the other classes—it was a black button in the back of the room. The other one was you got to go down to the basement and get the milk for everybody at lunchtime, little half-pints.

We rode an early 50s school bus. It was short and squat, and Russell Wollver was our bus driver. And it's not like it is today. If you misbehaved on the bus, I don't care if it was the middle of January, he'd pull off the road, you got off the bus, and you had to worry about how you'd get home. And you never sat on the left side of the bus in warm weather. Russell always had a big wad of Red Man (chewing tobacco). He used to spit out the window, and it would go all the way down the left side. So you kept your windows shut on the left side of the bus.

K. Frank Derr had the fifth and sixth graders, and he had a paddle that hung up. It had to be 30 inches long with holes drilled through it. The paddle's name was Clarence, and he was not afraid to use Clarence on you at all. You can't do that kind of stuff today, but back then, you could. I have one sister, Patty; she's three years older than me. We would get off the bus and run down our 230-foot driveway, run into the garage to grab our fishing poles and vest jackets, go to the refrigerator, grab our night crawlers, and get out on the creek and fish after school. And my mom would yell down, "Kids, dinner's ready." "Okay, Mom, just a minute," then about 15, 20 minutes would go by. She'd do it again.

"Okay, we'll be right there." The third time, my dad came out, and you knew it was time to come to dinner.

YPM
That sounds like an idyllic childhood.

Jack
There were no problems, no kind of abuse. They were wonderful parents. We were brought up going to First United Methodist Church. I was an Eagle Scout. For four years, I served on the Camp Kline staff, a Boy Scout camp on Pine Creek. So I had an excellent upbringing.

I went to Lycoming College, pre-dental biochemistry. I kind of stepped away from the Lord and got into the college frolicking. I guess you'd call it. I got my degree there. I was living with two fraternity brothers. One of the fraternity brother's fathers was very wealthy. He was a vice-president of Johnson & Johnson, and he bought Eric a house, and we lived there. So we were off-campus. There were parties there and this, that and the other. And I kind of got off track there. I went to work selling cars.

And then I went to work for a startup company called Computer Mail Order. We were the first in the country to manufacture IBM clones. And I stayed with them, and the company just grew and grew. By 1980, we built a beautiful facility in an industrial park. I was the corporate distribution manager. We would sell software packages and machines to educational institutions, colleges, and high schools. And we had an office out in Lake Tahoe.

I was walking down the hall, and I looked in the computer room as I went by. Computers were really big back in the day, and they printed on those tractor-feed printers. I saw this girl in her little shorts. "Look at that," I said, "I've got to ask her out." That was the beginning. And we've been together ever since. The Lord put that girl in my life for a reason.

In this atmosphere at that particular place, I was asked by an individual if I knew where he could get some cocaine. He told me he had a couple of lawyer friends looking for it, but they were afraid just to go out and try to find it. So they asked him if he would do something for them, and I knew where to get it. And I did, and he was wearing a wire. He was working for the district attorney.

YPM

How did you know how to get it? Were you using yourself?

Jack

Oh yeah. I used some recreationally. I didn't use it a lot, but I knew a guy who did it and figured, well, okay, I'll get it and make a couple of hundred bucks for doing nothing. You know?

YPM

You're married. Do you have children?

Jack

We called ourselves "Dinks"—double income, no kids. I was arrested when I was 34 years old.

YPM

You're 34 years old. You're married. You get some cocaine, and you deliver it to this guy, and he was going to pay you for it.

Jack

Yup. The guy who set me up paid me for it ahead of time. And it was marked money, and he was wearing a wire.

YPM

So were you arrested right away?

Jack

Pretty close to it. The guy had been arrested for, I guess, the cocaine. The district attorney was under the impression that the owner of MMI was so successful and had so much money because he was a drug king-pin. So he set this whole thing up so that I would turn this guy in and set up a buy with him. And I told him, "No," I said, "He's not. He's a good businessman. And we all work hard. And we have a great business. That's how he got wealth." They didn't believe it. Ernie Preate was the attorney general of Pennsylvania at the time. And the state had given $100,000 to the Lycoming County district attorney's office task force for the investigation.

After the fact when I got the transcripts, I found out they were sitting outside my house. They followed Cindy and me everywhere. They knew when we had lights on. We had automatic lights, and they shined out where we fed the deer. Every time the light went on or went off, they had it written down. We would go up to "Little Bears" to look at the stars. There's a fire tower up there. There's this big field where you have an unobstructed view of the sky. And we would see a meteor shower. So we would go up with a blanket and lay down there. They thought we were up there doing drug deals and followed us up there. And it's just a long, long story. But they came up with nothing because there was nothing else.

And I told the district attorney, "You know what I did. You know the whole story." They wanted me to go to our Christmas party at the Oaks Club and sell some cocaine to the president of the company—who was the best man at my wedding and the owner of the company—and another gentleman. I said, "I'm not doing it." And he said, "Well, Mr.

Schrader, you made your bed. You'll sleep in it." I said, "Okay." This was a Thursday. I said, "I'll tell you what, I will come in, and I'll turn myself in on Monday. I would like to at least have the weekend with my wife." He said, "Okay, that'd be fine."

So then, Friday night at home, I'm sitting in my pajamas, and so is my wife. We are sitting at the table, eating dinner, all of a sudden, there's a knock at the door. And my wife opens the door, and boy, they come in guns drawn, take her out in the living room. She's screaming and scared to death. They told me to get dressed and put me in the car. And the district attorney, I really shouldn't name, I went to high school with him. I knew him very well. And he looked like Kojak with a trench coat on. And he is sitting in the front seat of the police car and says, "I'm sorry, it has to be like this, Jack." And I said, "Well, it didn't. I told you I would have been in on Monday. Where am I running to?" I was making good money. In the early 80s, I made $38,000, which was good money back then.

YPM

So your wife is screaming.

Jack

Yep.

YPM

How are you feeling? All these guys had guns drawn, and you are in your pajamas. Are you angry? Are you scared? Are you crying? What was your reaction?

Jack

I was livid. I was livid with the way they did it. They put it in the newspaper, "Local Businessman, Drug Kingpin." I mean, they tried to make this big thing out of it because they had gotten all this money, thinking that they would get this big cocaine ring that never existed. And then they took me in my home like that and scared my wife like that. It was unacceptable. That's where I started, and I went to the county jail, and then I went from county to Camp Hill SCI.

YPM

So you had never been arrested for anything before in your life? Have you ever committed another crime?

Jack

I had a DUI. I was just over the limit. That was the only thing, not even a parking ticket.

YPM

So what are you going through in county jail? This is the first time in your life that a heavy metal prison door shut behind you.

Jack

Well, I guess I'm getting ahead of myself. I'm at the sentencing. You couldn't get any more people in the courtroom. They were even out into the hallway in support. They knew what was going on. They knew me. They knew how I was. And for my first offense, I got 8 to 16 years, first offense. So when I went to prison, it was a very strange experience. I didn't know at that point what my life was going to be like. I was upset. I was feeling disgusted. I was feeling like I let everybody down—my parents, my wife, my friends, my church—because I was involved in so much stuff, community service stuff. And you know, everybody knows me.

And then they put that on the front page of the paper. Then I went to jail, and of course, they had a report about the sentencing; it had to go into the paper. So there's all those emotions—anger, guilt, frustration—all those things. As I said, I didn't know what was going to happen to my life. I mean, the next thing you know, I'm in a jail cell. It's loud, and it's crazy in there. When I first come in, of course, everybody's yelling, trying to intimidate you. So I was there for maybe a month, six weeks, and they transferred me to Camp Hill. And my timing was good because that was right after the Camp Hill riots, where they burned everything that could have done them any good. Everything else—educational stuff, the library—was burned except the chapel. All that was left were the cell blocks and the church.

So I went there for classification, and I was there for probably another six months. It was a bad stop because the guards weren't in any mood. They would take us to the shower handcuffed together. And how are you supposed to wash, you know what I mean? And so you tried to soap as much as you could and then switched, and everybody had to switch hands and wash. Then the guards stood there and said, "Soap off," and hit the thing and scalded you to death with the hot water. Also, we were locked up the whole time, and there was a slot in the bottom of the cell door, and they would kick your food tray underneath it. They just treated us terribly there. So then, when I got classified, they sent me to SCI Dallas because of the length of my sentence at that time. It was mostly lifers and real long-term, 20-plus years, that kind of thing. Again my timing was excellent because that's when prison overcrowding was a big issue. SCI Dallas originally was a juvenile detention facility. The cells were very small, but they were single cells.

And the next thing you know, you're taking in some young snot-nosed kid. Maybe you've been in that cell for 25 years. That's your home; that's where you live. And now you've got to share it with somebody. So there were a couple of really nasty riots while I was there. There was one on my block where a lot of people were hurt very, very badly. A lot of guards were hurt very badly, but I just made up my mind when I got there. If I have to spend this time, I'm going to do something.

The best way to go through that system is to mind your own business and make good use of your time. So while I was there, I got a degree in business administration, summa cum laude from Luzerne County Community College. I was a Laubach literacy tutor. Then I got involved in the church again, and Chaplain Paul and I became pretty close. I was in the choir there. I went to a couple of different Bible studies there, and I got back into the Word. I saw God's hand all over things when I was there. There's no question things that happened or didn't happen were miracles in my life. There were just bad situations that could have been terrible for me, and I was protected.

YPM

How did you first come to faith in Christ? Did you always believe or was there a big decision day in your life?

Jack

I wouldn't say I wasn't saved. I went to church, but as far as accepting Him as my Lord and Savior, it wasn't until this happened. I remember at my house. I lived out on Route 87. My wife and I lived there for 23 years. I had 48 acres of land, plus three came with the house. We had a little bridge that went over a stream. After I was arrested, I remember standing on that bridge and looking at the mountain and just saying, "Lord, I don't know what I can say other than 'I'm sorry.'" I was feeling like I had let everybody down. I said, "Lord, I need forgiveness because if I don't get your forgiveness, then I don't know how I'm going to go through this whole situation I got myself into." And I accepted Christ right there as my Lord and Savior.

I always believed, but I wasn't dedicated. And I don't know if that's the right word, but I wasn't dedicated to Christ, His Word, His behaviors, His way of living. I studied the Bible cover to cover, but since then, it's been so overwhelming. You're forgiven all your sins, they're gone. They don't even exist. He doesn't even remember them anymore. That's where I accepted Him rather than just being a church-going guy.

YPM

So you had been arrested. You were at your house on this bridge looking at the mountain. And that's when you gave your life for real, not just your beliefs, but your whole body, your soul, your heart. You dedicate yourself to the Lord. Prison is awful; it's loud, it's chaotic. So now you experience this change in your relationship with Christ. How did giving your life to Christ affect you during those awful days?

Jack

I just felt this protection around me. There were two riots when I was there. One riot happened when the guard opened all the gates for the inmates to go to the yard. When all the other gates opened, somehow, mine and a couple of other people's cells went shut. Ah, come on. You know what I mean? You couldn't pull them shut. They're all automatic.

YPM

Other people are rioting, and you're locked in your cell.

Jack

Yup. And it was nasty. It was nasty. I saw things that were just terrible, terrible things. I saw people just get sliced and diced. There wasn't an inch of their body that wasn't cut. I saw terrible things, and He protected me the whole time. That was one instance. Something that could have happened that would have been bad didn't happen. There were educational opportunities that I was given. And my parents and my wife, our family attorney, Fred Holland, who was a civil attorney and had never done criminal work, was also a friend of the family. He took my case to the Superior Court in Philadelphia, a three-judge panel. And something didn't quite ring right with this situation. So they sent it out to the full nine-judge Superior Court in Pittsburgh. So my parents and my wife, Cindy, and my attorney went out there, and he pleaded the case in front of the full nine-judge panel. They decided that it was an illegal sentence. "Let the man go." So there again, God was at work.

YPM
How long had you been in prison when you were released?

Jack
Almost four years. So they let me out to a pre-release center. And my dad gave me a job because you either had a job or went to "work crew." You'd go down to the recycle center or ride a recycle truck and pick up stuff on highway cleanup or something.

My dad had started a business. He was the president of Lundy Lumber Company. And then Lundy Lumber bought Briggs Lumber in New York. So they had 14 lumber yards, and then American Maize bought Lundy-Briggs and took it public and made my dad president of Lundy-Briggs, a division of American Maize-Products Co.

Well, he didn't like it at all. He's not the jet-set kind of guy. He didn't like the corporate mentality where people don't matter. You just squash them. So he resigned and started with two other guys that were with him. They all resigned. They started their own company, LSM Enterprises, Lundy Schrader Miller, an overhead door company. They had Schrader Architectural Products, a spin off of Allied Building Products. So my dad hired me. Then he brought me into his office, and he said, "You know, I've always wanted you to work for me, but you had your career path. You were doing well." He also said, "Why don't we buy Schrader Overhead Door and split off from the homes' division, and we'll have RSJ Enterprises, Inc., Robert Schrader Jr.?" and I said, "Okay."

When I came to work in the office, the first day I came in, my office was here, and my dad's office was right there. I knew nothing about construction, about architectural products, about overhead doors, nothing! On the first day on the job, someone came into his office and asked him questions. He said, "You'll have to ask Jack. He's your boss."

And he kept doing it, and I was really upset. I was almost in tears after about a week. I said, "Dad, why are you doing this to me? Are you trying to punish me or what?" He said, "No, Jack, I love you." He said, "You're going to learn. And this is the way you learn. If you don't know the answer, you will figure it out." He says, "I'm not trying to punish you. I'm just trying to teach you how to rationally think through this business and how to handle employees." After that, I was a wreck. The first day at a job and the first week, I mean, people were just coming and asking me questions.

So it was tough love, but God's hand was all over it because that was 1994. And then, in 1997, my father was diagnosed with esophageal cancer. It was bad. They opened him up all the way, and they removed his entire esophagus, the top part of the stomach, and drug the rest of the stomach up and attached it to his throat. It was horrible. I watched him die for three years. So I had to run a business.

I don't know if he knew something was going on. If he hadn't done that, I wouldn't have been ready; I'm done. My mom thinks he knew something was going on, and he wanted to get me prepared. But it was very, very sad. He wasted away to nothing. He died on September 11, 1999, my best friend. He keeps his eye on me.

YPM

Take me back to Superior Court in Pittsburgh. Were you in a jail cell or were you actually in the courtroom?

Jack

I was in jail.

YPM

So your mom and dad and your wife Cindy and your attorney friend were there. You thought you would be in prison for 8 to 16 years? How did you hear that you were getting out in less than four years?

Jack

Oh my, as soon as I got the decision, oh my word, I was ecstatic. They asked my attorney and friend, Fred Holland, because there was some precedent, but it wasn't clear. So if Fred answered it one way, I'd have stayed in prison. That was it. But he had to answer it the right way. It was like a yes or no. And then they made their decision, and I think it was unanimous. They called me right away.

They vacated the sentence, and it was illegal. So we went back to the courtroom, and I had probably 10 letters from corrections officers at SCI Dallas. They're not allowed to write letters in support of inmates.

In prison, I never was in trouble. I had a letter from the district attorney that did this to me: he wrote a letter and said in all his years of law enforcement, I was the only person he felt deserved not only a reconsideration but a pardon. And I got a letter from the other judge. I had letters from the community, from community leaders. I had all kinds of support. And when I went to the resentencing, the courtroom was packed, and the whole sheriff's department was there in the back. It was just marvelous, that support that I had.

And I said to myself, I am never, ever gonna put myself in that position again. God was good. All those people stuck with me through this. Even though I disappointed them, they stuck with me. My wife visited me every Saturday. She drove from our house to Dallas every Saturday, rain or shine. She would bring sandwiches and stuff to the visiting room. And I got to the point at Dallas where I had the highest clearance. I used to go out to the main gate. They would throw me the keys to the pickup truck. And I'd go into the officer's dining room and get all the guards' meals and put them in stainless boxes. They let down a rope with a hook on it, and I hooked their meals to it. I delivered the mail to the superintendent. I had so much support there.

I spent a lot of time in Bible studies. That's where I got based in the Word and understanding it. I had a couple of really good Bible teachers. We might spend an hour on two or three verses. I never knew about Strong's Concordance or Vine's Bible Dictionary. I was introduced to commentaries. So that helped get me through that whole process, all that ugliness through all that. And then He let me get out. I had the support of my family, friends, and community. I think I had more support after I was in prison than before if you can believe that.

I promised myself, I promised the Lord, "You got me through some really, really terrible things." There were certain things that there's no way I had any control over. I knew where my help came from. And I just promised Him. I promised myself, "I will never, never put myself in that position again, whether you forgive my sins today, tomorrow, and in the future, you're not going to have to worry about that one anyway."

YPM

Go back to the corrections officers. You had some COs that treated you horribly, especially right after the Camp Hill riot. But you also had COs who wrote your letters of recommendation.

Jack

Yup.

YPM

As a person who's been an inmate, help me understand what makes corrections officers tick? Like all people, there are some good ones and some struggling ones. What are your thoughts?

Jack

Some younger ones you find are more cocky. They are more pushy. There are wisecrackers. The older ones, they've been doing it a long time. They've seen everything. They know how to handle situations. They know how to handle potential incidents without throwing gasoline on the fire. Some of the COs are muscle-bound, and they walk around and intimidate. The older, more mature corrections officers do their job. They know what's going on. They can just watch and know what's going on. They don't have to walk around. So it just seems like the younger correctional officers, a lot of them maybe got out of the service or something.

What brought them into corrections? I don't know. Because some corrections officers are there to get you through your time. You don't bother me. I'm not going to bother you. And then some got in it apparently for different reasons. I don't know why, but they're angry people; they're macho. They liked to intimidate. But all in all, the COs that worked with me and that I worked for or with, I just treated them with the respect that you should, as an authority.

Do what you're supposed to do. Use your time wisely. Don't get involved in everybody else's crap. Get as busy as you could be. So from the time you get up at 5:30 in the morning until the time you go to bed at 9:00 pm, you're so busy. Then when you go to bed, you're exhausted, and you go to sleep. And that's the only way, in my opinion, you get through prison. Those are the big things. Mind your own business, keep busy, offer respect to authority, and you'll be fine.

YPM

How did you get connected to Yokefellowship Prison Ministry?

Jack

Well, first of all, Nessie Whaley, she's the most spirit-filled woman I've ever met in my life. She was working at the time for Prison Fellowship. Gordon Barnes and Nessie would come in and do a weekend once a year, and you could sign up for it like a retreat. So I signed up for it, and that's how I met Nessie and Gordon and the whole family. The girls came and sang. That was my first meeting with Nessie. And then John Mosteller, the executive director of YPM International, also had a Christian clown ministry and came into the prison and did some guest preaching. So when I got out, I had working with YPM in the back of my mind.

I got involved with YPM locally. I've been a council chair for 20 years. I had to hire a new executive director. So I get the resumes in the mail. I'm looking through them. Oh my God, Nessie Whaley applied for the job—done, done deal! I love her. She is just a wonderful, high-energy, spirit-filled woman who God has blessed in an amazing way. And she just takes more and more on now. Now she just took a pastorship at a church in Jersey Shore on top of everything, on top of United Churches, on top of state Yokefellowship. She's just amazing. We are going to a board meeting, and we're going to have a light lunch, and she'll have a table eight feet long, all kinds of food, tables set for the holiday. She decorates the whole place. I wish I had that. She's so supportive of me with my health issues. She'll record prayers she is sending to me. She sends cards. I can't say enough about Nessie Whaley.

I just believe in Yokefellowship, in their small group meetings, and allowing the inmates to talk. You have conversations; you listen to them. You ask somebody, what would you want to talk about? Or maybe what are you struggling with? And they might say loneliness. So it gives you ideas. You can go back the next week and have all kinds of scriptures concerning that particular feeling out of God's Word. It's a small group discussion, not a Bible study, and I liked that concept. It got the inmate to interact, to open up, and then be able to take that and process it through the filter of God's Word. I strongly believe in Bible studies. Getting incarcerated people grounded inside is going to help them outside.

When I was released, I was fortunate that I walked out of the gates at Dallas, and my wife was sitting there in the car to pick me up. There was a guy I used to lift with in the yard. He was there for 23 years. He had nobody there to pick him up. It's heartbreaking that there are so many that just slip through the cracks. That's why I believe in preparation before you get out. If I can ever retire, I'd like to put time into working with returning citizens and make sure there's somebody there to pick them up and get them to a church and those types of things, so they don't end up back in prison.

I wasn't there 20 years, but I was there long enough to know. I saw the same people going out and coming back while I was there. When I was doing Laubach tutoring, there were people 50, 55, 60 years old who didn't know how to do a checkbook, didn't know how to read, didn't know how to do a calendar—all these basic, basic things that you need in life when you get outside. I never realized that there are guys that are faking it. I tutored, and all of a sudden, they assigned this guy to me in his late 50s who had no idea how to do any of that.

What the heck is a guy like that gonna do when he gets released? He doesn't know how to fill out a job application. He doesn't know how to get assistance. Then they bounce right back in, which is a thing that gets me a little bit because—and I don't know if I should be saying this—the staff "counselors" could give you a lift, but I don't know what they do. They process paperwork. Some of the classes they make you go to are an absolute joke. It doesn't do anything for anybody. If you get a write-up, it goes to the counselor. He'll call you in and chastise you a little bit or whatever.

But as far as counseling and trying to get people set up for potential release and stuff like that, they missed the mark. I think that's a real problem. Either call it a jail or a corrections facility. But if you're going to call it a correctional institution, then you should try to correct behavior and prepare an individual to return to society, in my opinion. Right?

YPM

Jack, you're a country boy from out in the mountains. You're a White guy. You're college-educated. You're not a career criminal. You haven't been in a gang. You've never been addicted. You have used drugs, but you weren't an addict.

Jack

Right.

YPM

A lot of inmates were different from you. What did you learn about your fellow inmates in those four years? What do you see when you look at inmates now? People have stereotypes about what prison inmates are. What do you think about those men you got to know in prison?

Jack

They are human beings. Maybe 2% of SCI Dallas were White, but it was mostly Puerto Rican and African-American. I became good friends with lifers who had done some pretty nasty things. I never had any problems with them because they saw how I handled myself. Inmates don't miss a trick. They might not know how to balance a checkbook, but I'll tell you what: they could tell you what you're thinking; they can tell you what you're going to do before you do it; they've been there for God knows how many years, and they have seen it all. So I think they looked at me. I don't know what the word is, but I never had any problems with any of them. Some of them were really bad actors and were in trouble, and the Puerto Rican community and the Black community were having issues. What I learned is that everybody is a human being.

There might be some people that have an evil heart. But I would say that the majority of inmates that I came across, they're human beings—they have soft sides, hard sides, personalities that they have to maintain, but they're all human. I think they're all reachable with the right technique. Some people are just evil. What are you going to do? But the vast majority can be rehabilitated if they have the opportunity—if they're prepared, have a good spiritual counselor, someone to stand beside them.

A lot of times, counselors are just agitating. They think of inmates as complete animals. We are subterranean, you know what I mean, off the planet, a stone? That's what a lot of them think. And it's the way they treat you. When that happens day after day after day, people get an attitude. But I think they're all reachable. And that's why I believe in programs to prepare somebody for release. And if inmates are not going to get out, they should have jobs. We had a mattress factory in Dallas.

They should have an intervention class or something that they would have a write-up to decide if they want to attend. There should be something available for inmates if they're having a problem. If you're having a problem and go to your counselor, that'd be all over the jail in 24 hours. So you can't go and spill your guts about how you're feeling.

So that's my opinion: inmates are human. I think most of them are reachable. When I was there, the inmates watched me every day. I went to the yard. I was a powerlifter. I lifted three times a day. I went to the library, I got a degree, and I'm going to classes. I'm in my bunk, they go by, and I'm not watching TV. I'm reading and studying. I just never had a problem with any of them. And a lot of them got to like me a lot. And I didn't think anything would happen to me. The Lord had my back during this whole thing. And that's why I say there were so many instances where things could have gone sideways, but by the grace of God, they didn't.

YPM

When you first were arrested, you felt bad about what you did to your wife, parents, church, and everyone else. You were feeling ashamed, guilty. But now you have come out, and you're the owner of a business. Your community, your church, and your neighbors saw you on the front page of the paper. How has their attitude towards you been, and how has that changed? First, all those people knew who you were, and then they knew you as an inmate, then you were a returned citizen. How is that going for you?

Jack

I don't think their opinion of me changed. I think they knew the Jack Schrader that went in, and when I came out, I had so much support. I've taken a very small business and turned it into a pretty good-sized business. I've purchased a big building with showrooms. I've added probably 50 different lines of products. I got the humanitarian of the year award from the International Door Association. I got the Hickson Award from Kiwanis. I got the Small Business of the Year Award from the Williamsport-Lycoming Chamber of Commerce. I'm on the president's advisory council for the overhead door corporation. There are only 10 of us throughout the country, and there are 455 distributors. I've become good friends with the president, CEO, and senior executives at the corporate level. I've got people that work for me, and they stay. I treat my people well. I pay them well. I pay 100% for health insurance. I pay 50% for dependents with dental and life insurance. The commercial manager Dick Ferguson was hired by my dad when he was 18 years old. He just passed away. He was in my office the day he passed away. Dick was in his 52nd year with the company. The residential manager was there for 22 years. Most of the people here have been here for a number of years. I try to treat people the way I want to be treated.

I'm not a stickler. I'm pretty easygoing. Somebody needs some time to do something as long as they do their job. I don't care. And I have a very comprehensive employee handbook for employer liability insurance which is good. So everybody knows the rules, but they're my rules. So if somebody needs extra days when somebody needs this or that, that's fine. People want to do their job better when you're treating them and their families with respect. Add value to them, and that reciprocates, and that's why people stay. I have been blessed. I am not some super guy or anything like it. My father gave me a chance. The bank gave me a chance when I bought this place. I went through the process. The Industrial Properties Corporation sponsored me through the chamber for a PIDA loan, Pennsylvania Industrial Development Authority.

So I could get going, excuse my language, but I didn't have a "you know what" or "a window to throw it out of?" So I went down there, and I had my business plan. I had all my ducks in a row, and my PIDA application was two inches thick with 15 tabs. It was nine months of hell. My attorney usually represents the state in these things. He had to recuse himself because of our friendship, but he said, "Jack, 95% of people that start this process throw their hands up." You had to have a letter from the bank saying that they would lend you the money.

So my local bank here took a chance on me, and they gave me a letter of commitment that they were going to give me the money, which took nine months. And secretary Yablonsky would still call and ask me for additional information. And when you get called down to Harrisburg, you go in, and it's like a courtroom, but the tables are set up like a "U" and Secretary Yablonsky, he's in the middle. And there was a little desk like you had in elementary school sitting in the middle with a microphone on it. And when they call you up at that point, they can ask you additional questions about your business plan. What would you do in this industry or whatever? And three people that were ahead of me all got denied. You go through all this stuff for nine months, and you don't know until you're there. I went up again, and the Lord was there. Secretary Yablonsky says, "Everybody's had time to review Mr. Schrader's application. Does anybody have any additional questions for him?"

No one had questions. They vote. It was unanimous. Bang. I got the money. And since I got the money from PIDA, the Small Business First program gave me money, and the Williamsport Industrial Properties

Corporation gave me money at 2.75% fixed for 15 years. This is back in 2000 or 2001, when interest rates were like 15%. So that was like free money.

So again, God was with me. I've been so fortunate, and so many people I was incarcerated with don't have the support on the outside or anything else. It's sad. That's why I say I'm not some super guy. I just do my best for my fellow human beings. I know what I've done. I repented, and I moved forward. And by the grace of God, I had support outside, a good wife to visit me every week, good family support when I got out, good church support. When I got out, I was in the choir for 25 years. I was the finance chair at a large church, too. With Yokefellowship and all these different things, you know, He has a plan. He has a plan for every single person. And He worked miracles in my life.

There are people that we still write to. They're lifers, some of them are trying for commutation or parole, and we're doing our darn best to help them out. But people think of prisoners as the scum of the earth, and they aren't. They're human beings. They have emotions. The majority of them can be touched in some way if they're afforded that opportunity. There's that attitude—throw away the key, throw away the key! When I was trying to get a halfway house started, I went to the city council. The attitude was, we don't want them in our neighborhood.

A lot of people have that opinion of prisoners. Before I went in, I thought they were all just bad people that belonged in jail. Then I went to prison. I think God wanted me to experience that. He wanted me to repent. If I'm going to put you through this, I want you to learn something. And I learned a very valuable lesson about human nature. I have a whole different opinion about my fellow man and prisoners than when I went in.

YPM

Jack, as you look back on your study of the Bible, is there a story, verse, or theme in the Bible that connects to you in terms of your journey?

Jack

Oh boy. Well, a guy named John Pugh had a Bible study. He was one of the two I went to, and this guy he dug deep. One of my favorites was the Book of Isaiah. It was the one that affected me the most. He would talk about the plan in Isaiah and all the prophecies that were fulfilled. You can't make that up! There are no coincidences involved there. It's clear as crystal about the Messiah, how He would come and how He would suffer, the whole deal. And I thought to myself, that's thousands of years before! And then just getting to see how the church started. The Holy Spirit came in Acts chapter 2, and then the church scattered to the ends of the earth, the missionary journeys of the disciples.

But one thing I never understood in all my studies is why every one of the disciples, except for John, had their heads cut off. They were stoned and stuff. The Bible says you're going to be persecuted for your faith. The Lord taught that. But He let John be exiled at Patmos and write the book of Revelation. And I think that's the only way he made it. That's something I can ask when I get there. But I think Isaiah was putting that all together, the Old Testament, the New Testament, and the prophets. It made it crystal clear that this is no Big Bang theory. This is not coincidental. This is prophecy. And it's been mostly fulfilled, with a lot more to come. I did a very comprehensive study of Revelation. I love that book. It's hard with all the symbolism and everything else, but if you have a concordance, you can make sense of some things. But the bottom line is we win. We win! That's the bottom line.

YPM

I'm so glad that you won a victory with the Lord's help, Jack. We're writing this book with people who've gotten free and stayed free. And it seems to me you were free before you went to prison. That night on the little bridge, looking out at the mountain, you were freed spiritually, and it took some years for you to get physically free. But, you've stayed free with the Lord's help and the help of a lot of other people. So, your story is going to be an encouragement to others.

Jack

I hope so because I've been on a journey. I never in my wildest dreams growing up would ever think that I would end up where I ended up. Then when I was in prison, I never thought it would end up where it has ended up. So God always has all these surprises, and He has plans for your life, but it's all a plan. Everything is a plan, and I've come to believe that there's a plan that God has for every life, and He'll direct your path. And you should be able to direct others.

YPM

Well, thank you, Jack.

Jack

Yeah, I'd like to grab lunch or something sometime when you are up this neck of the woods.

Jack Schrader
Chairman, Upper Susquehanna Valley Area Council, Yokefellowship Prison Ministry
First United Methodist Church, Williamsport, Pennsylvania
jrs32@schraderproducts.com

Biblical Reflection

You could understand if Jack Schrader became a bitter, angry, ungrateful man. He was the victim of a sting. The district attorney laid out the bait hoping that Jack would lead him to a much bigger fish, and Jack took the bait. But there was no bigger fish to be had, and Jack got the full weight of the law for procuring cocaine for two imaginary lawyers, a sentence of 8 to 16 years in prison, and very public humiliation as a "drug kingpin."

Far from being bitter, angry, and ungrateful, Jack became repentant and reflective. He knows he made a terrible choice. He knows the consequences of his decision also fell on his spouse Cindy and his parents and friends and church and community. He accepted Christ as Lord and Savior and lived in prison in a respectful way that blessed his fellow inmates and the prison staff.

When he gets to Heaven, Jack wants to ask the Lord why all the disciples of Jesus—except John, who was exiled to the island of Patmos—died a martyr's death. He could just as easily ask the question about himself: "Why did this ordeal happen to me?" But Jack does not ask that question because he believes that God has a plan for every life and that "He'll direct your path." (Proverbs 3:6)

God had a plan for His Son laid out by the prophet Isaiah long before it happened. In Isaiah, the "Suffering Servant" offers his back to those who beat him and does not hide his face from those who mocked and spit on him. "Because the Sovereign Lord helps me, I will not be disgraced." (Isaiah 50:7a) God had a plan for His Son that included humiliation and crucifixion. Sometimes God's plan for us includes humiliation and suffering.

Because the "Sovereign Lord helps us," Jack Schrader knows we can endure suffering even if we do not like it or understand it. You can survive and grow during incarceration when you know that God is with you every day. Even if you remain in prison for the rest of your life, you are part of God's plan. You can rejoice because the bottom line of the last book in the Bible is, as Jack says, very simple: "We win!"

Chapter 8
Randall Schieck

Hearing Randall Schieck describe his early life tightens your throat and brings a tear to your eye. No child, no young person should experience what Randall did. You can understand why it has been difficult for him to learn what it means to be a man. "I had so many things that had happened to me, and nobody taught me what it means to be a man. And I gotta be honest, I'm 65 now, and I'm still learning." God has compassion for children like Randall. In Luke 18:16, Jesus says, "Let the children come to me, and do not hinder them, for the Kingdom of God belongs to such as these." (NIV) But God is righteous and just, as well as compassionate. So a tragic and difficult childhood does not shield us from God's wrath when we sin. Randall's wife, Barb Schieck, joins us during this interview to help us better understand his story.

YPM

Please tell me about your early life, the kind of kid you were, your family, your circumstances growing up.

Randall

I was born in Davenport, Iowa. My mother committed suicide when I was 4. And then, from 4 to 8, I was with different relatives.

YPM

Was your father with you?

Randall

He was, but I didn't see him a lot because he worked at Oscar Meyer in Davenport. And when he wasn't working, he did a lot of drinking. He remarried. My stepmother was abusive in just about every way you could probably think of. He said that he married her "so Randall would have a mother" because he felt bad about how I was tossed around from different relatives.

She wasn't a good mother. When he found out about some of the things she was doing, he kicked her out. She would chain me up to the bedpost. During one of those times, I got bit by a mouse or a rat. I was bleeding all over the floor, and she didn't do anything to help me. She would say she was giving me a peanut butter and jelly sandwich, but it was peanut butter and Tabasco sauce. She abused me sexually. I'm not going to go into it. She was a bad mother. She was bad.

YPM

What age were you when she came into your life?

Randall

Maybe 6, something like that. When I was 8 years old, my dad put me into an orphanage called the Iowa Annie Whittenmyer Home. And the reason that he put me there was because he felt with his work and just the way he is or was, he didn't think that he would make a very good father to me. And I know I was hard to handle. I'd gone through so many things by that time. I didn't know who to trust. I had a lot of abandonment issues. I had a lot of anger, a lot of bitterness. When I was at the orphanage between 8 and 15, I had 14 different foster families.

And I spent probably five and a half years at the orphanage. The rest of the time, I was with foster families, and a couple of those families were very abusive. There were house parents at the orphanage, one, in particular, that was very abusive. I went through emotional, physical and you could call it sexual abuse again. There was a janitor that was abusive to me. Some of the kids in a foster family abused me when I was 15. I ran away, and I just started staying wherever I could on the streets, trying to find friends. I didn't finish school. I got into fights in school, and I got picked on. I got kicked out.

YPM
Why did you leave your last foster family?

Randall
I left because the father, in particular, and his older daughter were abusive to me. I did get one good thing from that family. The father took me to a Chicago Cubs game at Wrigley Field. I don't know if you remember Hank Aaron, who beat Babe Ruth's record for home runs. I saw him hit his 725th home run that day. The crowd stood up and applauded him for like 15 minutes. He was down there on the field just crying and waving. I didn't realize it at the time, but that particular incident showed me what a man is supposed to be like—that baseball player, Hank Aaron. It didn't click at the time, but I'll never forget that incident. After that, I started wondering about myself. I had so many things that had happened to me, and nobody taught me what it means to be a man. And I gotta be honest, I'm 65 now, and I'm still learning.

After I ran away from that home and wound up on the streets, I started doing drugs, drinking a lot, and sleeping around with women and girls. And there was a guy—a street evangelist—his name is Jerry Bennett. Now Jerry could write a book. He's known pro wrestlers. He knew David Wilkerson. He took me off the street. He found me when I overdosed on acid, DMT, and strychnine, but I didn't know all of that. The doctor said if he hadn't taken me to a hospital, I would have been dead within an hour. So he took me to a hospital. I was in and out of a coma for three days. And when I got out, he let me stay with him in his place. He started taking me to this Christian coffeehouse called the Outlet. The Outlet was in Rock Island, Illinois. That's where I first started hearing extensively about the Lord and about being a Christian and following Jesus.

When you first become a Christian, some changes need to be made in your life. And He was trying to help me walk me through some of those changes. I rebelled, and I ran away from him too.

Before I go further, there's one thing that I want to say. When he took me in on the very first night, Jerry told me that he just stayed by my bedside and prayed for me throughout the night. I slept for 14 hours straight. When I would try to go to sleep, I would have nightmares. I was afraid to go to sleep a lot of times. Before I went to sleep that first night, Jerry said, "I'm going to pray for you, and I want you to close your eyes and tell me what you see." I said, "Okay." And what I saw was just a cross. All I saw was a wooden cross. After that, I slept for 14 hours!

YPM
How old were you?

Randall

I think I was 15 because I was still in the foster care system, but Jerry Bennett petitioned them to allow him to keep me. There's a couple of things I'm missing here because my mind just forgets. When Jerry found me, I was on a bridge called the Bicentennial Bridge. It goes between Davenport and Bettendorf, Iowa, over the Mississippi. I was going to commit suicide on that bridge. Jerry found me, and the police came at the same time. Jerry had a rapport with the police; he would help kids get off drugs to try to get them stabilized. So the police knew him, and Jerry just put out his hand and said, "I'll take care of this," and they let him do it. So Jerry and a friend of his took me to the hospital.

So that was backtracking a little. I'm sorry. When I ran away from Jerry's, there was a Christian tent ministry called "Christ Is The Answer." The guy that was in charge was named Bill Lowery. As far as I know, they've started up again here in the states, and they have 10 teams throughout the world. But I thought, well, I'm going to try to find these guys. And I ran away, and I heard they were in Decatur, Illinois. So I got a Greyhound bus, and I went to Decatur. All I had was one of those army duffel bags.

I got there, and they said come over, and we'll find you a cot. They had a big tent for the brothers. They had another tent for the sisters. They had campers for married couples. They had Peterbilt tractor-trailers. One of them was a shower. One was a kitchen and a laundry room. Another one held all the materials for a five-pole tent for their meetings, all the chairs. We just lived off Greyhound buses. I went to Decatur, Nashville, and Indianapolis. This is during the Jesus movement. And I learned how to go out on the streets and talk to people about the Lord and invite them to the meetings and live that kind of communal lifestyle.

And the guy that was in charge, Bill Lowery, had to go because they were going to start a team in Norway. And while he was gone, there was some fornication within the camp and a few things that weren't good. And when he came back, he got really upset and indignant. He started treating the whole place like a boot camp. He was kicking people out left and right, laying down the law about what would be done and how we would be punished. I was a young Christian and rebellious, and I couldn't handle authority. So I ran away from that too. There's a pattern here. I've been doing a lot of running. I wound up back in Indianapolis. Jerry, by the way, has passed away. So he's no longer with us, but we did find him. I lost contact with him for 30 years.

I wound up back in Indianapolis. I met a guy named Marty Miles. Marty is a Christian worship leader. We still keep in touch from time to time. He had a place called a "Flophouse," where people could stay. It wasn't a negative thing. He liked to help homeless people. He liked to help addicts. So I stayed there. And then, I guess, after about three weeks, he says, "Hey, I know somebody up in Elkhart, Indiana. He's a deacon at a church called Maranatha Fellowship. And I want you to go up there and stay with him. He said you can come up." The guy's name was Phil Barns. Phil had three daughters, and he had another worship leader staying with him, named Ross Mo. They all lived in a trailer home, and it was tight.

But Phil had a problem with Christian music like Andre Crouch and the Disciples. Rock music was the devil's music. So anyway, he says, "There's this place in Goshen, Indiana, called Teen Haven. I'm going to take you over there." And Teen Haven is associated with a quartet group called Gospel Echoes. And I don't know if they're still doing anything or not, so I went there, and Mel Shetler was the director. He's a pastor now in Goshen. He's still there.

While I was there, I met a girl, and I got her pregnant. The baby named Jennifer was adopted, and she grew up and found me years later. I don't know where she is right now.

After I was with Mel, I stayed in a funeral home with some other guys, and they were from a church called Zion Chapel. And that's where I met my wife, Barb. This was 1977; we got married in 1978. One of the things that I appreciated about Zion chapel was they had Bible study in-home meetings and small groups. I started learning and growing. I worked at a couple of different places until about 1980. And then we moved to Pennsylvania. Her dad had a dairy farm, and he needed some help. I didn't know anything about cows. I hated them. I learned how to milk cows.

YPM
That's hard work, dairy farm work.

Randall
I never really had a good family. I met Barb's mom and dad, and I thought they were really, really good people.

Barb Schieck
It was a stable farm family.

YPM
Randy, you grew up in abuse. And it seems to me that you were running away from that, but you kept running towards people like Jerry Bennett. And you're trying to run towards Christ. Now you've found a good family, a good person. But everything is not all right. So we need to get from here to whatever happened that sent you to prison. So what's that next stage? It seems like you're heading in the right direction. So how do we get from here to where you got incarcerated?

Randall

Well, for starters, I had a lot of baggage. I had a lot of issues even though I had come to the Lord. I never really took the steps I needed to take to deal with my past. I brought that into the marriage. Not that I noticed. Barb didn't notice right away.

Barb

He told me the story right away. So I knew, yes, but I knew he was a Christian.

YPM

Did you have a sense of the baggage at that time?

Randall

No, I didn't know how things affect people, that residual stuff; I didn't know about that.

Barb

I knew he acted in certain ways because of his past.

Randall

Her family was traditional Mennonite. The church they went to had a lot of the same kind of people, farming families. My background was not even close to where they were. I felt like I was a black sheep or not a black sheep so much as an outsider. I didn't know how to talk to people about my past. I just kept stuffing it down. I kept things inside me. We started having children. We have five kids—four boys and one girl—and nobody taught me how to be a dad. I mean, nobody teaches you. You just kind of learn it as you go. But because I never saw how a good family was supposed to function, I felt like I was just winging it. I was trying to do the best I could. I didn't have any foundation to fall back on. I wasn't taught well. So all this frustration, anger, and stuff just kept piling up inside me.

Barb
When was it you lost that last job?

Randall
In 1994, I felt like my life was slipping away from the Lord. So when we got here, I tried to act like a Christian, the best that I could. They let me be a worship leader at the church.

So things just kept piling up, and they let me help out with the youth. There was a girl in the group, and the more I slipped away from the Lord, the more I started thinking about her and less about Barb. I got into drinking a bit. I tried to hide it. I tried to find ways not to go to church or family events. I was just separating myself from what was really important and what I really needed.

I had a nervous breakdown. I abused this girl. So for a whole year after that, it was just eating away at me. I just felt like I was tortured. The kids would come home from school. They would find me crying in the living room. I couldn't talk to Barb. I couldn't talk to anybody about it. I knew that what I was doing was wrong. But I had gotten to where I was hard, and I didn't want to change. I didn't know how to change. I didn't know how to talk to anybody about what I was going through. So in 1998, she told somebody, I think she told her mom.

Barb
No, she had told a boy.

Randall
The boy told his dad. Anyway, I got found out, and they arrested me.

YPM

Where did they arrest you?

Randall

They arrested me at our home.

YPM

How old were the five children when you were arrested?

Randall

The oldest was 17, and the youngest was 7.

YPM

How long did your behavior with the girl go on?

Randall

It was only about six months.

Barb

Then she wanted to break it off, right?

Randall

I kept saying I did too.

YPM

Tell me about your arrest. Where did they take you?

Randall

I went to Schuylkill County in Pottsville. I was there for probably 120 days. And then they took me to Camp Hill near Harrisburg.

YPM

What was the sentence?

Randall

Five to 10 years. I did the whole 10, but there's a lot of good stuff that happened while I was in prison.

YPM

You had all this buried stuff inside that you knew very well, but you hid from Barb and everybody else. And Barb, you knew about Randall's past, but you didn't know about this, and you didn't know he was going to be arrested.

Barb

We knew something was wrong because of how he was acting, but we didn't know what. My daughter was 16 at the time. She and I went to a counselor; we knew something was wrong. We never knew what until he got arrested.

YPM

So now everyone in the family learns what's wrong. Barb, you know, the children know. Randall, take me through your emotions. What were you feeling, sitting there in the county jail and waiting for trial? What was your emotional state when you got to Camp Hill?

Randall

I was a mess. I was crying. I was crying just about every day. I was filled with remorse, guilt, and shame. And I thought I had lost everything, my whole family. I didn't know if I would get out of jail alive. I mean, three COs in the county jail were abusive to me. They didn't hit me or anything.

It was just a mess. I was suicidal before I got arrested. And I had thought about it while I was in county, but then I thought, you know, even though I did something like this, I can't commit suicide because that would not be good for Barbara, the kids. I was just messed up mentally, emotionally, and spiritually.

YPM

Talk about your spirituality. Where were you in your relationship with Christ?

Randall

I didn't have a relationship. I didn't have a relationship with the Lord. I thought, you know, this is going to send me to Hell for sure. God is just. He's not going to want anything to do with me, and He's done with me. That's what I felt.

YPM

Were you reading your Bible, or was that beyond you?

Randall

Not at that time, no.

YPM

You weren't physically free. You were in prison getting ready to be sentenced, but you were not spiritually free either. So they send you to Camp Hill. What happened?

Randall

While I was still in the county jail, I met a pastor.

Barb

The pastor that we were counseling with went to visit Randy. He was a good counselor.

Randall

He came to me in county jail, and he took me to Jeremiah Chapter 17. And he said, "Look at you, you think you have control over everything. You can't even control yourself." This guy is Russian, and he's got a gruff voice. And he got right into my face, very frank and very direct. And he shared Jeremiah 17 with me. After he left, I thought about what he said. And I remembered before I got arrested, my youngest boy, Joel, came up to the bedroom one night. He said, "Dad, there's something I want to ask you, but I'm scared." And he started crying, and I said, "Come over here and sit down, and you don't have to be scared. You don't have to cry. Ask me what you want to ask me." And he just cried. He said, "Why are you so mean to everybody?"

And I just held him, and I said, "Look, I'm going through some things that I don't understand. I don't know how to take care of them. I am having a really hard time. I need you to pray for me. Can you do that?" And he says, "Yeah." And I remember this while I was sitting in county after I met with the pastor. I believe that when Joel came in and asked me that question, it may have been when I started to change. So in county jail, after this pastor talked to me, I gave my life back to the Lord. I didn't feel like I was completely set free of everything that was going on inside of me or that I carried. But I did rededicate my life back to Him.

YPM

So you went to Camp Hill SCI in 1998?

Randall

I went there, and I went to the desk where they take you in, and you give them your belt and whatever else you got. I gave this guy my wallet. And I had a picture in my wallet, a family photo. So he starts taking stuff out. And he's looking at my family. He says, "Who's this?" I said, "Well, that's my family, my wife, and my kids." He just looked at me, and he said, "What are you doing here? What's the matter, man? You know?"

They put me on a suicide watch during the first couple of weeks. Generally, if you're doing a lot of time, they say it takes about two years for you to kind of find out where you fit within the system—how you're supposed to act and what you're supposed to do. For those first two years, I was so afraid that Barb would divorce me and forget about me, and the kids didn't want anything to do with me anymore.

I talked to a chaplain there—his name is Otha Bell—and he prayed with me. He counseled me a lot while I was there. And then, one Sunday morning during a church service, they had about 300 men that would go to this service. And I don't know if you've ever been in a meeting with 300 men before who love the Lord and are excited, and they're singing. And I mean, it was just amazing. I wanted to be there all the time. Some of these guys, I would trust more, and they made more sense than a lot of people on the outside. During the service, they were singing. And I don't know what happened to me other than just that the Holy Spirit fell on me. And I just went to my knees. I was crying uncontrollably. Others came around me and laid hands on me, and they were praying for me. And I had no idea at all what was going on. I was there for maybe 10 minutes on my knees, just crying. I was shaking.

I didn't ask the Lord for anything. It just happened. I don't know how to explain it. When I got up, I felt such a weight had been taken off me. Wow! I just felt so much peace. And that felt like the Lord was saying to me, "You're going to be alright; we're going to be alright." I didn't know that the whole time I was in prison, God had been helping my wife in many different ways with our finances, work, and kids. He just met her needs left and right. I didn't know. I didn't have anything to offer. Everything I had or I could've offered, I just, I threw away. But the Lord didn't leave her alone. And while I was in prison, she was praying for me. She would write me letters from time to time. I saw the kids a couple of times.

Barb

I didn't visit as much as some people do, just when I could get a free Saturday because it's two hours from where we lived.

Randall

In prison, they found out that I played guitar, and I knew a whole bunch of scripture songs that Barbara and I used to sing at Zion Chapel in Goshen, Indiana, back in the 70s. And I write songs, and they asked me to help. When people first come into prison, they're dressed in "blues"—blue shirts and blue jeans. If you're going to do a lot of time or life, or if you're going to be at that prison and not going to be transferred somewhere else, you're dressed in "browns." I was asked to go to two blues Bible studies. Volunteers come in and do Bible studies with the inmates. I was asked to share music and talk about the Lord with them. And I thought, why me? Why do they want me to talk to them about the Lord?

I'm not a teacher. I'm not a pastor. I can do music. I can share stuff with them. I can do music, so I did. And that lasted for a few weeks. And I guess then some people moved on, so they decided to end it. So I taught another group of people in browns after being there for a while. These guys were with a Yokefellowship Prison Ministry. And there's a brother from Harrisburg who's a YPM volunteer, and his name is Larry Lingle.

So Larry said, "I think the Lord wants me to buy you a guitar." I used the church's guitar every time they wanted me to share something. So he bought me a guitar, and I started sharing music with the group. And it was a real blessing. I was a part of the Protestant band for our church services and the Catholic choir. God was helping me along while I was there.

I had been threatened a few times. There was a clerk at the chapel who was a Muslim. Now, this guy was huge, and he was a clerk for the Muslims at that chapel. One day two guys started giving me a hard time, and he walked up and said, "I know this guy. You touch him. You got to go through me." This guy was like my bodyguard. At the chapel, we would sit down and talk about things of God and banter back and forth. God helped me in different ways like that. I would get put with cellmates that were also Christians.

YPM

You haven't mentioned it, but did you have a more challenging time because you were a sexual offender?

Randall

Yeah, in county jail and state, some people gave me a hard time as a sexual offender. I was out on parole. I violated parole by talking to somebody I wasn't supposed to. I had an experience at Graterford SCI as well. Before they sent me back to Camp Hill to finish my term, they sent me to Graterford. Graterford was scary. It was really scary.

I could see, looking back, time after time when God just protected me, and He set things up in a way where I wouldn't have to go through a lot of hard times. He wanted me to focus more on Him and less on my experience. The experience was bad enough. But I think He wanted me to just focus on Him, so I did. I did everything I could. I went to a lot of Bible studies. I went to all the church services and the programs that would make you a better person, like choice theory or a parenting class and stuff like that. I made it a point to go to those.

YPM

The Muslim you talked to about God, you said it felt like he was your bodyguard, and you would talk about things of God. So here you are, a Christian, and you're talking to a Muslim. What did you two talk about?

Randall

I mentioned to him that Jesus was born of the Virgin Mary, and He was the Son of God, and He died for our sins. And then he starts telling me what the Koran has to say about Jesus. I asked him about his background and his upbringing, and we talked about mine. It wasn't so much deep theological things; it was more about our experiences. I told him about the tent ministry. He wanted to know about that. When Muslims are growing up, they're forced to read the Koran, and they have to memorize it word for word.

And if they don't, there's punishment. So I told him about the tent ministry. What we did in the tent ministry was get up in the morning and have breakfast. We would have a short Bible study and sing. Then we'd go out on the streets, and we would tell people about Jesus. We didn't have the whole Bible memorized. We shared our personal experiences of how we came to the Lord and what He's done in our lives. I asked him, I said, "Do you think you would ever want to leave Islam and come to Christ? Is that something you think you'd like to do?" And he said, "You guys are like really nice people, but I don't think I can ever do that because, in our faith, it's not a good idea. If they catch me, I think they could kill me." And I said, "I understand, that doesn't sound like a very loving kind of faith. It's a lot different than Christ." I don't know. He never came to the Lord. Well, I don't know—he may have.

YPM

And your gift guitar, did you keep it in your cell, or did Yokefellowship bring it in every time they had a service?

Randall

It stayed with me.

YPM

The prison lets you keep the guitar in your cell?

Randall

There's a company called American Musical Supply Company, one of the prison system's merchants. When the guitar came in, they checked everything to make sure there were no weapons. It had an Allen wrench that came with it, and they took that. They wouldn't let me have it. It had an extra set of guitar strings, and I didn't get them. It had a strap, and I didn't get that either. As far as I know, I'm the only guy that had that going on.

YPM

When you dissolved in tears at the church service and the men prayed for you, how long had you been in prison?

Randall

I think it was my third year. People talk about being delivered from demons and having healing and stuff like that going on inside. I think that's what happened.

YPM

So you were at Camp Hill for three years, with demons attacking you and your relationship with the Lord, and you were physically separated from your family. But you were spiritually free from the moment fellow inmates laid hands and prayed for you while you were kneeling and weeping in that chapel service, is that fair to say?

Randall

Yeah, but I think there are a lot of areas that I needed to grow in. And, even now, I'm still growing and still learning. I think when you say that you've arrived, that's a dangerous place to be. You are in spiritual recovery from what happened.

I didn't tell you about my testimony. I got into Satanism a little bit too.

YPM

You got into Satanism before you went to prison?

Randall

Yeah. But I have no desire for things like that. I have no desire to smoke. I have no desire to drink. I have no desire to commit adultery. I don't want to kill anybody for sure. I want more of the Lord, and I want more to be an example of Him.

YPM

The day that the Lord frees you from your demons and saves you is not the day that you're sanctified and perfectly holy.

Barb

That's never-ending for any of us!

YPM

So you got your physical freedom after 10 years?

Randall

I maxed out on June 18, 2008.

YPM

When you maxed out in 2008, what were your relationships like with your children and Barb? Is your family waiting at the door and throwing their arms around you, or was there repair work to be done?

Randall

Barb came to pick me up when I maxed out.

Barb

We talked about it for the last couple of years after he had gone back in after violating parole. So we were planning on him coming home.

YPM

So now that the kids were 10 years older, who was still living at home?

Barb

Only the youngest was home, and he was 17.

YPM

Home or not, how were all your children in terms of their connections to their dad? They must have gone through a lot of complex emotions too.

Randall

Of course, they were affected by all of this. Trust is hard to regain after it has been lost. Rebuilding my relationship with them has been an ongoing journey. For their sake, I will not go into every detail. I am doing what I can to do what is right for them, and our relationship has improved. My daughter was married and living in Portland, Oregon, when I got out. The two older boys were married as well. One of the first things that I wanted to do when I got out was to renew my vows with Barb. We planned that, so we did that. We went to the Lighthouse

Church, and our Pastor Bill Orf officiated. There's a song by Matt Redmon called "The Heart of Worship." I wanted the worship leader, Pastor Mark, to sing that for our renewal.

Barb

Our old friends were there, my family, all the kids were there.

Randall

And the reason that I wanted that song, it says, "I'm coming back to the heart of worship, and it's all about You, it's all about You. Jesus. I'm sorry, Lord, for the thing I've made it." I wanted that song to express how I wanted our marriage to be, which is a life of witness and testimony about what Jesus has done in my life, what He's done in my wife's life, and our life together. Because the way that I had handled things in the past was not good, to say the least. And I didn't want to go back to that again. So when we renewed our vows from that day forward, this hasn't been easy for me. I wanted to put the past behind me. My testimony is I did something wrong. I messed up, but the Lord took me back. That was an event in my life. It's not my lifestyle. And God does forgive. He does restore. He does deliver. God is a God of second chances. And that's what He's done for me. And one of the residual effects of this is that I have to register annually under Megan's Law for life.

Barb

That requirement prevents him from finding jobs.

Randall

When this started, I signed a paper that said I only had to do Megan's Law for 10 years, but they've changed things now. But God opens doors. That's the one thing I want to get out—when man shuts doors on you because of your past or because of what they see on paper, God has a way of opening another door so that you can be effective for him. That's what happened in our lives after we renewed our vows.

The following summer, we went to see our daughter. We went on a mission trip to Honduras. Then we went to Columbia for four or five years together. And then Columbia said, "You have a federal offense. You can no longer come into our country." But we keep in touch with a couple of people we know there. God has opened doors for us to be involved with prison ministries. Barb gets to go into the prisons, but because of my record, I can't. I was able to go into a county prison twice, but that's been it. They won't allow me to go into state prisons. They will not let me go into federal prisons. But I can promote, I can do things outside. I've led Bible studies for men that have been in prison. I'm involved in some men's groups right now that help hold me accountable, which I think is very important. We are with the Kairos Prison Ministry. We are with Yokefellowship Prison Ministries. I'm on the board for the Walk to Emmaus.

I have led worship in several churches. I lead worship at Mountainside Bible Church on the second Sunday of every month. I lead worship for our Friday night Bible study. I counsel people who have addictions and the homeless in Stroudsburg. I'm working with a group in Pottsville called Renew. They do the same thing. So that's my life now.

YPM

Barb, let me ask you a question. There's something wrong with your husband. You don't know what it is. You're praying for him. Then, all of a sudden, you have the police at your door, and he's gone for 10 years. You're left with five confused and traumatized children. The finances and the responsibilities, you're doing it all on your own. And your husband has been unfaithful to you. Randall fell to his knees and cried in the prison chapel. What happened to you? How did this hit you, and how did God help you through it?

Barb

One thing was that counselor, part of his ministry was counseling Christians with broken hearts. It's a long involved thing with lots of scriptures showing what that means. What is a heart, how does God use your heart, and what does that all mean in the Scriptures? So he goes through all that. But the basic thing is that we get broken hearts when we trust man instead of God because God says, "Trust me with all your heart." And we trust men—not just men but women too—and our hearts get broken because they will disappoint us.

I had gone through counseling pretty much by the time Randall got arrested. And when I called the counselor, I said, "Oh no, he just got arrested!" And the pastor said, "Oh good, now we know what's wrong with him."

YPM

Your counselor was a wise man.

Barb

It was freeing for me because it showed me God is working, and this is not a disaster. But it was a disaster. I was left with five children, and I had never worked full time in my life. I didn't have a career to fall back on. I had part-time jobs all the time.

But we went to a very good church, the Lighthouse Church, and I knew those people loved me. I had a loving Christian family, and I knew I would never be out in the streets. Somebody would help me out, and that's what happened. They did help me out. My oven went, and the church just up and bought me one at Christmas. People would randomly collect money from their Sunday school class for me or something like that. So I was sustained by that.

Right after this, my mother had died, and the inheritance came from her. And then, a few years later, my father died, and I got an inheritance. So that was how God provided some of the money for us.

And then I went to a Christian man at our church, and he advised me to go to the school and ask for an opportunity. I started being a substitute teacher, and then I became a teacher, which was a good salary.

YPM

You already had an education degree?

Barb

Yes. As far as the children, I think the Lord protected us. Why were they not devastated?

Randall

I don't know. They are smart kids.

Barb

The oldest was most affected. He knew the girl, and she had been one of his girlfriends. So he ran away from home for a while. He was a smart kid, and he came back, and he said, "I can't get anywhere without an education." He had already dropped out of high school. So he went back and got his GED and went and got a diesel mechanic certification. He was the most affected, I'd say; the others not as much. My daughter had gone to this counseling with me, and she was a very strong Christian. She went to Bible college a couple of years after this. She was involved in the youth group and church

YPM

And the second son?

Barb

He handled it okay too. Then the younger ones hardly knew what was going on. It didn't bother them so much that he was gone, I guess because Randall was often away from home when they were young. He kinda did his own thing—that was part of the problem with our marriage. He was off doing his own thing. They were good things, which is why we didn't realize the problem. He would go to Bible studies, lead youth, whatever ministries, he loved ministry. So he was often gone, and I was home with the kids. I don't know if that's why they weathered it, but they did; they did fine. It wasn't in the papers that I know of. Maybe a blurb in the police blotter, but it wasn't a big to-do in the town. I never heard a negative thing from anybody.

YPM

Did your church know about it?

Barb

Yes, the church knew that we were in trouble, but we were already looking for another church by the time he got arrested. By the time Randall was arrested, we were no longer in that church. We sort of attended it, but as soon as this happened, we said we couldn't go back there because the poor pastor has to deal with the aftermath of a youth leader and a youth and all that happened. So we didn't go back.

YPM

I understand. So the church that was giving you a new oven, giving you money from collections—they just knew you were without a husband? They didn't know why?

Barb

Right. I told select friends. People are divorced all the time, and most people don't ask. I told people who asked.

YPM

Randall, there was a point in your life when you weren't praying. But you said you asked Joel to pray for you. You couldn't pray, but there was enough faith inside you to ask your 7-year-old son to pray for you. You didn't think enough of yourself to pray for yourself, but you could ask your little boy to pray for you.

Barb

And he was the one that was still home when Randall got home.

Randall

Yeah. Our kids went to Quakertown Christian School, and they had gone to church pretty much ever since they were born. Yeah. I didn't know how to tell a 7 year old what I was going through. He understood prayer, and I felt like I needed his prayers.

I knew I had to reconcile with God, and I had to reconcile with my wife and kids and the youth pastor I was working with when all this had happened. To reconcile with somebody else, especially with what I'd gone through, I don't even know where to begin. You can say, I'm sorry. Yes, I'm remorseful. You know all the things that people usually say—it won't happen again and all that kind of stuff. But it goes so much deeper than that. When God forgives you, and He changes your heart, and you start telling other people about this, they're going to want to see it. Trust is a very hard thing to get back.

Barb

And if he would write from prison, he'd apologize in his letters to the kids. I think they thought, yeah, we'll see what happens when he gets out. They had to see for themselves. But I think they have by now—it's been 13 years.

Randall

More than anything, I want people to know that I love Jesus and what He's done for me. He can do that for them and more if they'll let Him. But I want people to know that I love my wife, even with all the stupid stuff I did. Deep down in my heart, I never stopped loving her. And I want my family to get that. I want God. I want our marriage to be the kind of marriage where people will look at us and say, "Hey, they've got something for each other—not just for each other, but they've got Jesus." I've had to go to each of my kids and talk to them individually about what I did and tell them how sorry I still am. I don't think it's something you can ever wipe away.

As Barb said, the hardest one has been our oldest boy, but after 13 years, I finally feel like I can talk to him and have fun with him. We just did the other night—it was his birthday, and we had a great time. We don't spend a lot of time together. We get to take their kids, our grandkids, to church now. They know about Jesus. Millie and Reagan, they're our grandkids. They've gone to Bible camp, and they've accepted Jesus. My daughter has nine kids, and her husband's a pastor, and all of them love Jesus.

The youth worker that I was with when this happened, I found out that he was working with Teen Challenge in Rehrersburg, Pennsylvania, and I made it a point to look him up. I knew I had to reconcile with him, and you know what? I found him. We sat down in his office. We talked, we cried. We shared Scripture for about an hour. It was so good!

He said, "Man. I love you. I forgive you. I'm so glad you came back to the Lord, and I'm really glad to see what he's doing in your life. Don't stop."

I mean, God has been so good to us. He's blessed our marriage. He's blessed our family. He's blessed us with a ministry, and I don't deserve any of it as far as I'm concerned. And He just doesn't stop. He keeps opening doors. There's a ton of stuff that I could tell you that I haven't said to you that He's done in our lives and us individually. And it just keeps going. And that's what I share with people. God can turn your life around.

Barb
Living for the Lord is a blessing. It's not a hardship.

YPM
Well, you two are an inspiration—what a remarkable story of reconciliation.

Barb
But I have had people say, "How could you take him back?" But I say, "Why not?"

Randall
I've had people call themselves Christians, and they're spirit-filled, and they've dogged me badly, a few of them. And it hurts, it hurts so much, but there's nothing I can do about it except pray for him and love him and forgive him just like Christ did for me.

YPM
Like the counselor's advice to Barb, you put your trust in God, not in the person. Sometimes people don't put their faith in God but in their

holiness. Everyone has feet of clay, and we all fail. What we're praying for is that these stories of people "getting free and staying free" are going to encourage others. We appreciate you sharing your hearts and sharing your story.

Randall

When I was in Graterford SCI, my daughter sent me a letter. She said I had hurt a lot of people, and it was going to take a long time to trust. But there is forgiveness, and she sent me a particular scripture, Isaiah 57:14-19. And basically, what that talks about is that the Lord will not be angry forever. Right? He will forgive, and He will restore, and He will heal the backslider and the heart. So she sent that to me, believing even while I was still in prison that God would do that. And it's happened.

YPM

When parents raise their children to know Jesus, it makes a big difference.

Randall

You know, I have to tell you, I've been very nervous about this interview. Thank you very much for your help. I wasn't quite sure how it was going to pan out.

YPM

Nerves come with life. I'm a little nervous, too, each time I start an interview, but the stories encourage me and strengthen my faith. So I might start a little nervous, but I am excited about what God has done by the end.

So Larry Lingle from Yokefellowship Prison Ministry got you a guitar, but you also went to their Bible studies, right?

Randall

Yes.

YPM

Everybody in the book has been touched in some way by YPM.

Barb

That's who I minister under now.

Randall

When Larry Coleman was the executive director of Yokefellowship Prison Ministries, he asked me to share music and give a short testimony. I didn't go into a lot of detail because I was on parole at the time.

This doesn't have to be part of the book, but can I tell you something real quick? While I was in prison at Camp Hill, I walked into the chapel one day, and there was a Bible study going on with Second Chance Ministries. I was at the back of the chapel. I saw a couple of men upfront. I noticed one of the men was talking to another guy, and then he made a beeline for me. Well, back in the 80s, I did some music for the Full Gospel Businessmen's Fellowship of the Lehigh Valley a few times. And I worked with this guy, and all of a sudden, he saw me in prison.

He says, "What are you doing here?" And I told him, and he laid his hands on me and said, "I got something that God wants me to share with you, pray over you." And I said, "Okay." So he started praying for me, and he prophesied. He said the Lord spoke through him. He said that there would be no case of divorce or adultery in my family, not with my wife or any of my kids. It won't happen. I said, "Oh, that's good, good." I didn't even tell him this, but my dad had been married three or four times. He was a womanizer. I was a womanizer. I didn't tell him any of this. And he says God will not allow this to happen in your marriage or your kids' marriages. I thought, wow! And I haven't seen him since. I just think that was a God moment right there. Oh my goodness, powerful stuff. Our kids have successful marriages. They're all doing well.

YPM

Thanks very much for your time and have a good day.

Randall

You too, thanks.

Randall Schieck
Advanced Fellowship Ministries
rgsafm@yahoo.com

Biblical Reflection

Revival begins with repentance. Revival starts with people on their knees. In revival, people deal with the truth about who they are and their past. John 1:9 does not say God will forgive our sins; John 1:9 says, "If we confess our sins, God is faithful and just and will forgive us our sins and purify us from all unrighteousness." (NIV) If we confess, God forgives. Randall Schieck had not truthfully confessed his past. "I had a lot of baggage. I had a lot of issues even though I had come to the Lord. I never really took the steps I needed to take to deal with my past. I brought that into the marriage. Not that I noticed. Barb didn't notice right away."

The problem with not dealing with the past is that it has consequences for our present. "So all this frustration and anger and stuff just kept piling up inside of me." Randall was leading worship and helping with the youth at church, but at the same time, he was hiding and separating from his family. He was drinking and hiding that too. And Randall began to think about this girl in the youth group, and the thoughts became a reality. And then there was more separation, hiding, a nervous breakdown, an arrest and conviction, and all the devastation inflicted on the young girl and her family, on his spouse and children, on the church. So how does a compassionate, just, and righteous God help? He sends a good counselor with a good word.

Barb was going to see a Christian counselor. Part of his ministry was working with people who had broken hearts. When Randall got arrested, Barb called the counselor. "Oh no, he just got arrested!" And the pastor said, "Oh good, now we know what's wrong with him." Randall was finally out of hiding. The counselor came to visit him. "He came to me in county jail, and he took me to Jeremiah Chapter 17. And he said, 'Look at you, you think you have control over everything, you can't even control yourself.' This guy is Russian, and he's got a gruff voice. And he got right into my face, very frank and very direct. And he shared Jeremiah 17 with me."

Jeremiah 17:5-10 says that God will curse and punish those who trust in themselves and turn their hearts away from trusting in Him. But God will bless those who trust in Him. They will be like a tree planted by a stream with no worries in years of drought. Randall was cursed and punished, but he fell on his knees and confessed his sin. While in Graterford SCI, his daughter sent him a letter pointing to Isaiah 57:14-19. In that text, God says He lives in a high and holy place, but He also lives with lowly and contrite people. God will not punish them forever. The Lord will not always be angry. Instead, he will restore them and bring comfort. Sometimes we need and deserve God's punishment. But we always need and never deserve God's grace. He gives us grace anyway.

WILL YOU HELP ME
DEDICATED TO YOKEFELLOW PRISON MINISTRY

VERSE 1

Some may never notice, and some have never heard
That I've been here in prison
Just praying and reading God's word
I need a reason to go on living
I need a friend that will never fail
I need someone who will do more than sign to pay my bail

CHORUS

I'm looking for love beyond these walls
I'm looking for support so I won't fall
Do I have to get on my knees and crawl? Will you help me?
You know I've run so far away from home
There is no one to turn to or call my own
I don't want to walk this road alone. Will you help me?

VERSE 2

No one comes to visit me, and no one answers the phone
Letters are few and far between
Am I forgotten? What does it mean?
I met a preacher who gave me assurance
That God would never let me down
And He's calling for those who will bear the yoke
Of the lost when no one's around

BRIDGE

Jesus can see the homeless
And those who live in poverty
And the prisoners that no one ever sees
And He says to you if you will only take the time to hear
When you've done it to the least of these
You've done it unto me

VERSE 3

They tell me that I'm worthless, that I don't amount to much
And I've left scars that will not heal
But I've felt the savior's touch
Now there's a love that will never let me go

Can you help me carry on?

Will you stand by me when everybody else has come and gone

END

I don't want to walk this road alone. Will you help me?

Chapter 9
Marsha Curry-Nixon

What is consuming enough to cause a mother to endanger the life of her children? Addiction. What is hurtful enough to fill a bright and talented young girl with anger? Physical and sexual abuse. What is evil enough to magnify the consequences of that torture? A forced cover-up. What is profound enough to heal those unspeakable wounds and bring forgiveness and restoration of relationships? The touch of God.

YPM

Please tell me about your early life, where you were born, your family, the kind of little girl you were? Where did it all begin for Marsha?

Marsha

I was born and raised in Philadelphia to two very young parents. I was my father's firstborn and my mother's third born. I did not meet my parents until I was about 5 years old. There's a story that my mother wanted to leave the parental obligations to my father, who, to my understanding, was caught up in an addiction to alcohol. So my parents gave their parental rights to my paternal grandmother, Francis

Lewis. So for the first five years of my life, I lived with her on 33rd Street in Philadelphia. I was a curious little girl. I lived a typical first five years of life with my Grams, and I had cousins and my father's brother I got to see a lot. He came to visit my grandma a lot.

I was a little girl that ran up and down the streets, a little tomboy-ish. I had a nickname early on, "Worrywart." And it's interesting, you know, out of my curiosity, my concern for my grandmother and the absence of my parents, I worried about a lot of things. Abandonment issues were probably an early onset for me. I remember having friends and playing in the streets with my neighbors. My grandmother had a best friend that lived across the street. She cared for four emotionally challenged girls—Alice, Carol, Susan, and Mary Jane. They were my playmates. They were emotionally challenged but amazing.

So our travels to go fishing, go shopping, and go to park events were done with these girls, my grandmother, and her best friend. We did a lot of things together throughout my beginning years of life. I remember catching the bus to Roxborough to go to the Woolworth's store. That was a weekly event that I celebrated because I always got a piece of taffy. That was my treat. And it was the first time that I'd ever gotten on the bus. We took public transportation to do those things. My grandmother was a hard worker. She worked at the laundromat, and she did a little bit of housecleaning for folks in the area. So when she was gone, I stayed with the neighbor across the street who was caring for the four girls.

YPM

Was it just you and your grandma?

Marsha

I do have a grandfather. My grandmother was married, but she was estranged from her husband, David Lewis, Sr. My grandfather lived just a few blocks up from grandma's house. And I went to visit him. He would visit. So they had a good, disconnected marriage if you will. They had three children. My dad was the second oldest one—Nita, David, and Daniel were their three children. My grandfather lived with his mother, Sally Lewis.

YPM

Were you in that situation until you were five?

Marsha

Or six if not, maybe a little longer. I went to my dad's wedding. My dad got clean and met a lady named Barbara Jean, who lived on the same block as my grandma's house. And they got married and became Jehovah's Witnesses. They stayed at her mother's house for a while, and then they bought a home in West Philadelphia not too long after the wedding. I have a picture of me at my dad's wedding all this time because of my skin complexion. My father's a little darker than I am. I thought my Uncle Daniel was my dad. I didn't feel anybody told me that he came more often because we were close. In my mind, I felt that that's what a dad was supposed to be doing. But I grew up with his voice. He did not have a daughter. He had three boys.

YPM

So, when you start school, your life at home changes; what happened?

Marsha

Well, I started school with my grandma. I went to kindergarten around the corner at Lehigh Elementary. I was still staying with my grandma.

My parents decided that was the way that my dad would see me. So I didn't start visiting my biological parents until I was 10.

YPM

So, you liked school and did well in school?

Marsha

I loved school! I did. And I enjoyed going to school and did well. The comfort of my grandma showed up in all these events. I just went around the corner to school. So for the first 10 years, things seemed normal for me.

YPM

So you're a worrywart, and it's challenging to grow up not knowing who your father is and living with your grandma, not with your parents. So what happens in the teenage years?

Marsha

Let's say the craziness started in my teenage years. I met my parents in a courtroom. My mom and dad went to court to get custody of me. And I didn't know what any of that meant. I just wanted to stay with my grams. But the court ordered that my parents have shared custody. So I ended up going to my mom's. Now all of this time, I didn't know I had siblings. My mother had four other children by the time I started to visit. And my dad married a woman caring for her sister after her mother died, which made her my aunt. And they had children—Sandra, Don, and later Nate. So they had had other children in their marriage.

My mother lived on Diamond Street, just a few blocks away from my grandma. My dad lived across town. You had to catch a bus to get to my dad's house. I went to middle school with my sisters and my brother. The abuse started with my oldest sister.

Just to bring things into a full circle, I was abused, raped, and involved in molestation and incest in both households from the age of 10 to 14. The abuse began with my oldest sister and then with one other sister and me. We were all protective of one another. As a result of these encounters, my sister got pregnant.

Mom decided to keep the secret. We were abused. I mean, really abused in that household. We kept a lot of secrets. And she made us tell certain stories. And my sister's story was that she went out one day and hooked up with some guy and got pregnant. She would not let her abort the baby. So my sister gave birth to a baby boy. And mom raised my sister's baby as her son. We took turns skipping school to help take care of the baby.

I remember a rape happening to me and Children and Youth Services coming in in the midst of that trauma. My mother's boyfriend had assaulted me. Talking to the police and talking to social services was traumatic for me. I think what happened after that is they gave permission for me to spend some time with my dad. So I have memories of going to grammar school while living with my grandmother and then going into middle school while sharing custody with my dad and my mom. I ran away a lot at that age. After those incidents, I started running away.

I always went back to my grandma's house. That's where I felt safe. But of course, they would come and get me. I did that for a while. I turned from a happy, loving school kind of child to a very bitter, very broken, very hurt, traumatic little girl. I did things to get attention. I took money from my stepmother. I would take the change out of her room.

I frustrated her with my running away. I started back talking. I was just angry. I was like, dang. I turned into this angry little girl. And my dad was abusive. He started drinking again; he thought it was under control, but he abused his wife. That was traumatic. And her reaction to dealing with his abuse was to abuse me.

I got beat with an extension cord when I was in my father's home. She would beat my naked body and then put me in a bathtub with salt. That was supposed to heal the scars on my body, which went on for a couple of years. Finally, I figured the public transportation out, and I ran away a lot.

YPM

How old were you during those years?

Marsha

I was 11, 12, 13, 14. At 14, with all that was going on in my life, we ended up back in court. Children and Youth Services had been coming through. I loved my siblings at my mother's house. I struggled with my relationship with my siblings at my father's house because of the restrictions they had based on their religious beliefs that I didn't believe in and the abuse that I experienced during that time. When we went back to court, his wife insisted that I be put out. And so we went back to court, and once you get to a certain age, the child can speak to the court and say how they feel about being at these places. And I got an opportunity to do that. I had an advocate stand with me, and I simply explained what was going on in my life.

YPM

So you told the truth to the court?

Marsha

The judge asked me what I wanted, and I said, "I want to go back to my grandmother's house." They gave custody to my grandmother. I graduated from eighth grade. My mother, grandmother, and sister's grandmother were all in a photo at our junior high graduation. I went to my grandmother's house and went through high school at my grandmother's house. I walked to the local high school. I got accepted into a really good vocational-technical high school. And I then started to live what I believe was a normal teenage life. I remember seeing my parents but not staying with them. I did an overnight at my mom's once, but her behavior patterns hadn't changed. She was still getting drunk. She still had drunk boyfriends. My baby sister's father was the best man that came into my mother's life that protected me and cared about me. We called him Baba. He was a Black man who met my mother in treatment for psychiatric illness.

So they met in the psych ward. They got together, and of course, made my baby sister. But he became a part of the family there. When he was there, I felt safe. He thought it necessary to protect his daughters. He did call us his daughters 'til the day he died, which was just a couple of years ago. We have always been connected so he cared for me as a father. My father did not come to my graduation. He had some resentments. His wife had some resentments. They had rules because I wasn't a Jehovah's Witness. Their interaction with me was limited. Barbara Jean felt I lied about her. But I didn't. I told the truth. But she didn't like that. So the relationship with them had been estranged.

But I graduated from high school. I celebrate that because it was probably one of the most exciting things in my life, considering all the other things I went through. I went to prom. My mother had some sisters that lived in the area. Her sister did my hair for the prom, and her sister's girlfriend made my dress. I thought that was amazing. I just dismissed some of the unhealthy parts of my life.

YPM

What did you do with the angry girl you had been as a junior higher when you were in high school? Did you just bury all that? Did you change?

Marsha

I buried it. Those were secrets. I became a different person when I entered high school. I wasn't promiscuous. I wasn't physically engaging with boys, but I was flirtatious in high school. I did have some boyfriends. Everything was kind of supervised. I went to events. I went to the school dances. So I was pretty popular. I joined the debate team. I was pretty bright and very talented. I was also on the drill team. I was the water girl for the wrestling team. I just put all of that stuff somewhere. I just wanted to be normal. Nobody knew my secrets. I just wanted to be me. I traveled to Washington, D.C., with my debate team. My uncle paid for everything I did. I traveled to Washington, D.C., on a class trip. I got to go to the events at the school. All those things were provided for me. My uncle knew my secrets, but nobody else outside the house did.

YPM

So you're trying your best. Like a lot of us, you got hurt, and you buried it, but it's still there. So when does it emerge? When does it come out? When does keeping those secrets lead you to even more hurt? That's the way life works. What happened that got you into prison?

Marsha

At 17 or 18 years old, I started sneaking out to basement parties in the neighborhood, and I started exploring marijuana and what is it called, opium? They were doing drinking little coolers. I met a guy at the house parties who went to Glen Mills. Glen Mills is a facility where bad boys go, a juvenile center. So I fell in love with the guy in Glen Mills and ended up getting pregnant. I kept it a secret. I was disappearing. Grandma thought I was just going to be with the girls. And I was disappearing. So we had some words, and then I told Grams that I thought it was time for me to move.

I went, and I stayed with this young man. He had a room in West Philadelphia, and I stayed with him. We had a very unhealthy relationship. We lived in a room where you could lock yourself in, and you can lock yourself out. So when he would leave, he would lock me in. Everything I needed was in the room. So it didn't bother me. You could knock on the door to get out of the place, but to me, it was okay. I had the TV. I had the bathroom. He would always come back. I believe he was drinking and or stealing. But he would always come back. His name was Steven. I tried to look him up.

I wondered what had happened to him. We didn't communicate after this incident I'm going to tell you about. Steven left one day, and I think I was about four months pregnant, not showing and keeping it secret. Steven went out one day, and I think he got arrested and never came back. So I lay in that space, getting sick and hungry and dehydrated. And then one day, I started banging on the door and asking somebody to get the door open saying, "I can't get out!" So someone finally got a hold of the property manager. They came up and opened up the door, and I was a mess. And at that point, I wasn't using anything. I was just dehydrated. They called the ambulance and took me to the hospital. I had lost the baby; I miscarried the baby.

So I went to my grandma's for a little while. And my mom moved back down to North Philadelphia. I went to where my sisters and brothers lived just to visit. I tried to get back into my normal things to do. My mom was getting ready to get a place with my baby sister's dad. They were moving into a nicer neighborhood. So I went along with them. That didn't go well. I ended up going back and forth seeing my grandma every week. At 18, I feel like I'm grown. I can come and go as I please. I started roller skating because the roller skating facility was right there.

That's where I met my son's father. I snuck off with him one day, and we got into a relationship that lasted six months because he was involved with a whole lot of other girls. He's got 11 children. But I got pregnant with him. My mom did not put me out. I stayed with her. Something happened, and she broke up her relationship with my sister's dad. And we ended up going to West Oak Lane in Philadelphia, which we call the big house. It's a three-story house. My mother is one of 17.

So I moved up there with her. I gave birth to my first child when I was in her home. My son, Timothy, was born in March 1984 when I shared a room with my mother in her family's home. While I was carrying him, I remember helping my mother cook in the kitchen, and I got this first-degree burn on my body. I spilled a pot of spaghetti on myself and got rushed to the emergency room, and they grafted my skin. During that time, I was no longer in a relationship with my son's father, who was living with his mother on the other side of town.

YPM

Wasn't it your mom's boyfriend and your half-brother who had abused you? But now you go back to live with her anyway?

Marsha

Yeah, I felt as though I had disrespected my grandmother. I valued my relationship with my grandmother, and I put her through so much. I just felt at that point that I no longer wanted to be an embarrassment to her.

YPM

So you lived with your mother, but you weren't feeling wonderful about it. You were pregnant, and you had to go somewhere.

Marsha

Right. And it was acceptable. Our relationship was still strained, but I was 18 years old, and I could make adult decisions. And in this house, I had cousins who had similar life experiences.

YPM

So what got you into prison?

Marsha

In a couple of months that I was at my mom's place, I met a guy. I came in looking for a way out and didn't plan on staying. One day, a guy walked past the house while I was sitting on the porch with my son, who was just a couple of months old. And I started talking to him. His name is Greg. And we got into a relationship. I started hanging out at his place, just a couple of blocks away. Our relationship got physical, and I got pregnant again. My son, Timothy, was six months old when I got pregnant. He asked me to move in with him, so I moved back to North Philadelphia in a house with him and his two brothers.

I got introduced to a life that spiraled into prison. I had a history of drug abuse, addiction, and domestic violence that spiraled for the next 10 years of my life back and forth, living with him, getting into other relationships, reconnecting with him, going into and out of rehab. I got addicted to crack cocaine at the age of 20, and that was merely because he kept taking my money, and I told him he couldn't. And said if he didn't take me with him, he wouldn't get my money. So he took me to a crack house, and I started getting high from that point. I continuously got high with him. He went back and forth to prison. I met my children's father Abdul on the street corner while I was out on the street prostituting and looking for drugs. I got pregnant by Abdul while Greg was in prison. So that behavior, all of that continued to transpire for the next 10 years. I didn't get arrested until 1994.

YPM

How old are your children when you do get arrested?

Marsha

The kids were stairsteps. When I got arrested, David was two. David is Abdul's son. I had been homeless that whole time, living in shelters. When Greg went to prison, I went into a shelter. I did years of shelter living, living on the street, homeless, and was hungry for years until Greg got out of prison, and we went to rehab. We got clean. I was clean for a year. We moved to the suburbs with all of the kids, and a year later, Greg started using again, started beating on me again. In January 1994, when I got arrested, and both of us were caught up in our addiction, we would leave the kids unattended. I would leave the kids with him. He'd be in the bathroom getting high.

And I'm going out trying to find ways to get more. So in this private subsidized housing community, the police came. The police had been to the house multiple times due to the incidences of abuse. But this was the first time they had come to make an arrest. I had left the house. The neighbors would keep after the kids, which they often did when they saw us leaving the kids. It got really bad. The house was in horrible condition. I had been on a binge for a while, and Greg had been missing. So when they came, he went out the back door, and I sat in the living room and had a conversation with the police. And at that point, they had decided that they wanted to press charges, endangering the welfare of a child. So that's what I went through.

YPM

When you went to prison, how many children did you have? What were their ages?

Marsha

There were six, and their ages were 9, 7, 6, 5, 4, and 2.

YPM

So now you are in prison. How long did they give you?

Marsha

One and a half to five years. I ended up doing two and a half years.

YPM

You were a person whose crimes came directly out of your addiction. Without being addicted or high, you would never have endangered the life of your children. Is that fair to say?

Marsha

Yes.

YPM

So now you get to prison and are breathing.

Marsha

I went to Montgomery County Prison. I went through my assessment and physical and found out that I was pregnant with my seventh child. Oh, my goodness. I had a baby in prison, the worst experience in my life.

YPM

What happens now with all the stuff you had buried? Now you are thinking about how you have been treating your children and your addiction. Now you are separated from your children. What is going on inside of you? What's going on in your body, your soul? Were you guilty, bitter, angry, broken, humbled?

Marsha

I was all of that and more. I cried for days. I had never been to prison. I cried for all of the pain of my past. I relived that for the six months I sat in that county jail, and this was an old school county jail where the doors slammed closed every time they opened them. And every time that happened, my skin shook. So I was an emotional wreck, and I had no one to blame but myself. And of course, I went through that cycle of blaming my parents, blaming my husband at the time. "Just what's wrong with you, Marsha. Why couldn't you get it together?" I got to see a psychiatrist while I was there, and I worked on some of the past, and I talked through the pain. I went to the NA (Narcotics Anonymous) meetings there. When it came time for delivery, I had a lot of physical pain because I wasn't taking care of myself.

I went to prison in January. I gave birth to a son, Christian, in May. They transported me to Lancaster County Prison in Pennsylvania. I gave birth to my son at Lancaster General Hospital. Twenty-four hours after I had my baby, they took my baby away. Then I went back into another cycle of depression, frustration, anger, and resentment.

I say to people, I was broken, but I was breathing. I had to accept it. They talk about that in the NA fellowship. I had to know what I could change and accept things I could not change. They took my kids. The judge told me in the courtroom that I couldn't have my kids back, that I was not worthy of being a parent, I had lost all my rights to my children. I could not have any contact with my children during my sentence.

But they had no authority over the child that I was carrying. So I was able to give the baby a name. I named him Christian Nathaniel. I was able to give him to a church family that I had gotten close to. They also took three of my other children. So I knew my kids were safe. Although the judge ordered me not to have any communication, they sent me letters. They sent me Bible studies. They sent me scriptures. They sent me photos. And so did the other lady that had two of the other kids despite what the judge had ordered. So I sat in the county for, I don't know, maybe a month before they transported me to the state prison.

YPM

So you spent six months at Montgomery County Prison, you have the baby, and then you go a month later to which state prison?

Marsha

I went to Muncy. That was different. I got accustomed to how they did things at the county jail. And I made a couple of friends in my 12 Step group. I got comfortable talking about my journey and dealing with some of my stuff, but Lord, have mercy. I got to this prison, and it looked nothing like the other prison I was in for the last seven months. And I have to start all over again. I think my fear level went way up because it just got real. Now I was in "jail jail." And there was no getting out. So I think I regressed. I tapped back into my anger. I was angrier now. They took my baby, and I was very angry about that!

YPM

When you were with your grandma, did you go to church? You weren't a Jehovah's Witness; that wasn't your faith. I'm assuming you were a

Christian believer, but how real was it in you? How mature was your faith? Did your faith help you, or had you forgotten all of that? Were you weeping for months? Were you praying as well? Where was your spirit and your connection to God during that time?

Marsha

I believe the foundation was placed at my grandma's at a young age. I'm still doing "lay me down to sleep" with my children. That foundation was set during my periodic moments of sanity. I want to say that I had an internal spiritual foundation. Yes, I knew how to pray. I knew to cry and pray. I did a lot of that in prison. I went to church while in prison. I listened to people tell me that I could be saved. I believed, and that helped give me substance.

YPM

You believed you could be saved, but were you saved?

Marsha

I got baptized when I first moved to Pottstown and immediately became involved in the church. When Greg got out of prison, we both had gone through rehab and were clean, and we did what they call a geographical change. We moved to what I call the suburbs in Pottstown, away from Philadelphia and addiction, and that's where the addiction resurfaced.

When Greg was gone, I went to church. I got connected with the Seventh Day Adventist Church. My kids were involved in activities. Corine and Eugene Smith became my mentors. They were spiritual parents. They visited me in prison. I was humiliated. I was embarrassed. But they encouraged me and informed me and kept telling me about the love of Jesus and the sacrifice that Jesus had made and that He died for me. They made that very clear all the time. When they came to meet with me, we did Bible studies. When I got letters, it was about forgiveness. I didn't feel worthy. I was still struggling to believe that after all I had done and particularly that I couldn't stay clean for the sake of my children. I didn't think that was a forgivable sin. And so once I got upstate, I struggled to the point that I lashed out at an inmate and got sent to the hole because I was so angry and bitter with myself.

It wasn't until I spent those 30 days in the hole that I got to sit still and really reflect on my journey and truly ask God to forgive me, to say I was so sorry. I wrote a lot of letters to my family, apologizing and continuously trying to heal. It wasn't until I got out of the hole that I made a commitment to God. I spent 30 days focused on the Word, reading the Word, speaking out loud about my convictions. I was confessing and asking God for forgiveness. I made a promise before I left the hole that I would do whatever I needed to do to regain God's trust in me, restore my relationship with my children, restore my relationship with my family, and work on forgiving myself.

They said that I had to forgive myself to feel free, to believe that I am forgiven. And that was a process for me. I came out of the hole and went to church. I signed up for every church service. I had a Muslim doula, and I dabbled in the Islamic faith. I went to Islamic services, and I went to Christian services. I needed to be spiritually fit. I was confused about who I was but needed to create every opportunity I could to find out how to heal. And so, for the next two years, I stayed focused on my recovery. I went through a treatment program in prison. I sang with the church choir.

I listened to a lot of spiritual music from the 80s and the 90s, which became my strength. I attended the Yokefellowship Prison Ministry. I did the Yokefellowship Bible studies. I went through all of the Bible studies by mail. You read the study, answer the questions, and mail out your answers, and they mail it back to you. I did all of that. I started to change the way I thought and felt about myself. And I started believing that I was delivered. I began to believe that I was a good person and worthy of Jesus's sacrifice for me on the cross. He did that for me.

So I started in my mind, and in my heart, through my actions, to believe that I was being transformed. My transformation started in prison. My recommitment to Christ happened in prison. That reality started for me there. When I was getting into the niche of being controlled by Christ, I had support from a lifer named Naomi Blount, who spoke to my spirit, and Gina Stocker, who was there for embezzlement. She reminded me of my grandmother and those women. Rocky Severpool, Naomi Blount, and Gina Stocker soaked into me the love of Jesus and the power that I could have if I stayed focused on my journey of becoming whole again. He promised to make me whole again, and I believed it. I took a class in photography because God confirmed with me that I needed to see the world through a different lens.

I was in my addiction for over 11 years. I had missed the beauty of this earth, this place, and the world I was living in because I was shut in by my pain, abuse, and trauma. So being behind the camera lens and producing the film in the lab, I produced my photos. I saw them come to life. I took pictures of trees and snow and flowers, things that I hadn't seen in all of the years I had been in my addiction because my addiction blinded me. I started to look at life differently. I saw that I could produce something great, something good, something of value.

When I graduated from that class, the Smiths came to the prison for my graduation, and I felt like I had accomplished something. I completed parenting classes, and I got a certificate. I did my Bible studies. I got a certificate. I felt that at that point, I was showing myself approved.

I was able to give God something back because, for some reason, He saved me. He didn't have to; I had three suicide attempts in my addiction. I had overdosed. I lost count of how many times I woke up on the side of a curb somewhere and how many cars I had gotten into with strange men. For some reason, He saved me. And I'm still trying to figure out why, but as things are starting to unfold for me, I see the value in my life.

They brought my son to see me when he was a year old. And I got to see him walk for the first time. That changed my life. Knowing that Christian and the other children that were in foster care with these church families were going to be a part of my life, whether physically or emotionally, gave me something to work hard for and helped me to believe that the lie of the Enemy is not the one for me. I kept seeing that judge's face telling me all of those mean things in that courtroom. I relived that over and over again, but that helped me dismiss the Enemy's voice and to believe that I am a good mother. I am a child of the King that died for Marsha Renae Curry. I knew that. So as I moved forward in my journey, I grew stronger and closer to the Lord. I knew that it would be important for me to survive once I got out of prison. Now that leads us to another situation.

YPM

Before you go into that situation, please take me back to your time in the hole. I've visited people in prison, but I've never been to "the hole." Those 30 days were a powerful kind of wilderness experience for you. Something happened to you. What was it like in the hole? What was your day like in that place? Could you hear other people? Could you see other people, or were you isolated?

Marsha

I could see other people, but I was isolated. I wasn't the only one in the hole, and you got to come out for an hour, and you got fed in your room. You couldn't go out into a public space. It was confinement, restrictive confinement. But you got to keep your Bible. You get out for a shower. Then you go back by yourself. I couldn't go to class, couldn't go to church—none of that, just me and God. I had my Bible and Bible study activities, all of which I could do. You could send mail out when you were in the hole. And I was able to write letters and get my studies out in their mail. You could go to medical. You could go to medical, but you're escorted. I was under psychiatric care, so I got to see the psychiatrist. And so it was awhile. It was a very difficult 30 days. It was a very much needed 30 days.

YPM

Before you go back to that other situation, can you talk about the Yokefellowship Prison Ministry? Pastor Larry Coleman, a former executive director of YPM, gave me your name. This book consists of interviews with people YPM impacted while they were inmates. What do you remember about Yokefellowship Prison Ministry?

Marsha

I had a mentor couple, Roy and Ann Zeiset, who came in from Yokefellowship to do my Bible studies. Back then, you could have meals brought in, and we had a picnic and talked about the Bible. They checked in and wrote to me while doing my Bible study series. When my son, Timothy, came to visit, my sister brought him to visit me. They stayed with Roy and Ann. While they came out to visit me at the prison, Timothy got to see some goats. I got pictures of Timothy and the animals on their farm. But it was through my relationship with them and doing my Bible study lessons that I learned more about Yokefellowship, learned more about the Bible, and understood my responsibility as a Christian. Those Bible lessons were what kept me motivated and kept me engaged in my biblical studies. I was a bright young lady before I picked up a drug. I loved to learn. I loved school. And I loved the whole learning experience. So I enjoyed advancing in my studies. There was a level of accomplishment and excitement about completing a study series, sending it in, and going to the next level. That was empowering for me. And part of the spiritual journey for sure.

YPM

You're going to church. You're into your Bible studies. You're into learning, and the Bible is becoming real for you. And then something else happens.

Marsha

I got transferred to Cambridge Springs SCI. Cambridge Springs is in the middle of nowhere, further from civilization.

YPM

Further from family and visits.

Marsha

I was devastated, but I kept my spiritual foundation. I was locked in. They wanted me to believe that this was a good move. I was in a maximum-security prison; Cambridge Springs was a minimum-security prison. They said that it would help me to move towards parole. I could have stayed, but I did not refuse to move. I was going to be obedient to whatever God had for me. So right at half of my sentence, they took me to Cambridge Springs. They said you have to do a year on state grounds before seeing parole.

I had already done my year at Muncy, and I was ready to see parole, and then they moved me. But at Cambridge Springs, I did go to see parole. I had completed my programs and did everything I was required to do for parenting, but I didn't have a place to go. No one would let me come to their house. The truth is that I didn't want to go to my mother's house. I wrote her a letter and shared my thoughts with her. That was not a healthy idea. My father didn't want me to go to his house. He wouldn't accept me anyway. So I sat in that prison. And that's how I ended up doing two and a half years because I couldn't find a home plan. One of the friends I had made in the Muslim community said she had a brother that she could connect me with. In prison, it's called a "jailhouse hook up," but here was the challenge. He lived in Harrisburg, and I had never been to Harrisburg. So what in the world am I going to do in Harrisburg? So I talked to Naomi. I spoke to Ms. Gina and asked for some advice. Then, of course, I don't need to tell you—I took it to the altar. I prayed about it, and I kept asking God what I was supposed to do? I'm ready to go home, whatever that looks like. I'm ready to go to the next level, the next step. I wasn't 100% sure that God wanted me to go this route, but I did it anyway. So I agreed to meet with this young man in the visiting room to explain my intentions, find out his intentions, and see if this collaboration would work.

He was a very nice, respectful Muslim man and agreed to allow me to use his address as a home plan to be released. I met with his sister, and she assured me that I would be safe. This arrangement wasn't about a relationship. This arrangement was about the connection that my Muslim friend and I made. Her brother and I had no intentions with one another. So once I felt comfortable with that, I prayed and asked God to forgive me if I've stepped out of line here, and if this is not your will, then do what you need to do. This was my third time going before parole. My home plan was approved, and I was off to Harrisburg.

So I was getting out. I wrote some letters and sent out some resumes to businesses in that area looking for work. I also contacted someone from a mental health recovery, my priority. Maybe a couple of months later, they knocked on my cell door, and I had been there for a year, and said that I was being released. They don't tell you your release date for the sake of security. They just knock on your door and say, "Curry, pack it up!"

YPM

What has happened to your life since then? What's your relationship with your children today? Where are they? That's how God got you free. How have you stayed free?

Marsha

I kept my commitment, went to church, and stayed in recovery. The second I got out, my first stop was an NA meeting. My second stop was at church. I went to the one on the corner, and I worked my way through there. I made some friends in the fellowship of Narcotics Anonymous. I was actively involved in church and church activities. I couldn't find a job. I had a criminal record. I was a nobody. I was new in the area.

Instead of sulking, a young lady agreed to sponsor me. Her name was Avis. Avis was a beautician who had a really strong recovery. I became friends with Avis, and I started volunteering at her salon. I started sweeping and cleaning. I became a shampoo girl for my first year at home. That was my life. That was my journey. But my little old self clicked in a year after I was home. I met a guy in NA and got into a relationship. I believed it was a healthy relationship for the first time with somebody in recovery. So I started dating him, and I got pregnant.

We were in church together. We were put into counseling, and we agreed to get married. We were going to consummate this family and this marriage under God. It didn't take long for that to happen. He was instrumental in the process of helping me on my next step. I had access to Timothy and baby Christian, but they didn't rush to give me them. They just came for visits. I didn't have a place where they could stay. I eventually left the guy's house, and Avis offered for me to move in with her. I didn't feel comfortable with the boys at this man's house. I had my first visit with the boys, and they stayed overnight.

I had a lot of assistance from my mental health therapists. I talked about my kids a lot, so I started working on a plan. I know many women who have lost their children to the system. I found out only by the grace of God that I did not lose my rights to my children, despite what the judge said to me. I had never relinquished my parental rights to my children. I didn't know that the whole time that I was in prison. Once that was revealed to me, I asked, what did I need to do to have interaction with my children? So I moved into a program called Delta Housing.

I got involved in Delta Housing which then transferred over to Brethren Housing. Brethren Housing was a facility run by the Church of the Brethren, and that helped me stay connected to my commitment to Christ. So I got involved and accepted into this program. They give you supportive services, and they connect you to your family. They provide you with a home and supervision. And so I started in that program. It took about a year and a half through this program.

I was required to go to McDonald's on Exit 22 to meet with Children and Youth Services, and my children and I did one-hour visits during those six months. I had to be committed to that consistency for my children. If I wasn't going to be able to do that, they didn't want me to see my kids because my kids needed to have the assurance that I would be the parent that I was committed to in this agreement. So I did that.

I had an amazing case manager, an awesome therapist, and a good church network with a strong spiritual foundation. And those are the key components that led me to make the front page of the Patriot News. When my children were returned to me—all of them, all of them—we made the newspaper's front page. At that point, I felt God was telling me the scripture that speaks about touching the hem of his garment. That scripture speaks to me needing to believe that my life could be transformed by renewing my mind and renewing my spirit. God created that in me, and I believed it. Life was not perfect, but I was committed to seeing it through. And as long as I stayed true to my faith and my belief in Christ, then all things would be accomplished through Him.

YPM
Did your seven children come to live with you?

Marsha
Yes, when we made the front page of the paper.

YPM
Did you have a place big enough for everybody?

Marsha
Through Brethren Housing, we had a big enough place. When I married, we got into a bigger place. I moved into a three-story, five-bedroom house covered under the program. The Section Eight program was expedited on my behalf because I needed to come out of the two-bedroom unit I was in with Timothy and Christian.

YPM

How did it go with everybody?

Marsha

It was great, listen, it was crazy! Be careful what you ask for. I mean, it was crazy. My kids had issues going back to when I was home. I had to deal with my mental health issues. I had to deal with their mental health issues.

I had an amazing case manager, Julie. God placed her in my life. Our family social worker, Susan, is still friends with me today. God put her in my life. She was a God-fearing and committed woman who was a human service provider. These two women, in particular, became a part of my family. They didn't miss graduation. They didn't miss a birthday party. They have been the foundation of my spiritual journey.

YPM

So, Timothy is your oldest, and Andrea is your youngest, correct? So, how old are they today?

Marsha

Timothy is 37, Andrea is 25.

YPM

My goodness. You should write a book, lady.

Marsha

I know. Can you write it for me?

YPM

Let me get through this one first.

Marsha

Honestly, I want to, and I want it to be spiritual.

YPM

The story of how you took all those children from all the different places they've been and experiences they've been through and brought them together is a story worth telling.

Marsha

That's amazing. It is only God. It had been a journey of struggle, triumph, and overcoming. We had a lot of challenges. They had picked up behaviors that were not meeting my expectations, not to mention they had picked up very dangerous behaviors. Malcolm had attempted suicide while in foster care. David was impulsive and angry. It was a lot for me to handle. I would not have been able to handle it without a lot of prayer, church support, and mental health counseling. But we did it. And you know, today I have eight children. After eight years of marriage, we divorced.

I started dating a man who was a local pastor and a banker. I did not know he was a functional addict. I don't know how I missed that. I fell in love with my eyes. I knew enough to do better. He was a man of the cloth. I was a first lady (pastor's spouse) married in the church, and he was getting high on the weekends. But we somehow survived that. I got divorced again and then became a single woman and said, "Okay God, I'm focused. Let me figure this out. What should I do next?" I turned 50 and was fully engaged in the church and fully engaged in Yokefellowship. I was doing my part to keep my kids connected until they turned 18 and could tell me that they didn't want to go to church.

My kids went to college. I have three college graduates. They either went to college or business school or learned a trade. I give honor to nobody but God on that journey. Several of them work alongside me in Amiracle4sure and have become a part of God's vision for this work. So I had a vision. However, I struggled with finding a job. So I went to volunteer at a women's facility where women were coming home from prison called Promise Place. I met Larry Coleman from Yokefellowship Prison Ministry; he was in YPM leadership. His wife, Judith Coleman, was on the board of Promise Place, which was a transitional house for women coming home from prison.

I was a mentor in that program and volunteered in the house with the women coming there. That was when the first seed was planted in me for what I wanted to do in the future. I prayed, and God led me to school. I went to college with eight kids at home. God led me to believe that this would be doable for me. It was the next step I had to take to live out my dream of becoming who I am today. So I committed to going to school and learning what I needed to know to start Amiracle4sure. I graduated in 2010 with my master's degree.

I knew I was brilliant. I knew I had skills. I just didn't realize how to tap into them. I didn't know I had to go through this life experience to see it come to fruition. I knew that I had messed it all up. But God brought it full circle. So in 2010, in my master's program, I developed and designed Amiracle4sure. I did not want women to be in prison and not have a place to go.

So that's how it started. I wrote my thesis on the premature release of women to communities. I wrote about letting people out of prison without giving them what they needed to stay out of prison. I learned how to do that. And by the time I graduated, I had been home for years and had not returned to prison. So I wrote that model, and I created a program. And I called it Amiracle4sure because that's what I am. But I realize that I am not the only one. So my goal, responsibility, and commitment to Christ were to reach souls like me and give them the hope that somebody gave me. And so that's what we do every day. It's developed a bit. I got a contract with the same institution, the same state system where I was an inmate. In 2013 I signed a contract with the Pennsylvania Department of Corrections to be a pre-approved facility for men and women to come to for help. And I've been doing it ever since.

YPM

You are an inspiration, an amazing person. I thank God for the work He's done in your life and for what you've done with your life. The way you've given back is remarkable.

Marsha

Thank you so much. I appreciate it.

YPM

You're welcome. All right. Take care.

Marsha R. Curry-Nixon
Founder and Executive Director of Amiracle4sure
amiracle4sure@gmail.com

Biblical Reflection

The crowds were so great they almost crushed Jesus (Luke 8:42b-48). But a desperate woman being crushed herself by the crowd came up behind Jesus and touched the hem of his cloak. Jesus asked out loud, "Who touched me?" Peter was perplexed. Many people were touching Jesus. But Jesus knew someone had touched him in such a way that power had gone out of him.

In Leviticus 15:19-30, the Hebrews were given detailed rules about ritual cleanliness. During her monthly period, a woman would be considered unclean. Anything she sat or lay on and anyone she touched would also be unclean until washed. When she was finished with her monthly discharge, she needed to wait seven days and then bring two doves and two pigeons to the priest at the entrance of the Tent of Meeting, and then he would "make atonement for her in the presence of God." Then she was clean again.

The woman who touched Jesus had been bleeding every day for 12 years! She could touch no one. She was ashamed, separated from family, separated from God, and barely hanging on to hope. But in her desperation, she made her way through a jostling crowd, touched Jesus, and was instantly healed. Jesus said, "Daughter, your faith has healed you. Go in peace."

Marsha Curry-Nixon felt unclean and unforgivable. She was separated from her children. Her anger got her sent to the "hole" for 30 days. But in that place of solitude and confinement, she reached out to touch God. "It wasn't until I spent those 30 days in the hole that I got to sit still and really reflect on my journey and truly ask God to forgive me, to say I was so sorry. I wrote a lot of letters to my family, apologizing and continuously trying to heal. It wasn't until I got out of the hole that I made a commitment to God. I spent 30 days focused on the Word, reading the Word, speaking out loud about my convictions.

I was confessing and asking God for forgiveness. I made a promise before I left the hole that I would do whatever I needed to do to regain God's trust in me, restore my relationship with my children, restore my relationship with my family, and work on forgiving myself."

Marsha was released from prison. After years of separation, she was reunited with her children. She reflected on a desperate woman who managed to touch Jesus when He was in a crowd. "At that point, I felt God was telling me the scripture that speaks about touching the hem of his garment. That speaks to my needing to believe that my life could be transformed by renewing my mind and renewing my spirit. God created that in me, and I believed it."

Chapter 10
Doug Hollis

You are an angry, wild 16-year-old who has lived a troubled, violent life. You have made a string of terrible choices. You commit the most serious of crimes. You take the life of a person God created. You are sentenced to spend the rest of your life in prison. You are released 42 years later. What kind of person do you expect you would be after living a life like that? How would you think, how would you speak, how would you relate to others? What would you believe about life and death and the purpose of your existence? Would you believe in God? Would you be truly free, or would you be living in a prison without bars?

YPM
How did you get started in life?

Doug
I was born and raised in Philadelphia. Both my parents were alcoholics. Well, maybe alcoholic is a bit strong, but they both engaged in drinking rather heavily. My mother had children when she wasn't ready. She was still a child herself. I am the third of four children. I have an older

brother, an older sister, and a younger brother. I was the only one to get caught up in the criminal justice system. It is crazy because I was always looked at as the smartest kid.

YPM
Was your family together all those years? Did your mom and dad stay together despite the drinking?

Doug
We were the typical dysfunctional family. My mother raised us; she was the primary caregiver until I was 10 or 11 years old. Then I was placed in foster care. My little brother was born in 1968. We were living in North Philadelphia. My sister had taken the purse of a Spanish woman who lived a few doors up from us. When the police came and saw the conditions, they said we were "abandoned children." My mother wasn't there because she did a lot of partying and drinking in those days. So they placed my sister, my younger brother, and me in the Stenton Childcare Center in Mount Airy.

Then they split us up. My sister was placed in a foster home in one section of the city, my little brother was placed in a foster home in another area, and I was placed in another foster home in South Philly. I didn't see my older brother, mother, sister, or little brother for two years. I had some difficulties with the foster parents that I was living with. So they placed me in the foster home of Mrs. Alima Walker in North Philly, which was about a mile from my father's. I stayed with Mrs. Walker until I completed the sixth grade. Then they sent me back home with my mother. My sister and younger brother had been returned to my mother by this time, so she had all of her children back.

YPM
What about your older brother?

Doug

He had been in the juvenile facility in Cornwells Heights. When they brought us all back together, my mother lived at 19th and Venango. She decided she was going to move to the Richard Allen Homes. That's where I first got involved with street gangs. My brother and I became members of the 12th and Poplar Street gang. That's when my life took a downward spiral. As I told you earlier, I was always considered smart. I was voted most likely to succeed when I graduated from sixth grade.

YPM

So what happened to your smarts when you got in the gang?

Doug

They went somewhere, but I don't know where. I got caught up in that life. There was no discipline at home. My teacher became the street, and that's where I stayed. I literally lived in the streets. I was in the streets all day long. I would sleep in hallways, cars—you name it, I've slept there. There was no parental guidance for me.

YPM

Were you going to school?

Doug

I was going to a combined elementary and a junior high. And as I told you, I got affiliated with gangs, and they were the thrust of the neighborhood. But I would get chased home by the rival gang, both my brother and me, and my mother said to me, "Boy, one of these days, they gonna bring your scraps home." And I said, "I'm not going back to school." My mother said, "You're going to school, boy!" Little did she know. But I used to just meet up with the gang at 11th and Brown, go up to the state store on 12th and Poplar and get a half-gallon of Thunder Bird wine and drink all day until it was time to go to gang war. But life got so bad for me during that time that I recall going down to City Hall in Philadelphia. Frank Rizzo was the mayor at the time. I had lunch with his bodyguard. I told him I wanted to be put back in foster care because my life was just so bad, and I just didn't want to deal with it. I was kinda worried about dying and all those things.

YPM

How did you get to have lunch with Frank Rizzo's bodyguard?

Doug

Well, I went down to the mayor's office in City Hall, and I wouldn't leave. I wanted to be put back in foster care. I didn't want to spend another day living my life the way I was living. So they put me in another foster home in South Philadelphia, which didn't work out either because it was a bad scene. I was torn up as a kid. I was mixed up in all the wrong things. I was stealing from my foster parents and doing stupid stuff, and it didn't work out, so I left the foster home and went back to Richard Allen projects. I went back to where I was running from, and it was just this downward spiral, a cycle of insanity, doing the same things over and over. It never got better.

YPM

Tell me about your relationship with your father. Where was he?

Doug

Well, my father was a good man when he was sober. And you couldn't ask for a better father in his sobriety, but unfortunately, my dad drank every day. I don't know if it was a result of his being involved in the war. I think it was World War II or the Korean war. He was a soldier, and I don't know if that put him in the mode of drinking, but he used to drink. He was what I call a functional alcoholic. He worked at Philadelphia General Hospital as an orderly.

But he always embraced us. My younger brother has a different father. So our father embraced my older brother, sister, and me. And my stepmother welcomed all four of us. My dad would take care of all four of us, and even though my younger brother wasn't his, he still cared for him. But we were in the custody of my mother, and we were with her until she got tired of us. I remember one Christmas, she just took us and left us on my father's doorstep, rang his bell, left us, got in the car with a boyfriend, and drove off.

YPM
Your mother did this?

Doug
Yeah. Our mother dropped us off at my father's and just left us. And I mean, it was cold. We were just standing there crying. "Mommy, mommy, don't leave us, mom." My father always took us in. He always cared for us until my mother decided to come back and get us. And it was that kind of life that we kids were dealt. I have one thing I want to make clear, though, I made a lot of poor choices in my life as a kid, and I don't ever want to blame that on my parents. I could have had a better childhood. I could have had a better life, but I made a bunch of poor choices back to the point with the foster parents—stealing from them, taking stuff. I didn't have to do that.

I was just a kid making stupid decisions out of ignorance. It was just stupid. And because of my smarts, they sent me to a place called George Junior Republic. You're supposed to be smart to go to George Junior. And they sent me there. I met Franco Harris and Rocky Bleier when I was there. I was really into sports, and I was good. So I was on George Junior's football team, and they brought professional football players in and introduced me to them. And they tried to encourage me to stay in athletics. But I was a kid caught up in stupidity. I'm going down my way. I'm hanging out with my guys. I don't care.

I'm a kid. I played basketball. So they gave another kid and me $10 and a bus ticket to basketball camp in Scranton, Pennsylvania. I take the $10 and buy a bus ticket to Philadelphia, going back down to Richard Allen homes in my youthful ignorance. There was something special in my family in the tragedy of all of this. My mother's brothers were people of the cloth. My uncle Luke was a pastor. He passed away in 1998 or 1999. I lived with him when I was little, but my mother didn't have anybody to take care of my little brother, so she took me from an uncle, and my life just went all to, you know. My uncle Larry, who lives over in Jersey, he's a lay pastor. There were just so many people in my family that could have helped us grow in Christ as a family if we only were smart enough.

YPM

Well, you were smart enough. It wasn't the lack of intelligence. It was youth and the lack of guidance. When you're a kid, you don't have experience or wisdom. What about faith? Did you ever go to church? Did you have a belief in God? Were you Christian?

Doug

I'll give you the story of my evolution here. When I lived with my Uncle Luke, he took me to church every Sunday. We went to a church in West Philadelphia called Bible Way Baptist. But when I went back to my mother, the church wasn't a part of our life. I don't want to say that I would have turned out differently if I had been more grounded in the church because God knows what I don't know. Sometimes God allows you to go through things.

YPM

So did you learn, did you grow?

Doug

I think that was a part of my life. My life was like Jonah's. God came to Jonah and told him to go to the people of Nineveh and speak to the people. But Jonah said they were wicked; they were corrupt. He didn't want to do that. So he ran from what God wanted him to do and ended up in the belly of the whale. In my case, because I didn't know God's calling on my life, I was in rebellion. And the belly of the whale for me was a prison until I humbled myself and cried out to God and His mercy and forgiveness. Then like Jonah, God released me from the whale and restored me to life. And now I have a purpose. Everything is about Him.

YPM

So you are with your buddy, and you do something dumb. What got you in big trouble?

Doug

We were both 16. I was born in October, and he was born in November. He came and asked me to commit a robbery with him. We're both part of the same gang. We are both stupid kids. We go to commit this robbery. As we walked down Franklin Street, we saw three elderly people, Mrs. Inej, her husband, and a friend. We attempt to take Mrs. Inej's purse. It falls to the ground. So I asked my co-defendant for his knife. I just want to intimidate them, scare them, thinking that'll work. But when Mrs. Inej saw the knife, she screamed. And when she started screaming, I panicked, and tragically Mrs. Inej was stabbed four times. The stab wound in her back went through the fatty tissue and into her heart, and that's what caused Mrs. Inej's death.

YPM

You're the one that stabbed Mrs. Inej. How did you know her?

Doug

I didn't know her. I didn't know any of the people involved. I say the name to be respectful to her. She was somebody for somebody. So I try to put a name with her because she deserves it.

YPM

So now what's happening with the other two people as she's lying on the ground.

Doug

I think the one guy, Harry, was stabbed in the arm. Nothing happened to Mrs. Inej's husband. The last thing my co-defendant or I ever wanted was to take someone's life. We can attribute it to youthful ignorance. It was a pity. It was the culmination of poor decisions by a kid. I made a bunch of poor decisions as a child, and I don't abdicate my responsibility in any of this stuff. Yeah.

YPM

I hear you. So it was Mrs. Inej and her husband and another man. And they're older people and the one man, the friend, was hurt, but she died. So what happens, what happens the next day? Were you caught right away?

Doug

No, no, no. The next day the police sweep the project. They're going door to door, arresting people. And someone came to me and told me that the police were looking for them. I was helping Darline Liner paint her apartment. And the police came up there and arrested me. That was on May 29, 1975. They took me to the police administration building and charged me with murder, robbery, criminal conspiracy— the general charges associated with something like that. My co-defendant had been arrested before me, so he was already in custody.

They offered him a deal to testify against me. They would give him 5 to 10 years. He refused. And subsequently, he was sentenced to life, just as I was. We were both juvenile lifers. Wow! We had separate trials, but the attorneys didn't put up much defense. It's really difficult to defend the indefensible. I don't harbor any animosity towards the attorneys or the district attorney. It was youthful ignorance. You can blame other people for your shortcomings, but at the end of the day, it's my shortcomings.

It took me some time to get to the point where I can sit here like I'm talking to you and say with a sense of reason, I made the mistakes. It was Doug Hollis that did all these things. If Doug Hollis doesn't go out to commit this robbery with his friend, Doug Hollis isn't in prison. Right? Doug Hollis made another poor choice asking for the weapon. It's by God's grace that I can look at my life. I can look at who I am and go forward and try to do better. Right?

YPM

You're a 16-year-old kid that made a string of bad choices. That doesn't take away the gravity of what you did, but you are a 16-year-old kid. You had a tough life, and you made many bad decisions. So you're convicted, and you didn't go right to the state prison because you were still a juvenile, right? Or were you already old enough to go?

Doug

I went from the police administration building in Philadelphia to E1, a wing at the House of Correction for Juveniles waiting to be certified as an adult. I was sentenced to life on June 21, 1976. So I'm still 17 at the time. On June 22, I was transferred to Holmesburg Prison in Philadelphia. On June 23, I was issued my identification number at Graterford Prison. After lunch that day, I went to Camp Hill State Prison. I stayed at Camp Hill from 1976 to 1983.

YPM

You're 17, and they put you in a state prison?

Doug

I was certified as an adult so they could send me to an adult prison. That's one of the tragedies of our judicial system; it sends children to adult institutions. You're surrounded by a bunch of barracudas and piranhas and all those other things. There was no way to get ahead.

YPM

So tell me what happened. All these barracudas and piranhas are surrounding you in prison. You're a 17-year-old. How did you respond in that atmosphere? Did you get worse before you got well? What happened next?

Doug

Well, let's go back a little bit. You'd asked me earlier about my religion and those kinds of things. When I came into the prison system, I thought of myself as a Christian. I was raised going to church with my uncle and those kinds of things. But when I came to prison, I was so cantankerous, I was so out of control that I needed some form of discipline, and I got that discipline in Islam. I was a Sunni Muslim for about a year and a half, maybe a little longer, but that's where I got disciplined.

YPM

How did the Muslims do it? How did the Muslims take an angry, cantankerous young man and discipline him in a way that worked? How do they do that? They must have a method.

Doug

If you're hungry for change, some of the things they do instill discipline. You're not supposed to commit suicide. So I'm not going to commit suicide. Why am I smoking cigarettes? You sort of break down and start breaking away from the bad habits that otherwise control you.

YPM

I'm curious, why did you listen to them? You are a big guy. So it wasn't just physical intimidation. Why did you do what they said? Why did you listen to them?

Doug

You're missing the thing here. I wasn't a follower in those days. I was a leader. I wasn't somebody that was just doing what they said. I got involved because I wanted discipline. I wanted to have more of a structured discipline. And I learned discipline in the process.

YPM

So it wasn't a sincere connection to Allah or the Islamic faith?

Doug

No.

YPM

What was it if it wasn't that?

Doug

I don't know. I'd call it a self-imposed belief where I know I'm doing what's right. I'm following a God that I believe in. What woke me up to the realization that it was false was in 1978. The Supreme Court denied an appeal that I had. Muslims pray five times a day, but this appeal was denied. And I found myself reverting to my undisciplined ways. In retrospect, that told me that I was not in the proper religion because when you meet trials and tribulations in life, they should bring you closer to your God, not further away.

YPM

So that's what you were thinking. That was the thought process at the time.

Doug

That's why I stopped being involved in Islam.

YPM

Didn't you pay a price for that?

Doug

I'm a big guy. So even if there's a lot of them, it's okay.

YPM

So you're a big guy, and you're strong enough to walk out, and you do not worry.

Doug

Well, here's the thing, when I was a kid, I was wild and had no discipline. And a lot of the people I engaged with in Islam knew me before I was a Muslim. They knew me when I was the renegade, the guy running around doing stupid stuff. People ask, how did I deal with the piranhas? One day at the House of Correction, I was in the mess hall eating, and there's a guy named Rick who came down from Camp Hill. I'm big now, but I was skinny then. My nickname was "Bones," that's how skinny I was.

And my voice is a little deeper now as an adult. When I was a kid, it was really soft. And so we're sitting at the table in the dining hall. They give you metal trays, and he's taking people's crackers off their trays. They used to give us little packs of crackers. And I guess he thought I was some type of chump or pushover or whatever. And he says, "I want those crackers." I said, "Okay, so do I." He said, "I'm taking them crackers. You ain't gonna do nothin." And I said, "Okay, you can take them as long as you can take what comes with them." He said, "You ain't doing nothin." And he took the crackers, and before he could get his hand back, I smacked him with the metal tray and just started beating him with it. That was how in my mind, I'm letting people know you're not going to take advantage of me.

You know, I'm not going to be the guy you come in and just take his crackers. The next thing you know, you'll be taking something else. Because that's how prison operates. People feel like they can take from you, and they just keep doing it. And ironically, that's what led me through the system because people know they can't do that to me. They used to call me a crazy young buck. I wasn't crazy. I just wasn't going to put myself in a position where people could take advantage of me. I just refused.

When I was in Islam, I was what they called the emir of security. And the emir of security is third in command. So you got the imam, the first emir, and the emir of security. The only people who didn't answer to me were the imam and the first emir. Everybody else answered to me. And I gave all that up because I was wrong. My belief system was tainted.

YPM

So you're an intelligent man and a brave man, and a strong man. But being smart, brave, and strong does not prevent us from sometimes doing dumb things. Everybody that goes to prison is not smart, brave, and strong, but you are. So now you're not in Islam. What then? What do you do? Where do your mind and your heart take you?

Doug

I started reading my Bible. I started going to church. I started doing the things that get you closer to God.

YPM

Did you do this on your own? Did you go to the chapel?

Doug

Other people helped me even before I knew Christ. I just didn't embrace Christ the way I should have because I had—even as a child—ignorance. I would have been grounded better because one of the things that we learned growing up in your family when you're learning the scriptures, you always hear John 3:16, "For God so loved the world that he gave his only begotten son that whoever believes in him should not perish but have everlasting life." As a child, you're not paying attention when they teach you the Lord's Prayer. You say, "Our Father who art in heaven" and so on. But the thing that none of us ever really holds on to is the key part of the whole Lord's Prayer, "Forgive us our trespasses as we forgive those who trespass against us"—like harboring ill will toward other people, but we want God to forgive us. And that was a part of my healing process, learning to forgive first and foremost.

YPM

It's pretty incredible. You're this angry kid, and you're stuck in prison. You're there for life. They deny your appeal, and you make this turn. How old were you when you made the turn from Islam back to Christ?

Doug

About 20 or 21.

YPM

So at age 20, you're turning back to what you knew but hadn't embraced. So tell me more about that spiritual journey.

Doug

When I come back to scripture and Christ, it is a slow learning process. It's not so much that I don't know the Word, but how did you apply this to your life? There's a bunch of people who say, "I'm a Christian." So who are you following? I'm not following any of the people following Christ. Some people are encouraging me in the Word, but I'm following Christ because they're going to leave me at some point. That's why Psalm 146 says, "Put not your trust in princes, nor in the son of man, in whom there is no help." They'll lead you wrong. So, I mean, while many people counseled me, I've got an understanding of the Word. What is Christ saying to me? What does He want from me?

How does He want me to live my life? Because at the end of the day, that's what this is about. How does Christ want me to live? What do I have to do? You read 1 Corinthians 13, the "Love Chapter." And it says what? Maybe I can speak to the languages of men and even of angels, but if I have not love, it does me no good. So while I can do all of these things, I hate this guy because he's White. I hate this guy because he's Hispanic. I hate this guy because of his crime. That's not love. God wants us to get to a point where we can love people, irrespective of what they've done. I tell people all the time, who am I to judge? I took someone's life. My crime is no better than yours. I'm a sinner saved by God's grace. I didn't earn this. My being here talking to you is by God's grace. Doug Hollis didn't do anything. God showed respite to me allowed me to come out of prison and begin my life anew.

YPM

All right, you're 20 years old, and you're growing in your faith. You're getting some spiritual wisdom. You're saying wise things, but you're still a young man without a family, without a good education, stuck in prison without freedom. Were you miserable, or were you happy? How did you react? How did you approach all that?

Doug

Well, here's one thing I know, this has been true most of my life. God has used me to help other people. When I went to Camp Hill, one of the things they told me when I went to the PRC, the Program Review Committee, was "You're going to be the problem inmate in housing, education, and employment. So we're going to send you to J block." In those days, J block was called the "animal house," the roughest part of the jail. I'm a 17-year-old kid, and he's telling me this. So that was my fuel to change. I used what they said I couldn't. I said I could. And the only reason that I could was because of Christ. And at the time, I didn't know that because I was involved in Islam. I understand now that it's by God's grace that I could navigate my way through those early years and do things that He was calling me to do.

YPM

It's hard for me to believe Jesus could pray for the people who crucified him. And it's hard for me to believe that you had this much peace when your life had been pulled out from underneath you. You're just 20 years old. You've got no future except prison. So are you happy? Are you hopeful? Or are you depressed?

Doug

I've always been optimistic. I've had friends say I wear rose-colored glasses, but that optimism comes from my faith. It's not because I'm a guy that sees everything working his way, but this is from faith that has grown over the years because of my investment in Christ, because of

His investment in me. Because if God doesn't invest in me, I'm never going to be this man if God doesn't see the man I am.

YPM

So you're trying to show God that you're His man.

Doug

He's showing me that I'm His child. I'm just living out what God wants me to show.

YPM

So you aim to be God's child, God's person, God's servant. You want to help other people.

Doug

Pastor Jim Newsome said, "Go where God wants you to go, do what God wants you to do, and be who God wants you to be." And that's what I'm trying to do daily. Sometimes the struggle is difficult because you don't want to take yourself out of the way. You always want to inject yourself in the way when God says to do something.

YPM

So was it a steady, upward climb, or did you have some setbacks and disasters where you screwed up?

Doug

There's been hills and valleys; nothing's ever straight because life is a series of trials. And I think how we respond to adversities is what builds us, is what makes us. As I told you, when I got denied in that 1978 appeal, that was a point of adversity. And I began to backslide. I began going backward. Now, when I've had adverse moments in Christ, I've run to Christ. I hold onto Christ.

He has helped me through so many difficult moments in my life. I didn't get to this point of faith just by saying that I wanted to be a Christian and do good. I got to this point because God has shown me, "I got you," in the midst of a storm; He's there.

YPM

What were some of those storms? Were you there during the riot at Camp Hill? Or are you gone by then?

Doug

I was at SCI Huntingdon. The Camp Hill riot was in 1989. Sometimes I wonder how my life could have gone. A part of God's grace is my wife. When I met my wife, I was 23 years old.

YPM

What's your wife's name?

Doug

Dianna.

YPM

How did you meet her?

Doug

She was a nurse at Camp Hill, and I was an inmate orderly. I was 23 years old. Crazy. Now I'm 63, and we're still together, again by God's grace.

YPM

Tell me that story.

Doug

Dianna started working at Camp Hill in 1982. I was working in the dispensary. I assisted the nurses and the doctors with wraps, eye drops, and nose drops—all the medical attention inmates needed. And we just sorta got close, closer than we should have gotten because she was staff. I was an inmate. She tells me I used to pontificate, get on my soapbox and talk about things. But God put her there for a reason. And she's been the biggest blessing in my life outside of Christ; there is nothing bigger in my life than her.

YPM

Did she lose her job over your relationship? What happened?

Doug

She resigned from Camp Hill. And that's why I was transferred from Camp Hill, because of our relationship. I was transferred to SCI Huntingdon. I guess a part of the administration's desire at the time was to create a wedge in our relationship. Because Diana is White and I'm Black.

YPM

Was that their main issue, or was it the fact that it was an inmate and a staff person? Or do you think it was a racial thing?

Doug

I think it was because it was an inmate and a staff person, but that was exacerbated by the fact that I'm Black and she's White. If we were people of the same ethnicity, they may have sent me to SCI Graterford or SCI Dallas, something like that. They sent me to SCI Huntingdon. At the time, Huntingdon was, I'd say, the most racial state prison at that time.

YPM

What do you mean by that?

Doug

I'll give you an example. When you go to "Mainline" to eat, the Blacks sit on the left-hand side of the mess hall and the Whites on the right-hand side. And if you're alright with me and I'm alright with you, we'll sit in the middle. The showers were like that. The movie hall was like that.

YPM

Was that because the prison authorities made it that way, or because the inmates made it that way?

Doug

I think it's twofold. I think both parties played a role in that. I think it was started through staff and carried on through inmates. It's hard to get a policy like that in place unless it's coming from the top. When you're going to have segregated dining halls, movie theaters, showers, that's something that has to come from the top. Over time it became just a natural occurrence.

YPM

So you're in Huntingdon. Dianna's separated from you. Does she keep visiting you? What's happening in your relationship?

Doug

You were allowed six visits a month, and she was there every visit.

YPM

So Dianna is visiting you at Huntingdon. And your relationship keeps growing?

Doug

Our relationship kept growing, and some things were designed to separate us. I had a guard getting in my face so close, screaming at me about kissing her. If I had turned around to look at him, I'd have been kissing him. That's how close he was in my face—screaming at me. I truly appreciate how I made it through the system by God's grace without becoming this angry, bitter, rebellious person. I went through things in the system because of my relationship with Dianna that nobody should go through. But you know I got through by God's grace.

YPM

Tell me why you didn't become an angry, bitter person. Some inmates are angry and resentful. I understand that. The miracle is that by God's grace, you weren't lashing out at everybody. So tell me about the men you must have known who were full of resentment, blaming everybody else for their problems. Is there a way to reach those guys? I know God reached you with grace. But it's not easy when somebody's full of bitterness and anger. I'm interviewing people who have gotten free and stayed free, not just physically but also spiritually. How many people come through prison spiritually free without anger and bitterness? What do you think is the difference? How would you try to reach men like that?

Doug

I think the best way to reach people like that is by example. People in prison, out here in society, look at other people to garner strength or encouragement for how you deal with situations. I used to teach a class on character development. I would tell guys that someone's child is looking to you to be an example. They're looking at you. They want to emulate you. What is it that you want them to emulate? Because if you don't want them to emulate you as this prisoner, as an inmate, you have to give them something better to see. And that's something that God pressed on me. You say you want to be better. If you want to be better, you have to do better. You can't be better if you're not willing to do better. That's impossible. I've always tried to exemplify the better part of what it is to be a man going through trials.

YPM

So the key is a good example. Can you think of inmates whom your example helped turn that corner, helped them move away from selfishness and anger to Christ? Can you think of men that tried to emulate you?

Doug

There are a lot of guys that I know even now that have come home that will tell me that my impact in their lives helped them get through that process. But I did it one day at a time with God's help. I'm not a finished product. God is still working on me. It's a continuous process. You see some of what God has done? He's still doing yet more. I want to make sure that people know that I am nothing without Him. So when you hear me talk about God and His grace and His mercy, it's because He's shown it to me. I know beyond a shadow of a doubt that if God doesn't intervene in my life, I would be one of those barracudas, piranhas that were in prison. God intervened.

YPM

Here's what this makes me think. God did not put you in prison. Your choices put you in prison. But God used you in prison in a powerful way. Imagine if there weren't men like you in prison? What would prison be like if there weren't some people like you there for others to emulate, optimistic people, people who had hope? Prison would be a thousand times worse than it is. But the fact is that people inside the prison system are going through the same things they are, and they can see these people are different. What a powerful impact that has on the inside of correctional institutions.

Doug

Here's something else I used to do. I was in the hole one time, and I was a little distraught. And my wife sent me this little thing called "Adversity." And I read it and applied it. And what it was saying is that there was a girl who had experienced so much trauma in her life. And all she ever did was complain. And her father was a chef. So he took her in the kitchen one day, and he put three pots on the stove and filled them with water. And in one pot, he put eggs; in another pot carrots; and in the third pot, he put coffee beans.

I use this when I speak to men that are incarcerated. I say this is a simplistic way of looking at the eggs, carrots, and coffee, but there is a moral to the story. And that moral is the ease of those items. They had the same adversity, the boiling water. Men who are incarcerated all endure the same adversity. We each respond to it differently. The egg had a hard exterior, but it was malleable and hardened. So many men go into prison and become hardened. Then you have those men that go into prison hard, but they come out like the carrot, soft because after the adversity, that's what happens to the carrot. The coffee beans were different in that the coffee beans changed the color of the water, but they also changed the flavor of the water. They remained the same. I tell people that's what we should aspire to do—change our environments in a positive way. We can impact people's lives in so many ways. Lead people to the right things to make better choices. Or we can lead them down a dark hole and let them be crazy following in your stupidity. Those are the choices.

YPM

Where and how did you get connected to Yokefellowship Prison Ministry?

Doug

Yokefellowship came on Saturdays. They'd have little groups where we talk about scripture. Over my years of incarceration, I truly appreciate the men and women who came in and gave us encouragement and inspiration and fed us because so often, when you're incarcerated, you're forgotten. But like Christ said, "What you do for the least of them, you do for me." (Matthew 25:40) Part of that is visiting those who are incarcerated. They came in. They lifted us. They fed us the Word of God.

YPM

Those volunteers are special people. They may not have the influence that you do with other inmates. Inmates know that you know what they are going through. You have been "in the pot" with them. But every person I've interviewed has told me that having somebody come in from the outside, even if they don't know everything about prison, is such a powerful force. You just said it, when you do it for one of the least of these, you do it for Christ. When volunteers visit someone in prison, they might as well be visiting Christ. It's great to hear somebody like you say that because volunteers who do the paperwork, get approved, give up their time, go into prison, encourage inmates, and let them know they are not forgotten, should know that their witness is compelling.

Doug

Absolutely. But here's something that you should know. Those volunteers have the same influence that I have. They influenced me. Without their influence on my life, I can't influence other people's lives.

YPM

I understand. I go to visit in prison and what do I know? I've never been incarcerated, but I hear you. The reality is I am there. That says something to an inmate. When a person takes the time to visit consistently and bring "Good News," it is a strong influence. Unfortunately, the COVID pandemic has cut off those kinds of ministry visits, and that is a tragic loss.

Doug

If we don't have people like yourself—John Rush, Jim Newsome, Roger Napper, all these people coming in and lifting us—how do we maintain our spirits? How will we maintain that drive to look at Christ and his Word? These people are the positive examples that we need.

YPM

I hear you. That's a good word. So now you're in Huntingdon. You and Dianna have this relationship, she loves you, but you're a lifer. So what do you do with that? What happens next? Tell me the story.

Doug

The love that Dianna had for me and has for me fueled a lot of the desire for me to grow and change. I don't want her to spend her life out here, working hard, struggling to make ends meet while I sit in prison and just sponge off her. She made a lot of sacrifices for this life, and they weren't easy sacrifices. One of the things that stood out was Dianna is an only child. And when our relationship was in its inception in its beginning, her parents were opposed to it. Her parents didn't even want to speak to her. But she endured. She held on.

YPM

Her parents must have thought—we love you, daughter, but sweetheart, he's a lifer. So what are you going to do?

Doug

People thought she was crazy, and sometimes I thought she was crazy because there were some difficult moments in this relationship. I was recommended to Governor Casey to have my sentence commuted in August 1992. I was denied in March 1994. Governor Casey said no. But the governor signed the commutation of a guy named Reginald McFadden. I don't know how much you know about Reginald McFadden, but he went to New York and raped and killed two women. And that's why the commutation process in Pennsylvania has become so arduous. I could never be recommended to the governor again because the board wouldn't hear my case. They wouldn't give me a merit review or give me public hearings. I could never get back to that pinnacle of being recommended.

The board refused to hear me point-blank. No questions asked. Dianna came to see me, and she was distraught—I mean, just distraught. She didn't understand why the board turned me down. And to be honest, I didn't understand either, but you know, when you do everything you can, the only thing left to do is trust in God. All you can do is what you can do. Then you have to leave the rest to God. And I told her, "I don't know, but don't worry, God has a plan." She said, "But why, why, why not? Why, why wouldn't they give you an answer?" "I don't know, but God has a plan. We just have to trust God for a plan." And the other painful part was another guy that I know that went up with me, who got a public hearing and was subsequently recommended to the governor.

This guy had just got a misconduct while he was waiting, and it still went through, and he's still got a favorable review. And here I am, a facilitator. I helped to save an inmate's life. I was president of inmate organizations. I did everything that a person could do in prison to better himself to do the right things. And it was like I was getting slapped in the face. But as I told her, we just have to trust.

Like when Moses was up against the Red Sea, what did he say to the Israelites? When they were screaming and crying, Pharaoh was coming and going to kill them. "Be still and see the salvation of the Lord." (Exodus 14:13). And that was my message. We've done all we can do. Now we have to wait on God and trust in him. And in January 2016, you have the Montgomery vs. Louisiana case where the United States Supreme Court says that you cannot send a juvenile to life without the possibility of parole.

And it applies to all the incarcerated people because Pennsylvania denied that in 2012. So here we were in 2016, and the U.S. Supreme Court is saying, no, it applies to all of them. And that was God's work, God's plan. And I didn't see it at the time, but I trusted that God had a plan. I knew that there was a plan, and it came to fruition. So, you know, you go from January 2016, I get re-sentenced December 2, 2016, I get released from prison March 3, 2017. And God continues to bless me. I talk about Jonah and the whale, but I was like Joseph in prison, who was innocent. I wasn't innocent, but God's favor was on me all my years of incarceration. Because if his favor weren't on me, I'd have been running around like a chicken without a head doing all kinds of crazy stuff. But God's favor was on me. It can be seen in everything.

YPM

It wasn't just that God's favor was on you. You believed God's favor was on you. Even in adversity, you ran to Him. When Dianna was distraught, you said, no, we've just got to wait for His plan. God's favor was on you, but there was faith in you. You had "...the assurance of things hoped for..." (Hebrews 11:1). You believed. A lot of people have God's favor, but they don't have that kind of faith. They don't believe in a Savior. When something terrible happens, they say, "That's it, there's no God. I'm done!"

Doug

I told you the one scripture, "Put not your trust in princes, nor the son of man...." Psalm 146. And there is Psalm 121 that I would always tell people, "I will lift my eyes unto the hills, from whence cometh my help. My help cometh from the Lord." The other passage that always helped me when things were rough, and I was unsure, or things weighed heavy on me was Philippians 4:6-7, "Be anxious for nothing, but in all things through prayer and supplication with thanksgiving let your requests be made known to God." That kept me straight, that kept me from backsliding or going stupid. Even to this day, I believe that God is in control of all things. No matter how difficult the road is in front of me, God is in control.

YPM

Well, you're encouraging and inspiring me, Doug. But just to bring the story to a close, what happened when you got out? Did you walk out the door, and Dianna was standing there? What happened the day you were released and had your freedom?

Doug

She was at the prison waiting for me. And it was bittersweet. It was more sweet than bitter, but I went to prison when I was 16; I came home at age 58. Wow! There were so many men I had grown to care for genuinely and love as a family that I was now leaving behind. And I think that's why I do the kind of work that I do. Since I have been out of prison, I have worked for three years as a re-entry coordinator and mentor for Sound Community Solutions. It's helping returning citizens who come out to try and keep them out of prison. I want them to realize and understand that I'm nothing special. What God did for me, He can do for them. But they have to believe. A part of belief is an investment. Unless you are willing to invest in yourself, invest in trust in the Lord, this isn't going to work.

Why is it that when your day of freedom comes, you'll sit your Bible on the table in the day room and walk out? That makes no sense. If this is what kept you doing the right things while you were incarcerated, why would you leave it? Why would you leave God's Word in prison and re-engage life without it? That's your sword and shield. You leave the full armor of God in prison when you should be taking it with you because the battle is greater out here than it was in there. And I never really understood why people do that. But you know, I'm blessed that God has kept me here.

YPM

Some of the people I have been interviewing tell me that when they first went to prison, they were not reading the Bible five minutes a day or five hours a day. They were living in the Bible every waking hour. They knew they needed God. But when life gets better for you, I think it's easier to say, "I'm doing this on my own. You don't feel like you need God so much."

Doug

Here's the thing, here's the challenge. We have to learn to turn to God when things are good or bad. That's a part of growth. That's a part of learning that God is the same. He's always the same. We're changing. And in the midst of our storms, that's when God is most available if we reach for Him. But when you're engaged in a challenge the easy thing to do is walk away. That's the easy thing. When something goes wrong, when something happens that's adverse or contrary to what you want, it's easy to say, man, I'm done with that. God ain't looking out for me, man, I'm through. But, no, that's when you press on. That's when you truly hold on to God. Because sometimes, as James says, consider it all joy when faced with trials and tribulations, because they're meant to build you up, not tear you down. During a struggle, that's what it is.

God is building you up for something, and you have to look for what God is showing you at that moment.

YPM

In sixth grade, you were voted the most likely to succeed. I believe you have succeeded. You can't give back the life you took as a 16 year old or undo some things you did—none of us can. But under the most trying circumstances and adversity, some of your own doing, you have succeeded. Not many people could go through what you've gone through and come out the other side the way you have. In a spiritual sense, there's no greater success than that. So whoever voted you to be most likely to succeed, they were right. You have succeeded. You're not a millionaire, but that's not the most important thing. But you have become a new person in Christ, and it's very inspiring to hear you talk.

Doug

The thing is, I thought about this interview today. And I prayed, and my prayer was, "Let it be Your words, Lord, out of my mouth, not mine." It's easy to pat myself on the back and say how well I've done, but I couldn't have done any of it without Him.

YPM

It is God's doing, but Doug, you believe God is with you and have faith and hope. So many people who had an early life like yours, who grew up with trials and struggles, wind up incarcerated. But they don't all finish as you have. That is God's success. I grant you that. But God uses imperfect people like you and me. And God has used you. And that's a success worth celebrating. You've allowed God to use you. You cooperated with the Holy Spirit. That's a pretty remarkable life, my friend.

This book we are working on is a part of a series of books about people who have been incarcerated but have gotten free and stayed free. And this book, in particular, tells the stories of people impacted in some way by Yokefellowship Prison Ministry. How does a person in prison get physically and spiritually free? How does that happen? It is miraculous. It is God's work when that happens. The people we are talking to could have gotten bitter and angry, turned away, become selfish, and spent their lives taking what they thought they missed out on and blaming others for their troubles. But that's not who they are. They are humble, grateful people who give all the glory to God for "getting free and staying free." Grace is not forced on us. It's a gift you have to accept. You said yes to the gift.

Doug

When you're in the storm, and everything's coming down on you, you have nowhere to go but to God. You can go back to the devil. It can snowball—going down the hill, just keep rolling and rolling, everything gets worse and worse and worse. But the true test of who we are in God is not when everything is going our way. When I can get up, pray, and be thankful for the life that I have, even in the face of adversity, even in the moment of challenge, I have passed the test.

Let's say you get fired from a job. That's an adverse moment. You're struggling to deal with it, but you can be thankful that you're alive. You can be thankful that God brought you through. You can try to find another job. Or you get in a car accident, and you can get up and walk away. The car can be replaced. You can be thankful that God allowed you to walk away because you could have been like the car. I could have been destroyed like that car, but for God, I can get up and walk away. I can walk out of that prison. If it weren't for God, I wouldn't have walked out of there. He protected me. I'm a big guy, and people knew this and that, but God protected me because even big guys are tested in prison.

God protected me. He put that hedge of protection around me. He shielded me from all the arrows that came my way. God did that. You know the racism of the system, the challenges of being called different things. One of the things that people understand in prison is a person who embraces God, grows and does all the right things. They're no longer Dougie from the "way" (neighborhood) or Freddie from there or any of that. They say, "He's a sellout. He's a company man. He's a bootleg." They say an inmate who embraces God is everything but who God says he is—a child of God. You have to be strong enough to endure those negative things that are going to be said about you. Because if you can't, you won't make It. People talked about Jesus in such ways that you can't even compare what they say about us. But knowing that He endured and He didn't give in, you have an example to follow. All you have to do is follow it.

YPM
Doug, thank you so much for sharing your story.

Doug
Well, thank you for wanting to hear my story.

Doug Hollis
Salem Evangelical Lutheran Church
dughollis@comcast.net

Biblical Reflection

When Jesus was on the cross, he cried out, "My God, my God, why have you forsaken me?" a direct quote from Psalm 22. When suffering comes to Jesus, He wants to know why. When suffering comes to us, we want to know why. Often in life, we do not receive a clear, satisfying answer. But followers of Jesus trust that God has the answer even if we do not. Disciples of Jesus trust that God is in control and that trust impacts the way they live their lives.

Doug Hollis believed that he could see his life reflected in the life of Jonah. "My life was like Jonah. God came to Jonah and told him to go to the people of Nineveh and speak to the people. But Jonah said they were wicked and corrupt. He didn't want to do that. So he ran from what God wanted him to do and ended up in the belly of the whale. In my case, I didn't know God's calling on my life, so I was in rebellion. And the belly of the whale for me was a prison until I humbled myself and cried out to God and His mercy and forgiveness. Then like Jonah, God released me from the whale and restored me to life. And now I have a purpose; everything is about Him."

Christians believe that they can triumph over suffering the way that Christ triumphed over a cross. An inmate triumphs despite incarceration and "gets free and stays free" by believing that God can use imprisonment to do good things and prepare us to do good things for others. Doug Hollis points to James 1:2. The trials and tribulations are there to build us up, not tear us down. "God is building you up for something, and you have to look for what God is showing you at that moment."

APPENDIX

The Essence of Yokefellows

- **Caring Fellowship**—The first goal of a Yokefellow group is to create a warm, accepting, and caring fellowship where persons feel comfortable and free to participate. This is Christ at work in the midst. His Spirit is present, bringing a sense of love, understanding, and care to the group. He creates a unity in which discussion, sharing, and mutual support work toward the stimulation of spiritual growth. Without this essential atmosphere, the group is little more than a glorified discussion group.

- **Disciplined Living**—Jesus' word of invitation to "take my yoke and learn of me" in essence is a call to discipleship. The Word tells the story: Disciple—learner; Discipline—a commitment to learning; Christian Discipleship—learning Jesus' way. Yokefellows seek to challenge persons to exercise their discipleship by seven basic disciplines of the Christian faith. A Yokefellows group receives a call to accept these disciplines and practice them.

- **Intentional Ministry**—All who follow Jesus are ministers of His Kingdom. Jesus' yoke is also His mission—to redeem all of life and to transform persons and society into a divine community. D. Elton Trueblood, founder of the Yokefellows International movement describes it as a ministry in the common life, i.e. make every aspect of life an arena in which we interpret and apply the ways of the Lord.

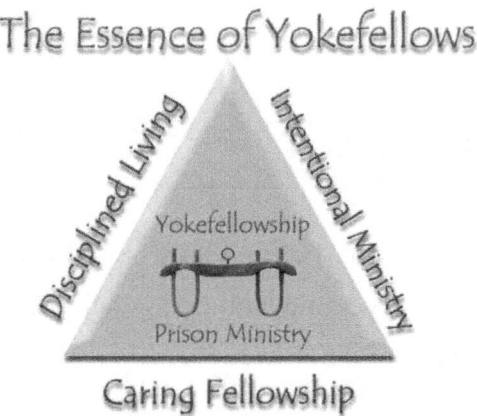

YOKEFELLOWSHIP

PRISON MINISTRY

The Marks of a Yokefellow

There are five traditional "Marks of a Yokefellow." These marks make it clear that those involved in the fellowship have joined together voluntarily for the promotion of a vital Christianity.

- **Commitment**—A Yokefellow is a disciple of the divine Lord, Christ, and is committed to the work of His Kingdom among people. A disciple's belief is not a closed affair, but one that is unafraid of inquiry or scrutiny. Disciples know that to be vital, their faith must grow; it must likewise be made relevant to their life and work.

- **Witness**—A Yokefellow knows that faith in Christ is not a private affair: to be kept it must be shared.

- **Ministry**—A Yokefellow is willing to be used by the Holy Spirit as a means of opening the doors of people's lives to God's love and grace.

- **Fellowship**—It is impossible to be a Christian and to choose to be a Christian in isolation. A Yokefellow finds or produces a redemptive Christian fellowship.

- **Discipline**—A Yokefellow voluntarily accepts:
  » **Discipline of Prayer**—pray daily.
  » **Discipline of Scripture**—read reverently and thoughtfully a portion of Scripture daily, following a definite plan.
  » **Discipline of Worship**—to share, at least weekly, in the public worship of God.
  » **Discipline of Money**—give a definite portion of my income to the promotion of Christ's cause as an act of worship.
  » **Discipline of Time**—use my time as a sacred gift, not to be wasted, striving to make my daily work, whatever it may be, a Christian vocation.
  » **Discipline of Service**—daily lift some human burden.

Resources

Yokefellowship Prison Ministry in Pennsylvania
Info@yokefellowship.net
www.yokefellowship.net
PO Box 531
Reedsville, PA 17084

David M. Lewis
Author, Chair of the Board,
   Yokefellowship Prison Ministry
   in Pennsylvania
davidmlewis8118@gmail.com

Carl Geissinger
Executive Director,
   Yokefellowship Prison Ministry
   in Pennsylvania
pastorgeis@gmail.com

Rich Jacobs
YPM Volunteer Coordinator,
   Get and Stay Free Publishing
www.getfreeandstayfree.com

John Rush
Former Prison Chaplain, Pastor,
   and YPM Executive Director
Founder of New Person
   Ministries, and Freedom
   Gate Ministries
Co-founder of Justice & Mercy,
   Inc.
rushjoes@aol.com

Dr. Tom Zeager
Co-founder and President,
   Justice & Mercy, Inc.
tzhz@ptd.net

About the Author

Pastor David M. Lewis served 43 years in pastoral ministry including most recently 30 years as senior pastor at New Hanover United Methodist Church in western Montgomery County, Pennsylvania. He was the organizing pastor of this new congregation which grew to become one of the largest United Methodist Churches in the northeastern United States. Prior to that, he served as a pastor in Wheaton, Maryland, and in Mt. Carmel, and Norristown, Pennsylvania.

Dave grew up in Philadelphia, is an Eagle Scout, served in the U.S. Marine Corps in Vietnam, graduated from Temple University, where he was on the rowing team, and Wesley Theological Seminary in Washington D. C. He is married to Nancy (Schuckert) Lewis. He has three grown children and their spouses, six grandchildren, and two "bonus" daughters with Nancy. Dave is the board chairman of Yokefellowship Prison Ministry in Pennsylvania. He enjoys ministering at a local prison, supporting the work of Urban Promise International, hunting, fishing, biking, hiking, kayaking, and puttering around the house.

A Message from Get Free and Stay Free Publishing

Are you currently in prison and have a story of hope and transformation?

Would you like to share your story of change and renewal with fellow prisoners and others—family, friends, those formerly incarcerated, and stakeholders, such as policy decision makers and lawmaking bodies that impact the criminal justice system? If so, we encourage you to send your story to Get Free and Stay Free Publishing.

Get Free and Stay Free publishes stories of hope and transformation told only by those who are or were in prison. As an all-volunteer team, we will do our best to scan your submission and post it on our website www.GetFreeAndStayFree.com.

Your story doesn't require perfect grammar and punctuation…just make sure it is legibly written so it can be read. If you can access a typewriter, that's encouraged as well. Write your story as short or as long as you like and give it a title.

If your submission is selected by our team for one of our upcoming book publications, we will contact you for your permission to publish it.

Submit your story by mail to: Get Free and Stay Free Publishing, PO Box 326, Gilbertsville, PA 19525.

Made in the USA
Coppell, TX
20 August 2022

81743165R10181